D1251872

FREESTONE & WEBB

1923-1958
THE STORY OF
A BRITISH COACHBUILDER

MICHAEL SEDGWICK
MEMORIAL TRUST

Freestone & Webb, 1923-1958 – The Story of a British Coachbuilder is published with the financial assistance of the Michael Sedgwick Memorial Trust. The M.S.M.T. was founded in memory of the motoring historian and author Michael C. Sedgwick (1926–1983) to encourage the publication of new motoring research, and the recording of Road Transport History. Support by the Trust does not imply any involvement in the editorial process, which remains the responsibility of the editor and publisher. The Trust is a Registered Charity, No 290841, and a full list of the Trustees and an overview of the functions of the M.S.M.T. can be found on: www.michaelsedgwicktrust.co.uk

Published in 2021
by Herridge & Sons Ltd
Lower Forda, Shebbear
Beaworthy, Devon EX21 5SY

© Copyright James Taylor 2021

Design by Ray Leaning, MUSE Fine Art & Design

All rights reserved. No part of this publication may be reproduced in any form
or by any means without the prior permission of the publisher and the copyright holder.

ISBN 978-1-906133-98-6
Printed in China

FREESTONE & WEBB

1923-1958
THE STORY OF
A BRITISH COACHBUILDER

By James Taylor

Herridge & Sons

FOREWORD AND ACKNOWLEDGMENTS

There have been surprisingly few books devoted to the great British coachbuilders, and historians have typically treated the work of these companies as secondary to that of the primary beneficiaries of their efforts – the Rolls-Royce and Bentley marques. So this book deliberately looks at the work of one of those coachbuilders, treating the chassis manufacturers as secondary to the narrative.

The first time I took an interest in Freestone & Webb must have been somewhere around late 1957 or early 1958. Reading my parents' newspapers, I was fascinated by the name of the Honeymoon Express, the spectacular car on Rolls-Royce Silver Cloud chassis that had just been shown at Earls Court and was to be, as it turned out, their swan song. The other thing that caught my eye was that name: Freestone & Webb. I found it unforgettable.

So, more than half a century later, and having become a motoring historian and journalist, I decided it was time to do something about that interest. As there were no books available about Freestone & Webb, I decided to write my own.

Doing so has taken me on a fascinating voyage of discovery, digging into old magazines, obscure archives and the works of other authors, and – of course – scouring the internet for nuggets of obscure information. It has been massively enjoyable, and I hope the result conveys some of that enjoyment as well as providing a sensible and readable history of one of Britain's leading builders of bespoke car coachwork in the 20th century.

The basis of this book is of course the list of bodies that Freestone & Webb constructed at their works in Brentfield Road, at Stonebridge Park in north-west London. No full list of these bodies existed when I started work, although fortunately the coachbuilder's order book that survives does cover the period from 1933 to 1958. I have therefore compiled the list for the period from 1923 to 1932 from such evidence as is available through other sources. Although I think this list is reasonably complete, I have no doubt that further information will come to light in due course. I thought it was at least worth collating what is known so that further research has a solid foundation to build on.

By my calculations (see the panel below), Freestone & Webb built fewer than 1000 bodies in the 35 years of their existence as a coachbuilder. That puts a perspective on the rarity of those that still survive thanks to the care of enthusiasts. Long may that survival continue.

Although this is the first book devoted entirely to the coachwork of Freestone & Webb (at least, as far as I am aware), it owes a debt to many existing books, of which several focus on the Rolls-Royce and Bentley marques. I am also very grateful to the many suppliers of photographs (who are credited individually in the captions), and to the following individuals and representatives of organisations who have made their own valuable contributions in one way or another:

John Bath, Martin Bennett, Tom Clarke, John Fox of the Alvis Owner Club, Len Cozzolino of the Lagonda Register,
Mark Garfitt of the Frazer Nash Car Club, Philip Hall of the Sir Henry Royce Memorial Foundation,
Malcolm Jenner of the Crossley Register, Bernard King, Will Morrison, Roy Pollard, Klaus-Josef Rossfeldt,
Ian Scott of the WO Bentley Memorial Foundation, Nigel Smith, Nelson Thorpe of Club Hispano-Suiza, Lionel Whitehead.

I have done my best to identify the origins of all the illustrations used in this book, but will be pleased to make amends in future editions if I have made any errors or omissions.

James Taylor
Oxfordshire,
December 2020

FREESTONE & WEBB BODY TOTALS	
These figures are based on the tables in this book, and are subject to the same caveats.	
1923-1929	264 bodies
1930-1939	410 bodies
1946-1949	111 bodies
1950-1958	211 bodies
Grand Total	**996 bodies**

CONTENTS

Chapter One

BUILDING A REPUTATION, 1923-1929

Founder AJ Webb probably learned the coachbuilding trade with Windovers before moving on to Sizaire-Berwick. This picture shows him at a formal dinner after a motor show in the early 1950s, when Freestone & Webb had been awarded one of their nine consecutive gold medals for coachwork.

Between 1923 and 1958, Freestone & Webb were known as one of Britain's top bespoke coach-building companies. The majority of their work was on Rolls-Royce and Bentley chassis, but they were never afraid to work with the more exotic imported types or with chassis from what might be called the second division of British manufacturers – makes such as Alvis, Daimler and Lagonda. They had a reputation for top quality work, and were regular exhibitors at the annual Motor Show in London, where they won a Gold Medal in the private coachbuilders' class for nine consecutive years.

The two men who founded the company, Messrs VE Freestone and AJ Webb, met while working for the Sizaire-Berwick concern, which had begun as the British importer of French-built Sizaire chassis. From 1915, its premises were at Park Royal on the northern edge of London, and from 1920 it manufactured both chassis and bodies there. However, changes at the French end of the business seem to have created some uncertainty about the future of the British subsidiary towards the end of 1922, and during 1923 British motor magnate Herbert Austin gained a controlling share in Sizaire-Berwick.

The company's employees must have begun to wonder how secure their jobs were at this stage, and it seems likely that VE Freestone and AJ Webb decided it was time to strike out on their own. Both men would have been in their early forties, with around two and a half decades of coachbuilding experience. They had a shining example to follow: William MacDonald Park and Charles Ward had also worked at Sizaire-Berwick, and in 1919 they had left to establish coachbuilder Park Ward in nearby Willesden. Park Ward was already a notable success.

There was every reason to set up the new Freestone & Webb business in the same general area. London was expanding under the provisions of the 1919 Housing and Town Planning Act, and both new housing and new industrial areas were springing up on its northern outskirts. Several other coachbuilding businesses were already established in the area, so there would be no shortage of skilled men; it is very likely that Freestone & Webb were able to persuade a number of former Vanden Plas employees to join them, as that company (located at Kingsbury nearby) was going through a difficult period in the first half of 1923. They may have brought some former colleagues with them from Sizaire-Berwick, too. It also made sense to open up near a chassis maker that was likely to provide a source of work. Messrs Freestone and Webb would have been very much aware of the rapidly growing success of Bentley, which had recently been established at Cricklewood and seemed to be exactly the sort of chassis manufacturer that might need their services.

One of the new industrial areas that was opening up on London's northern outskirts was at Stonebridge Park, where the local council had originally planned to build 1000 new houses but had halted the scheme in 1920 after building just 260 of them because of drainage difficulties. When the North Circular Road was driven through the middle of the planned estate, new industry followed, and the Stonebridge section of what had earlier been Dog Lane was renamed as Brentfield Road. It was here, on a three-acre site which became numbers 101-103, that Freestone & Webb set themselves up in new premises that were known as Unity Works.

The new workshops at Brentfield Road must have taken several months to erect, and it is very likely that the first Freestone & Webb bodies were constructed while building was still going on around them. We do not know for certain the identity of the company's first creation, but the earliest known Freestone & Webb body was a saloon on a Bentley chassis that was completed in October 1923.

As already explained, Freestone & Webb's new premises had been established just a few miles from the Bentley works at Cricklewood, and this relatively young company was an obvious target for the new coachbuilder. WO Bentley had set up his business in 1921, hoping to build a high-quality sporting chassis, but it had soon become obvious that there were many customers who wanted the Bentley 3-litre but did not want the typical open sporting bodywork of the day. What they wanted was enclosed saloon bodies (much to WO's annoyance), and Freestone & Webb seized their opportunity.

Those first few saloons – barely a handful – were coachbuilt in the traditional way with metal panels attached to a wooden framework, as were the substantial-looking barrel-sided tourer types and a few two-seaters that were built on Bentley chassis. However, Freestone & Webb took out a licence to build fabric-panelled bodies to the Weymann patents very early in their existence, and by 1924 the company had begun to turn out Weymann saloon bodies. These no doubt appealed to WO Bentley because they were lighter than the traditionally panelled type, and by October 1924, the Freestone & Webb Weymann saloon was among the bodies promoted in Bentley's own catalogues.

Most important, perhaps, was that these early bodies seem to have established a reputation for quality of construction, and by the autumn of 1924 word was spreading. That October, Freestone & Webb delivered their first body on a Rolls-Royce chassis, a saloon on the new "small" Twenty chassis. It would be the first of very many for Britain's most respected motor manufacturer.

Weymann coachwork

Freestone & Webb had opened for business just at the time in 1923 when Weymann body construction patents were being introduced to Britain. Like many other coachbuilders, they recognised the potential advantages of the Weymann method, and for the next five years or so a majority of the bodies constructed at Brentfield Road would depend on the Weymann principles.

A problem with early car bodies was that they rattled and squeaked as the rigid joints in their timber frames coped with shocks transmitted through the road wheels. To avoid this, French former aviator Charles Terres Weymann developed and patented a way of building bodies that depended on special metal joints

---

MESSRS FREESTONE AND WEBB

Victor Ernest Freestone was born at Lavendon in Buckinghamshire in the first half of 1881. In some comments published in *The Motor* of 14 October 1930, he claimed to have been a boy apprentice with the coachbuilder Arthur Mulliner in Northampton, and to have been one of those who helped make the first motor body ever built in England. He also claimed to have built with his own hands the first cabriolet body sold in Britain. By 1901, he was certainly an "apprentice coachbuilder".

At the time of the 1911 Census he was living in Sevenoaks, Kent, where he had become the manager of a motor works. Some accounts have him working for Crossley Motors at some indeterminate point after this, which would have taken him to that company's headquarters in Manchester. By about 1920, however, he was working for the body department of Sizaire-Berwick in London – and it was here that he met AJ Webb.

Arthur John Webb was born in September 1882 at Paulerspury in Northamptonshire. His father was a farmer and his brothers stayed in the family business, but by 1901 Arthur was boarding in Huntingdon and working as a coachbuilder. It is very likely that he was working for Windovers, and it may be that he subsequently worked at that company's Paris depot. In 1907 he married Cornelia Dickson, and by 1911 they were living in Balham, south London, and had one daughter, Violet Ethel. Arthur was then the manager of a motor works. A second daughter, Joan, was born in 1917, and in later years she worked in the office at Freestone & Webb.

Some accounts have AJ Webb working for a French coachbuilder, and these versions of the story may arise either from his possible time with the Windover branch in Paris, or from the fact that the Sizaire of Sizaire-Berwick was a French builder of chassis.

One way or the other, it appears that AJ Webb was working in the body department of Sizaire-Berwick when he met VE Freestone.

(These accounts of the two founders draw on research done by Will Morrison for the 2012 issue of The Roycean, *which is used here with grateful acknowledgement.)*

Freestone & Webb quickly earned favour from Bentley Motors with their lightweight coachwork that met customer demand for closed bodies without hindering the performance of what was, after all, a sporting chassis. This Weymann-bodied six-light saloon dates from May 1925 and is typical of the company's output at the time.

FREESTONE & WEBB ANNUAL PRODUCTION TOTALS, 1923-1929

The annual figures shown here should not be considered definitive. Like all the figures in this book for the period 1923-1932, they have been compiled from a variety of sources. These include references in the motoring press, surviving vehicles and, above all, the records of the Bentley and Rolls-Royce companies on whose chassis Freestone & Webb built a large proportion of their coachwork.

These figures are nevertheless the best currently available. They relate to calendar years.

1923	2
1924	25
1925	52
1926	45
1927	44
1928	43
1929	53

The overall total for the company's first seven years was therefore 264 bodies. If the 1923 output is discounted, as it represents a period of less than a year when the company was starting up, there were 262 bodies over six full years, which gives an annual average of just over 43 bodies.

that allowed the wooden framework to flex. Instead of traditional metal panels, fabric outer panels were stretched over the wooden frame, aircraft-style, so reducing weight. The seats, meanwhile, were mounted directly to the chassis frame rather than to the body.

To make curved external corners, small metal panels were inserted between the outer fabric and the timber body frame, and there were straining wires inside the doors to hold them in shape. The frame itself was then covered with muslin over chicken wire, with a thin layer of cotton wadding to span larger areas. The outer fabric layer – typically a pigmented synthetic leather – was then stretched over this, and aluminium mouldings were used to cover any exposed joins in the fabric. The Weymann method of construction also made car bodies considerably lighter, which of course was welcomed as a way of improving performance.

The earliest Weymann body known to have come from the Brentfield Road works was a six-light saloon on a Bentley 3-litre chassis in May 1924. The car became a demonstrator for Bentley themselves, and was used by Sales Manager HM Bentley, WO Bentley's older brother. Shortly after that, the company was asked to construct a similar body on an experimental six-cylinder Bentley chassis that was the ancestor of the later 6½-litre model.

Like these two, most of the early Freestone & Webb

Weymann saloons were six-light types, with a tall and somewhat square-rigged design. The basic shape may well have been drawn up at Cricklewood; Bentley did this kind of thing quite a lot in the early days, to avoid the problems caused by inferior designs. These bodies were certainly elegant, usually enhanced by contrasting upper panels in *Tôle Souple* (which translates roughly as flexible panelwork); this expensive feature involved the application to the fabric panels of layer upon layer of paint that was sanded down to give a glossy finish. They were generally similar to contemporary six-light Weymann designs from coachbuilders such as Park Ward and Gurney Nutting, although a practised eye could spot the slightly shallower windows favoured at Brentfield Road.

Weymann construction remained popular for most of the 1920s, but it did have considerable drawbacks. The fabric outer skin generally had a matt finish that made it look dull alongside coachpainted metal-panelled bodies. It was also readily damaged, which could lead to the timber frame and cotton wadding being exposed while pieces of fabric flapped in the breeze as the car was being driven. Another problem was that the fabric-on-timber construction afforded the occupants very little protection in an accident.

So within a few years, Weymann coachwork had become discredited. By the time of the 1929 Paris Salon, Weymann himself was looking at alternative construction methods, and had developed a semi-rigid method of construction using aluminium. The French company did not survive the economic crisis of 1930, although its British branch turned very successfully to building bus and coach bodies. By this time, Freestone & Webb had already begun to build coachwork with conventional metal panels once again.

The Olympia Show

The annual Motor Show had been a fixture at the Olympia exhibition hall in London ever since 1903 (although there had been some gaps during the 1914-1918 war). Always held in October, it marked the start of the motor manufacturers' "season". It was at this show that new models and new coachwork designs were previewed in the hope of attracting customer interest and orders for the following year, and as a consequence it was a very important event for the motor trade in general.

Freestone & Webb did not take a stand at Olympia until 1926, by which time they had been in business for three years. Perhaps the plan was purely to attract more business, but it is also undeniable that there was a certain cachet about having a stand at Olympia. If the company was to become firmly established among

COACH CRAFT

"*The Hall Mark of Quality Coachwork*"

Weymann Saloon by Freestone & Webb Ltd., on a 6-cyl. Bentley chassis.

See really beautiful coachwork on Stand 81

AT the Motor Exhibition we are showing two typical examples of our work—one a special Weymann Saloon on a 37.2 h.p. Hispano Suiza chassis ; the other, an open touring body on a 16/60 h.p. Voisin 6-cylinder chassis—and we hope to have an opportunity of discussing them with you and proving that our reputation is not only the result of the finest craftsmanship, but also of the exercise of a keen sense of beauty. Just as the hall-mark on silver is a definite proof of sterling quality, so the symbol " F. & W." is a sign of the very finest coachwork. Let us discuss your personal needs.

FREESTONE & WEBB LTD.,

UNITY WORKS, BRENTFIELD ROAD, WILLESDEN, N.W.10
Telephone : Willesden 4017.

Showrooms : 2, HALKIN PLACE, BELGRAVE SQUARE, S.W.1
Telephone : Sloane 5111.

the top-quality coachbuilders, it could not afford to be absent from that show.

The Olympia Show in October 1926 would therefore have been a big occasion for Freestone & Webb, and the company's management would have considered carefully how to make the most of it. So it is very interesting to see that the two bodies they chose to display that year were not bread-and-butter Bentley models but were on expensive and exotic imported chassis. There was a four-door touring body on the Voisin 16-60hp chassis to illustrate the company's skills with open coachwork, while a Weymann saloon demonstrated its design for enclosed bodies on a highly prestigious 6½-litre Hispano-Suiza H6B chassis. The association with Hispano would have made very clear indeed that Freestone & Webb worked with the best of the best, and in terms of public impact would almost certainly have been more effective than showing a body on a Rolls-Royce chassis.

The overall effect of the company's appearance at Olympia in 1926 was probably a greater public awareness of its existence and of its abilities. It does not seem to have prompted a sudden rush of new orders for the 1926-1927 season, when it looks as if Freestone & Webb built a comfortable 40 or so bodies. However, the company's reputation at the time was made very clear in *The Autocar* of 3 June 1927, which published a picture of a newly-completed Voisin with its coupé de ville coachwork and commented that "the body bears the stamp of being a production of a firm accustomed to turning out really good work."

So began the Freestone & Webb tradition of taking a stand at Olympia every October and displaying on

This 1926 advertisement refers to the bodies on Hispano-Suiza and Voisin chassis that Freestone & Webb displayed at Olympia that year, and is illustrated with an impressive-looking saloon body on a Bentley 6½-litre chassis, number WB2557. By this time, the company had showrooms off Belgrave Square in London. (Tom Clarke Collection)

FREESTONE & WEBB LTD

The FIRST Weymann Body

produced in this country upon conventional British lines
was built by Freestone & Webb.
We hold a direct licence for the construction of Weymann Bodies,
and have specialised, and consistently built, this type of coachwork since its inception. We would like to emphasise the fact
that we supply this type of body direct, or through recognised
motor agents of standing; also, that we have no connection with
any firm who claim selling or manufacturing rights for this
class of coachwork. Let us submit suggestions regarding the
body of your new car. A discussion implies no obligation.

COACH-CRAFT

The Hall Mark of Quality Coachwork

"F. & W." is the sign
of the very finest
coachwork and
stands for all that is
best in Weymann
construction.

Showrooms:
2, HALKIN PLACE,
BELGRAVE SQUARE, S.W.1
Sloane 5112.
UNITY WORKS,
BRENTFIELD ROAD,
WILLESDEN, N.W.10
Telephones: Willesden 4017-4018.

C44

KINDLY MENTION "THE MOTOR" WHEN CORRESPONDING WITH ADVERTISERS.

"The first Weymann body produced in this country along conventional British lines was built by Freestone & Webb," according to this advertisement from The Motor *for 1 March 1927. The illustration shows a four-light Weymann saloon on Bentley 6½-litre chassis FW2609, delivered in September 1926.*
(Tom Clarke Collection)

it two or more showpieces that would exhibit the company's skills to the best advantage. At the 1927 show, a smart Weymann saloon on a Crossley 20.9hp chassis was displayed next to a coupé de ville on a Bentley 6½-litre. In 1928, a Weymann saloon on a 4½-litre Bentley chassis stood alongside a coachbuilt saloon on a supercharged Mercedes-Benz Type S, demonstrating that Freestone & Webb were now beginning to move beyond Weymann fabric-panelled construction.

By the time of the 1929 Olympia Show, the name of Bentley was very much in the public eye. The company had once again triumphed at Le Mans that June with a Speed Six in first place followed by three 4½-litres in second, third and fourth. Tim Birkin made use of the show to present the first of his supercharged 4½-litre cars, and Freestone & Webb sensibly chose to ride the crest of that wave of interest. Their stand displayed a two-door sportsman's coupé on the 4½-litre chassis, and a limousine on the 6½-litre chassis. Both bodies featured the latest Triplex safety glass, newly available from the Triplex Imperial factory opened that September at Eccleston, near St Helens in Lancashire.

Developments in the late 1920s

The vast majority of known Freestone & Webb bodies from the company's earliest years were tourers or Weymann saloons. There were odd exceptions – Bentley two-seaters in 1923 and 1925, a sunroof saloon on Packard chassis in 1925, a Bentley folding-head coupé in 1927 – but these were very much exceptions. Then from the summer of 1927 it looks

as if the company made a deliberate attempt to extend the range of its coachwork styles. De ville designs carried maximum prestige, and the body built on a Voisin chassis in June 1927 seems to have been the first such coachwork from Freestone & Webb. A coupé de ville followed soon afterwards on the Bentley 6½-litre for that year's Olympia Show, then a sedanca de ville on a Hispano-Suiza H6B, and in 1928 there were a cabriolet de ville on a Bentley and a landaulette de ville on a Rolls-Royce Phantom.

There were novelties of other kinds, too. During 1928, the company built a special roadster on a Mercedes-Benz chassis, although it seems reasonably certain that the customer had a large say in the design of that. Drophead coupés began to figure in the repertoire, with one on a Mercedes-Benz chassis in 1928 and another on a Bentley 4½-litre the following year. Then 1929 brought some two-door saloons on the six-cylinder Bentley, and a pair of notably original "Grafton coupé" bodies, again on the 6½-litre Bentley chassis.

Perhaps the most important development in the later 1920s, however, was that move towards conventional metal panelled coachwork. Among the earliest examples of metal-panelled car bodies were two bodies on Voisin chassis, a saloon and a dual-cowl phaeton that were built during 1927. Although fabric-bodied Weymann types were still being built at Brentfield Road, the indications are that there were some bodies that combined metal lower panels with a Weymann-type fabric-covered roof – a type sometimes described as of "semi-Weymann" construction.

There would have been good reasons for this development. The public was beginning to turn away from fabric bodywork, thanks partly to the poor durability of the cheaper types. In addition, Nick Walker notes in A-Z British Coachbuilders that "fabric bodies were just not as attractive to look at as metal ones. They were dull instead of shiny, and they had sharp corners and flat panels instead of seductive curves…. Even their earlier advantage of being easier to clean had been nullified by the advent of cellulose paints."

Freestone & Webb could not have made the transition to metal panelling without taking on a number of new skilled men. A fleet of a dozen delivery vans (a most uncharacteristic order) on Austin Twenty chassis in 1929 may also have helped the Brentfield Road workforce become more familiar with this form of construction. But by this stage the company seemed to be on a sound footing and its owners probably considered that the financial risk was worth taking. Even then, they did not make the transition all at once, but rather over a period of years. If the first metal-panelled bodies were built in 1928, the last Weymann types were still being built in 1931.

The Mercedes-Benz Connection

In 1926, Germany's two oldest car makers merged to form the Daimler-Benz Aktiengesellschaft (AG). The products of the former Daimler Motorengesellschaft and Benz & Cie were thereafter sold as Mercedes-Benz cars, and the new company was understandably keen to establish itself in overseas markets. Among those was Great Britain, where British Mercedes-Benz Ltd was set up at 37 Davies Street in London's West End to act as importer.

Most of the cars that were imported through the London concessionaire were complete vehicles built in Germany, but the company was obviously well aware that customers for the most expensive chassis liked to have coachwork built to their own specifications, and so several bare chassis were also brought in.

Freestone & Webb was certainly not the only British coachbuilder to form a relationship with British Mercedes-Benz, but it did start early in the game and it did body at least a dozen chassis between 1926 and 1929. The earliest known example was a Weymann six-light saloon with vee screen supposedly built in 1926. It was built on either a 400 or a 630 chassis; from the surviving photograph it is hard to tell.

There then appears to have been a flurry of activity in 1928. New that year was an eight-cylinder chassis called the Nürburg or 460, and the Brentfield Road works appears to have bodied one of these as a six-light Weymann saloon. The combination of artillery wheels (common on this chassis) with a roof-mounted luggage rack made this look a rather heavy and old-fashioned design, but the cars built later that year would be very different.

British Mercedes-Benz had also started to bring in examples of the supercharged Type S, which was a car aimed very much at the wealthy playboy who enjoyed high performance. Four chassis went to Freestone & Webb during 1928 for coachwork, and both coachbuilder and importer obviously thought that this achievement should be recorded for posterity. So Freestone & Webb's regular photographer, Charles Bowers, was summoned and three of them, all in a part-finished state, were wheeled out of the workshops to be photographed. The fourth car had already been delivered to its no doubt delighted owner, a Captain Morton who had ordered a very special roadster body for it.

By 1929, British Mercedes-Benz was also importing examples of the new and more powerful supercharged Type SS, and naturally the Freestone & Webb efforts

This was the Freestone & Webb works at Brentfield Road in Stonebridge Park. The main erecting shop is in the centre, with a glass roof to provide maximum light. The picture dates from October 1928 and shows a number of Bentley models in the background, with a completed Crossley and a bare chassis in the road outside.

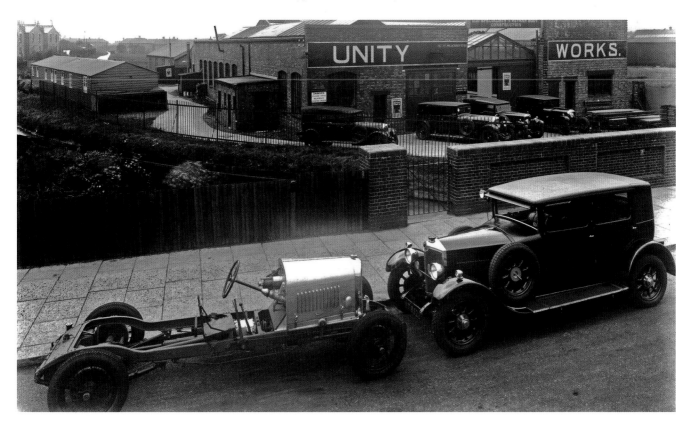

COACHWORK IN WHICH YOU CAN EXPRESS YOURSELF

◆ Freestone & Webb
are exhibiting at
STAND No. 70

1 The "Grafton" Weymann Coupé 4–5 seater on 4½-litre Bentley super-charged chassis.

2 The 4-door 4-light Weymann Sports Saloon with semi-bucket front seats and a removable drop-window division. Mounted on 6½-litre "Speed Six" Bentley chassis. A replica of this car will be shown at the Paris Motor Show in conjunction with Messrs. Rootes, Ltd.

The woman of to-day desires to show her individuality in the beautiful things with which she surrounds herself. Freestone and Webb ask her to let them help with expert knowledge and imagination in designing the coachwork for her new car. Come and talk matters over with their representative at Olympia.

Inspect for yourself the beauty and distinction of Freestone and Webb coachwork at Olympia

FREESTONE & WEBB Ltd.
Unity Works, Brentfield Road, Willesden, N.W. 10
Telephone: Willesden 4017-8

This advertisement from The Tatler *magazine of 16 October 1929 invites the lady of the house to have her say in choosing coachwork. The reference to the company's stand at Olympia is confusing – as Appendix A reveals, the Speed Six Bentley was not a sports saloon but had limousine coachwork. (Tom Clarke Collection)*

Also taken in October 1928, this was the back of Unity Works. Three Mercedes-Benz chassis are pictured, with their bodies in various stages of construction.

that year focussed on this chassis. There were at least three of them, and the importer displayed one – a fabric-panelled sportsman's coupé – on its own stand at Olympia in October 1929. This body was notable for its angled windscreen, accompanied by triangular glass side sections, and a similar feature appeared on Freestone & Webb's two-door tourer for an SS chassis that year. The third body on the SS chassis that year was a drophead coupé with a separate windscreen for the rear-seat passengers.

Probably the most interesting aspect of this relationship with British Mercedes-Benz was that Freestone & Webb had to design new bodies to suit the dimensions of the German chassis and used the opportunity to experiment with new shapes and styles. These bodies were symptomatic of the way the coachbuilder's horizons were broadening in the late 1920s.

Chapter Two

THE COACHWORK 1923-1929

Coachbuilding at Unity Works understandably got off to a rather slow start over the late summer and early autumn of 1923. It must have taken several months for the building works to be completed and for the new premises to be fitted out to suit the needs of the new company, and it is not hard to imagine the first bodies being constructed while all this was still going on.

We do not have a definitive list of the bodies that Freestone & Webb constructed in its first few months of existence in the second half of 1923, and our understanding of what went on has to be built up from scraps of information. Even so, it looks as if no more than two bodies were completed before the end of the year. Both were on Bentley 3-litre chassis. The first was probably completed in or around October 1923, which was the date when Bentley Motors issued the guarantee for the chassis on which it was built. All we know is that it was a saloon body; it must have been of traditional panelled construction, because Freestone & Webb had not yet taken out a Weymann licence to build fabric-panelled bodies.

The second body is generally thought to have been a two-seater, and Hay has suggested that it is the one pictured in a 1935 Freestone & Webb advertisement that refers to the company's long association with Bentley chassis. The picture is unfortunately too small to allow much to be deduced from it. That the body was a two-seater with a folding hood is clear; that the car was kitted out with wheel discs over its wire wheels is clear; but whether it had any other distinctive characteristics is simply impossible to say.

Sadly indistinct, this picture from a 1933 Freestone & Webb advertisement is claimed to represent an early two-seater body on a Bentley 3-litre chassis. It may well be the second car that the coachbuilder constructed.

THE 1923 BODY LIST

No body numbers are known for 1923. The bodies are therefore listed in order of their month of delivery, in so far as this is known. The "ID no" (Identity number) in the first column is a reference guide for research purposes only and does not reflect any numbering system used by Freestone & Webb. It is therefore shown within brackets. This list has been compiled on the basis of surviving evidence and is the most complete available, but it should not be regarded as definitive.

ID no	Type	Date	Chassis type	Chassis no
(23/1)	Saloon	1923, Oct	Bentley 3-litre	394
(23/2)	Two-seater?	1923?	Bentley 3-litre	Not known

Notes

(23/1) The saloon body on this car must have been built with conventional panelled construction, as Freestone & Webb had not yet taken out a Weymann licence.

(23/2) Michael Hay has suggested that a picture of this car surfaced in a 1933 Freestone & Webb advertisement, where it is described as "an early Bentley".

This picture comes from a Bentley sales brochure for the 6½-litre model, and actually shows the 1924 "Sun" prototype, its dummy radiator grille clearly evident. The body is a Freestone & Webb six-light Weymann saloon, probably selected by Bentley because of its light weight.

1924

Despite this slow start, Freestone & Webb seem to have been quick to get into their stride. During 1924, their first full calendar year, they turned out either 24 or 25 bodies. Of these, three were rebodies – that is, new bodies on earlier chassis – and the construction date of one of these is unclear, resulting in a question-mark over the total output for that year.

Although some of the 1924 Freestone & Webb bodies were of an unknown type, most of the known ones were Weymann saloons. In the October 1924 catalogue for the Bentley 3-litre, the chassis maker described Freestone & Webb's six-light Weymann saloon as follows:

"The Company's Standard Flexible Saloon has four doors, the front seats are of the sliding type and the screen is straight with a divided top half. The interior can be upholstered in leather or cloth to choice."

It went on to say that "a good variety both of colours and surface finish is available, from which a choice of panel fabric can be made." So although the basic design of the Weymann saloon for Bentley chassis may not have varied much, these bodies were by no means all the same.

Nevertheless, there was still a strong demand for open coachwork at the time, and the second most popular type from Freestone & Webb was a four-seat tourer. The known examples had a barrel-sided design, and shared a pair of characteristics with the saloons. One was the tool boxes sunk into the running-boards, and the other was a distinctive shape to the leading edge of

the front wings. In tandem, these two remain enough to aid the identification of a body as a Freestone & Webb product.

Of the remaining 1924 bodies, one was a coupé about which we know nothing because there are no known photographs, and the other was a two-door saloon. However, this was the rebody of questionable date, and might not actually have been built in 1924 at all.

Most obvious is that Freestone & Webb had already developed a good relationship with Bentley Motors. No fewer than 23 (or perhaps 22) of those 1924 bodies were on Bentley chassis, and by October 1924 the company's six-light Weymann saloon had become a catalogued option for the 3-litre chassis. Bentley had taken one as a demonstrator and had ordered a similar body for their prototype six-cylinder chassis (see below).

The association with Bentley chassis was clearly fundamental to the company's output during 1924. However, it was also broadening its offerings to include other top-quality chassis, and that year brought two commissions on Rolls-Royce chassis. One was a saloon on the Twenty chassis, delivered in October 1924, and the other was a body of unknown type on the now elderly 40/50 Silver Ghost chassis. Quite obviously, Freestone & Webb were aiming their business at the high end of the market and, on the face of it, were attracting the custom that they wanted.

The "Sun" prototype
When WO Bentley needed a body for the prototype six-

cylinder Bentley in 1924, he commissioned Freestone & Webb to build a six-light Weymann saloon for it. Some commentators have suggested that this was an odd choice, and that the body was deliberately ugly to deflect attention from the prototype chassis (which also had a dummy radiator grille proclaiming it to be a "Sun"). These opinions miss the point completely.

The fact was that the body on the "Sun" was very similar indeed to the six-light Freestone & Webb Weymann body on Bentley 3-litre number 648, which sales manager HM Bentley (WO's older brother) had ordered as a company demonstrator in spring 1924. This was exactly the right car for the job because it represented the type of body that so many Bentley buyers seemed to want – even though WO had envisaged the Bentley chassis as best suited to minimal sporting bodies. A big problem with traditionally-built saloon bodies was that they were very heavy and that this hindered the performance of the chassis, but Freestone & Webb's coachwork was known to be light in weight, thanks of course to its Weymann construction.

THE 1924 BODY LIST

No body numbers are known for 1924. The bodies are therefore listed in order of their month of delivery, in so far as this is known, and this is deduced from the date of the Bentley chassis guarantee that was issued after the completed car had been tested with its body in place. The "ID no" (Identity number) in the first column is a reference guide for research purposes only and does not reflect any numbering system used by Freestone & Webb. It is therefore shown within brackets. This list has been compiled on the basis of surviving evidence and is the most complete available, but it should not be regarded as definitive.

ID no	Type	Date	Chassis type	Chassis no
(24/1)	Tourer	1924, Mar	Bentley 3-litre	474
(24/2)	Unknown	1924, Apr	Bentley 3-litre	513
(24/3)	Tourer	1924, May	Bentley 3-litre	567
(24/4)	Tourer?	1924, May	Bentley 3-litre	593
(24/5)	Tourer	1924, May	Bentley 3-litre	603
(24/6)	Weymann six-light saloon	1924, May	Bentley 3-litre	648
(24/7)	Tourer?	1924, Jun	Bentley 3-litre	661
(24/8)	Weymann six-light saloon	1924, xxx	Bentley six-cylinder	EX1
(24/9)	Coupé	1924, Aug	Bentley 3-litre	700
(24/10)	Weymann six-light saloon	1924, Sep	Bentley 3-litre	778
(24/11)	Weymann two-door, four-light saloon	1924, Sep	Bentley 3-litre	779
(24/12)	Weymann saloon	1924, Sep	Bentley 3-litre	792
(24/13)	Four-seater	1924, Oct	Bentley 3-litre	791
(24/14)	Weymann six-light saloon	1924, Oct	Bentley 3-litre	768
(24/15)	Weymann saloon	1924, Oct	Bentley 3-litre	813
(24/16)	Weymann six-light saloon	1924, Oct	Bentley 3-litre	826
(24/17)	Saloon	1924, Oct	Rolls-Royce Twenty	GDK61
(24/18)	Tourer	1924, Nov	Bentley 3-litre	797
(24/19)	Unknown	1924, Nov	Bentley 3-litre	878
(24/20)	Weymann saloon	1924, Dec	Bentley 3-litre	875
(24/21)	Unknown	1924, Dec	Bentley 3-litre	927
(24/22)	Tourer	1924, Dec	Bentley 3-litre	939
(24/23)	Weymann six-light saloon	1924?	Bentley 3-litre	164
(24/24)	Weymann saloon	1924, xxx	Bentley 3-litre Speed model	470
(24/25)	Unknown	1924, xxx	Rolls-Royce Silver Ghost	62EM

Notes

(**24/6**) This is the earliest known Weymann body by Freestone & Webb, and it became a Bentley demonstrator.

(**24/8**) This was the prototype that was disguised as "The Sun" when on test in France over summer 1924.

(**24/11**) This may be a rebody of a later date than 1924.

(**24/23**) This was a rebody; the date has been estimated.

(**24/24**) This was a rebody that was carried out in late 1924; the car originally had an open four-seater body by Cadogan.

(**24/25**) The date of this body has been estimated from the chassis number.

1925

Freestone & Webb seem to have expanded massively during 1925, no doubt buoyed by a successful 1924. Although the total of 52 bodies turned up by research may not be completely accurate, it is unlikely to be very far away from the real total. This means that in 1925, the Brentfield Road works turned out twice as many bodies as it had in the previous year. It was a significant result that indicated the company was attracting plenty of custom.

It was good quality custom, too. Several more makes of chassis were now receiving Freestone & Webb coachwork, and all of them were expensive ones. From building only on the Bentley 3-litre in 1923, the company had progressed in 1924 to add a handful of Rolls-Royce chassis, and in 1925 had positively blossomed. Most of those 52 bodies were still on Bentley chassis, and there were three on Rolls-Royce types, one being a New Phantom and the others on the Twenty chassis. But there were many others, and a pair of Packards plus single examples of Bugatti, Crossley, Delage, Mercedes, Minerva, Panhard, Sizaire and Sunbeam were all among the 1925 crop.

During 1925, the company also expanded its range of body types. Although nine of that year's 52 bodies were of unknown type, there were at least nine types among the remainder if variations on the basic types are counted. Besides the most popular four-seat tourer and saloon types, there were a two-seat tourer, two Light Tourers (special lightweight bodies for the 3-litre Bentley), a drophead coupé, a cabriolet, a coupé, a sunroof saloon and a collapsible saloon, the latter with some sort of folding head arrangement. Clearly, Freestone & Webb were busily building a reputation for versatility.

This January 1925 picture by Charles Bowers, who worked regularly for several London coachbuilders, probably shows the body (here numbered (24/24)) that Freestone & Webb created to replace a Cadogan four-seater on Bentley 3-litre Speed chassis number 470. The contrast between the fabric of the lower panels and the highly polished "tôle souple" above the waist is very clear.

This reputation for lightness of construction is confirmed by a story that John W de Campi recounts in the January-February 2001 issue of *The Flying Lady* magazine. He explains that Reggie Beaumont-Thomas, the heir to a great steel fortune and a lover of fast cars, consulted London dealer Gordon Watney about coachwork for his new Rolls-Royce Phantom. "Reggie felt Hooper and Barker bodies were too heavy and degraded the performance of the car. It was Watney who recommended Freestone & Webb for attractive bodies that were lightweight and offered a 'good turn of speed.'" Reggie Beaumont-Thomas would go on to play an important part in the Freestone & Webb story in the early 1930s, and would remain friends with AJ Webb until the latter's death in 1954.

The six-light Weymann saloon design is familiar, but has been scaled down considerably for this small Bugatti chassis. It is a Type 23 Brescia Modifié, with a 93-inch wheelbase – considerably less than the 130 inches of a long-chassis Bentley 3-litre. This body is catalogued as number (25/20).

Very much in the same mould is the body numbered here as (25/21), photographed on the same day as the Bugatti, pictured left. The chassis this time is a Minerva.

Dating probably from July 1925, this neat two-door Weymann body on a Delage chassis has a semi-boat-tail feature that suggests growing confidence in design at Brentfield Road. The body is catalogued here as number (25/34).

Freestone & Webb built some standardised 4/5-seat tourer bodies for the Bentley 3-litre chassis, and this barrel-sided body is believed to show the example on chassis number 900. It is catalogued here as number (25/23).

The same familiar six-light Weymann saloon design sufficed for this Packard chassis, believed to be a type 336 with eight-cylinder engine. Body number (25/36) was probably completed in August 1925.

Remarkably, the original October 1925 six-light Weymann saloon body still survives on this Bentley 3-litre. Although the driver's door has clearly dropped, the handsome lines of body number (25/44) remain clear in this 2010 photograph. (via VintageBentleys.org)

The same basic six-light design was adapted to suit a Crossley chassis, probably a 19.6hp. This is body number (25/33), and was probably completed in July 1925.

There is a another truncated boat-tail feature at the rear of this Sports Torpedo body (25/40) on a Bentley 3-litre Speed chassis, probably NR522 dating from September 1925. In this case, the body is panelled rather than covered in fabric in the Weymann style.

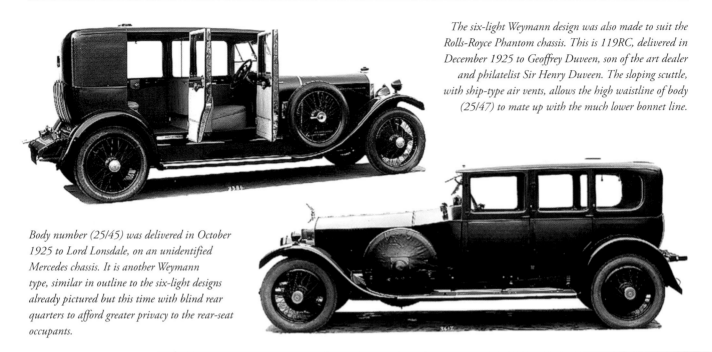

The six-light Weymann design was also made to suit the Rolls-Royce Phantom chassis. This is 119RC, delivered in December 1925 to Geoffrey Duveen, son of the art dealer and philatelist Sir Henry Duveen. The sloping scuttle, with ship-type air vents, allows the high waistline of body (25/47) to mate up with the much lower bonnet line.

Body number (25/45) was delivered in October 1925 to Lord Lonsdale, on an unidentified Mercedes chassis. It is another Weymann type, similar in outline to the six-light designs already pictured but this time with blind rear quarters to afford greater privacy to the rear-seat occupants.

THE 1925 BODY LIST

No body numbers are known for 1925. The bodies are therefore listed in order of their month of delivery, in so far as this is known. Dates for Bentley chassis have been deduced from the date of the chassis guarantee that was issued after the completed car had been tested with its body in place. The "ID no" (Identity number) in the first column is a reference guide for research purposes only and does not reflect any numbering system used by Freestone & Webb. It is therefore shown within brackets. This list has been compiled on the basis of surviving evidence and is the most complete available, but it should not be regarded as definitive.

ID no	Type	Date	Chassis type	Chassis no
(25/1)	Four-seater (or drophead coupé)	1925, Jan	Bentley 3-litre	911
(25/2)	Weymann saloon	1925, Jan	Bentley 3-litre	912
(25/3)	Weymann six-light saloon	1925, Jan	Bentley 3-litre	934
(25/4)	Unknown	1925, Jan	Bentley 3-litre	971
(25/5)	Weymann saloon	1925, Feb	Bentley 3-litre	920
(25/6)	Two-seater	1925, Feb	Bentley 3-litre	924
(25/7)	Unknown	1925, Feb	Bentley 3-litre	944
(25/8)	Tourer	1925, Feb	Bentley 3-litre	949
(25/9)	Tourer	1925, Feb	Bentley 3-litre	1000
(25/10)	Unknown	1925, Feb	Bentley 3-litre	1006
(25/11)	Tourer	1925, Mar	Bentley 3-litre	929
(25/12)	Tourer	1925, Mar	Bentley 3-litre	947
(25/13)	Tourer	1925, Mar	Bentley 3-litre	960
(25/14)	Weymann six-light saloon?	1925, Mar	Bentley 3-litre	1001
(25/15)	Saloon	1925, Mar	Bentley 3-litre	1021
(25/16)	Weymann saloon	1925, Apr	Bentley 3-litre	941
(25/17)	Tourer	1925, Apr	Bentley 3-litre	975
(25/18)	Tourer	1925, Apr	Bentley 3-litre	984
(25/19)	Unknown	1925, Apr	Bentley 3-litre	1010
(25/20)	Weymann saloon	1925, May	Bugatti T23 Brescia Modifié	Not known
(25/21)	Weymann six-light saloon	1925, May	Minerva	Not known
(25/22)	Flexible fabric coupé	1925, May	Panhard	Not known
(25/23)	Tourer	1925, May	Bentley 3-litre	900
(25/24)	Unknown	1925, May	Bentley 3-litre	1039
(25/25)	Weymann saloon	1925, May	Bentley 3-litre	1051
(25/26)	Unknown	1925, May	Bentley 3-litre	1053

Chassis-makers Packard appear to have called this body a Fully Collapsible Sedan. The fabric roof folded down at the rear, and the window pillars appear to have hinged inwards. The chassis was a 433 Six type and the picture of body (25/49) was taken just before Christmas 1925. Unfortunately, no relevant information is held in the Packard archives of the Studebaker Museum in South Bend, Indiana.

December 1925 again, and the six-light Weymann body is here adapted to suit a chassis from Sizaire Frères. The open rear door shows what must have been the coachbuilder's plate on the entry step of body number (25/48).

The six-light Weymann body was also adapted to suit this Sunbeam 3-litre chassis, which was photographed on the same day as the Packard in December 1925. This body is catalogued as number (25/50).

(25/27)	Tourer?	1925, Jun	Bentley 3-litre	851
(25/28)	Unknown	1925, Jun	Bentley 3-litre	1097
(25/29)	Tourer	1925, July	Bentley 3-litre	1105
(25/30)	Tourer	1925, July	Bentley 3-litre	1109
(25/31)	Unknown	1925, July	Bentley 3-litre	1124
(25/32)	Tourer	1925, July	Bentley 3-litre	1152
(25/33)	Six-light Saloon	1925, July	Crossley 19.6hp	Not known
(25/34)	Weymann two-door Saloon	1925, July	Delage	Not known
(25/35)	Tourer	1925, Aug	Bentley 3-litre	1130
(25/36)	Weymann? saloon	1925, Aug?	Packard 336?	Not known
(25/37)	Tourer	1925, Sep	Bentley 3-litre	1149
(25/38)	Weymann saloon	1925, Sep	Bentley 3-litre	1164
(25/39)	Unknown	1925, Sep	Bentley 3-litre	1182
(25/40)	Tourer	1925, Sep	Bentley 3-litre Speed model	NR522
(25/41)	Tourer	1925, Oct	Bentley 3-litre	1103
(25/42)	Tourer	1925, Oct	Bentley 3-litre	1150
(25/43)	Weymann saloon	1925, Oct	Bentley 3-litre	1155
(25/44)	Weymann saloon	1925, Oct	Bentley 3-litre	1194
(25/45)	Weymann saloon	1925, Oct	Mercedes	Not known
(25/46)	Weymann saloon	1925, Dec	Bentley 3-litre	1203
(25/47)	Saloon	1925, Dec	Rolls-Royce Phantom	119RC
(25/48)	Six-light saloon	1925, Dec	Sizaire Frères	Not known
(25/49)	Convertible saloon	1925, Dec	Packard 433 Six	Not known
(25/50)	Six-light saloon	1925, Dec	Sunbeam 3-litre	4198F
(25/51)	Cabriolet	1925, xxx	Rolls-Royce Twenty	GYK18
(25/52)	Saloon	1925, xxx	Rolls-Royce Twenty	GYK56

Notes
(25/32) This was a Light Touring model. The Light Touring variant of the Bentley 3-litre was introduced in summer 1925, was deliberately built down to a price (under £1000), and had a strict overall weight limit. It was a short-chassis model and the weight of 32cwt (3584 lb, 1625 kg) that Bentley imposed on it was intended to prevent customers from ruining its performance with heavy coachwork. Around half were bodied by Vanden Plas but the others attracted coachwork by various companies.
(25/40) Hay calls this a "sports torpedo" body.
(25/42) This was another Light Tourer (see above).
(25/49) This body has also been described as a "fully-collapsible sedan".

A good 80% of Freestone & Webb's 1926 output was for Bentley chassis, and this attractive four-light Weymann sports saloon was one of several similar bodies built on the short-chassis 3-litre in 1925-1926. This body is catalogued as number (26/8) and was pictured in March 1926, before delivery the following month.

Freestone & Webb were favoured by the British importers of the newly created Mercedes-Benz marque, and applied their six-light Weymann saloon design to this chassis, either a 400 or a 630, in April 1926. The vee-windscreen of body (26/11) introduces a subtle and no doubt fashionable difference. The car was for a Dr Cowan of Fitzroy Square in London.

1926

Bentley chassis predominated again at Brentfield Road during the 1926 calendar-year, accounting for 36 of that year's 45 known bodies. There were six of the new 6½-litre six-cylinder models as well as the familiar 3-litres. Although no more Rolls-Royce chassis were bodied this year, there was a single Lanchester, which was a very expensive and highly regarded make at the time. The other nine bodies were all on imported chassis, which therefore represented a little over 19% of Freestone & Webb's known business for 1926.

This work on imported chassis was clearly important, because when two cars were selected for display on Freestone & Webb's first-ever stand at Olympia in the autumn, one was a Hispano-Suiza and the other a Voisin. The Hispano was a hugely prestigious and expensive chassis, and was shown with a rather grand six-light Weymann saloon body that was broadly similar to the coachbuilder's contemporary offering on Bentley chassis; the Voisin was presented as a large tourer. These two bodies were very much representative of what Freestone & Webb were doing at the time, and were probably chosen for that very reason.

New chassis in the Freestone & Webb repertoire this year were the Voisin (of which there were three), the Hispano (two), and an Itala, which would be the only one the company ever bodied. There was a single Mercedes-Benz, a make which was of course new that year, having been formed by the merger of Benz & Cie and the Daimler Motorengesellschaft which used the Mercedes brand name. British Mercedes-Benz, the London importer, would go on to become a regular customer for Freestone & Webb coachwork in later years. A single Packard followed the two bodied in 1925, although Packard would not go on to figure regularly in the Freestone & Webb output. Then there was a single chassis that has been tentatively identified from photographs as a Delage.

Pictured in May 1926 was this two-door saloon (26/15) on a Voisin chassis. Despite the restrictions of the Weymann construction, the lines are very pleasing.

Only one Freestone & Webb body is known for an Itala chassis, and this is it. Once again the six-light Weymann style did the job admirably. Body number (26/19) was photographed in June 1926.

The longer wheelbase and deeper chassis of the Packard 333 Six required some adjustments to Freestone & Webb's six-light Weymann saloon design, which is nonetheless still readily recognisable. Pictured in June 1926, this body (26/20) has a folding roof section above the front compartment.

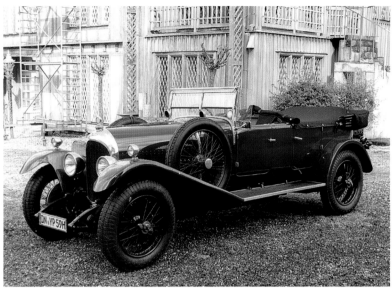

Excluding the 1924 prototype "Sun" chassis, this was the first Bentley 6½-litre to be bodied by Freestone & Webb. The scuttle ventilators lend distinction to body (26/25) from July 1926, and the wheel discs give an air of modernity – but this is still essentially the six-light saloon design introduced in 1924.

The barrel-sided tourer (26/22) with its metal panels was still in vogue for Bentley 3-litre chassis in 1926, and this one was new to an owner in South Africa in July that year. It has survived in astonishingly original condition as a rare example of Freestone & Webb's early coachwork. Now on standard wheels, it carries twin spares that show the size of the original wheels fitted for "colonial" conditions. (Klaus-Josef Rossfeldt)

A shorter scuttle and blind rear quarters helped this four-light saloon (26/26) on Lanchester chassis to look almost individual, although the basic shape was very familiar at Brentfield Road by July 1926 when it was photographed.

This four-light Weymann saloon (26/35) on the six-cylinder Bentley chassis successfully combined a sporting appearance with an integral luggage boot – quite an advanced feature for 1926 – although there was also a traditional folding luggage grid for good measure! It had a vee-windscreen and ship-type scuttle ventilators.

This six-light saloon (26/37) on the Hispano-Suiza 37.2hp chassis was destined to display Brentfield Road's abilities on the company's first Olympia Show stand. The design was typical of the company's work at the time.

This tourer body (26/38) on a Voisin 16-60hp chassis displayed Freestone & Webb's skills with open coachwork on the stand at Olympia in 1926. As with the six-light Hispano body on the stand, it was not radically new, and had some clear similarities with the tourer bodies then being produced for Bentley chassis.

This four-light body (26/43) introduced some new features and betrays clear American influence. The triangular glasses beside the windscreen are a novel feature and this body may have been the first one from Freestone & Webb to feature dummy landau irons. There is some question over the identity of the chassis: the Hispano-style stork mascot is misleading, and this is probably actually a Delage.

This stylish two-seater body (26/45) was built on a Bentley 3-litre with the standard 11ft wheelbase, and the panels in the top of the "bustle" suggest that it might have had a dickey seat. The body is of Weymann construction but was panelled in leather rather than in fabric.

Freestone & Webb proudly recorded the interior of their Hispano body for the 1926 Show. Its spaciousness comes across very clearly, and the body received praise in The Motor *for its interior decoration.*

THE 1926 BODY LIST

No body numbers are known for 1926. The bodies are therefore listed in order of their month of delivery, in so far as this is known. Dates for Bentley chassis have been deduced from the date of the chassis guarantee that was issued after the completed car had been tested with its body in place. The "ID no" (Identity number) in the first column is a reference guide for research purposes only and does not reflect any numbering system used by Freestone & Webb. It is therefore shown within brackets. This list has been compiled on the basis of surviving evidence and is the most complete available, but it should not be regarded as definitive.

ID no	Type	Date	Chassis type	Chassis no
(26/1)	Unknown	1926, Jan	Bentley 3-litre	HP377
(26/2)	Unknown	1926, Jan	Bentley 3-litre	HP385
(26/3)	Weymann saloon	1926, Jan	Bentley 3-litre	HP392
(26/4)	Weymann saloon	1926, Jan	Bentley 3-litre	HP397
(26/5)	Tourer	1926, Feb	Bentley 3-litre	AH1492
(26/6)	Unknown	1926, Feb	Bentley 3-litre	AH1493
(26/7)	Unknown	1926, Mar	Bentley 3-litre	HP391
(26/8)	Weymann saloon	1926, Apr	Bentley 3-litre	HP394
(26/9)	Weymann saloon	1926, Apr	Bentley 3-litre	SR1414
(26/10)	Weymann saloon	1926, Apr	Bentley 3-litre	SR1415
(26/11)	Six-light saloon	1926, Apr	Mercedes-Benz 400 or 630	Not known
(26/12)	Weymann saloon	1926, May	Bentley 3-litre	PH1452
(26/13)	Weymann saloon	1926, May	Bentley 3-litre	PH1458
(26/14)	Weymann saloon	1926, May	Bentley 3-litre	RT1529
(26/15)	Two-door saloon	1926, May	Voisin	Not known
(26/16)	Weymann saloon	1926, Jun	Bentley 3-litre	AH1487
(26/17)	Weymann saloon	1926, Jun	Bentley 3-litre	SR1416
(26/18)	Weymann saloon	1926, Jun	Bentley 3-litre	RT1530
(26/19)	Six-light saloon	1926, Jun	Itala	Not known
(26/20)	Sunroof saloon	1925, Jun	Packard 333 Six	Not known
(26/21)	Tourer	1926, July	Bentley 3-litre	SR1411
(26/22)	Tourer	1926, July	Bentley 3-litre	SR1413
(26/23)	Weymann six-light saloon	1926, July	Bentley 3-litre	RT1543
(26/24)	Weymann saloon	1926, July	Bentley 3-litre	DE1207
(26/25)	Weymann saloon	1926, July	Bentley 6½-litre	WB2557
(26/26)	Weymann saloon	1926, July	Lanchester	Not known
(26/27)	Weymann saloon	1926, Aug	Bentley 3-litre	DE1210
(26/28)	Tourer	1926, Aug	Bentley 3-litre	LM1328
(26/29)	Weymann saloon	1926, Aug	Bentley 3-litre	RE1382
(26/30)	Weymann saloon	1926, Aug	Bentley 3-litre	RE1385
(26/31)	Weymann saloon	1926, Sep	Bentley 3-litre	PH1464
(26/32)	Weymann saloon	1926, Sep	Bentley 3-litre	LM1340
(26/33)	Weymann saloon	1926, Sep	Bentley 3-litre	RE1380
(26/34)	Two-seater	1926, Sep	Bentley 6½-litre	TB2543
(26/35)	Weymann saloon	1926, Sep	Bentley 6½-litre	FW2609
(26/36)	Tourer	1926, Sep	Bentley 6½-litre	FW2616
(26/37)	Weymann saloon	1926, Sep	Hispano-Suiza 37.2hp	Not known
(26/38)	Tourer	1926, Sep	Voisin 16-60hp	Not known
(26/39)	Weymann saloon	1926, Oct	Voisin	Not known
(26/40)	Weymann saloon	1926, Oct	Bentley 3-litre	RE1384
(26/41)	Weymann saloon	1926, Oct	Bentley 6½-litre	TB2536
(26/42)	Saloon	1926, Nov	Bentley 3-litre	LT1583
(28/43)	Saloon	1926, Nov	Delage	Not known
(26/44)	Weymann saloon	1926, Dec	Bentley 3-litre	TN1554
(26/45)	Two-seater (Weymann)	1926, Dec	Bentley 6½-litre	TW2702

Notes

(**26/37**) This car was on the Freestone & Webb stand at Olympia in October 1926, which was the first time the company exhibited there.

(**26/38**) This car was on the Freestone & Webb stand at Olympia in October 1926.

(**26/43**) Pictures show that this car carried the stork radiator mascot associated with Hispano-Suiza, but that it was not a Hispano. The identification as a Delage is not confirmed.

1927

The Freestone & Webb output for 1927 remained healthy, and a total of 44 bodies have been identified as leaving the Brentfield Road works that year, just one less than in 1926. Most noticeable, perhaps, is that the cheaper tourer bodies had largely disappeared from the company's repertoire – there was just one, on a Minerva chassis – and that new and more expensive types were beginning to appear. That trend very probably offset

The single-pane windscreen was an advanced feature on this four-light body (27/4) for a Crossley chassis that was almost certainly a 20.9hp type. The body clearly has fabric panels, and retains the windscreen peak characteristic of closed Freestone & Webb bodies at the time.
(The Crossley Register)

This interior view of the same body makes clear that the landau irons were only dummies. There is a coachbuilder's plate on the sill at both front and rear, but neither carries a body number.
(The Crossley Register)

any financial shortfall from the slight reduction in the number of bodies that were completed.

The trend towards closed bodies was general in the motor industry in the mid-1920s, and there were only two open bodies from Brentfield Road in addition to that single Minerva tourer. One was a drophead coupé on a Bentley 3-litre, and the other an unusual dual-cowl phaeton on a Voisin chassis. By far the majority of the Freestone & Webb bodies built in 1927 were Weymann saloons, and most of those seem to have had the established six-light design. Nevertheless, some new ideas were appearing, and among those saloon bodies were some with a four-light design that had a far more sporting air to it. One of the four-light saloons was on a Crossley chassis for the 1927 Olympia Show, and another was on a 6½-litre Bentley chassis.

Weymann bodies with fabric panels were still Freestone & Webb's stock-in-trade, but it was in 1927 that metal-panelled bodies began to reappear. At least two seem to have been built this year, a saloon (27/21) and the dual-cowl phaeton (27/34), both on Voisin chassis. Did the British importers of Voisin perhaps have a special interest in metal-panelled bodies? The coincidence would otherwise be hard to explain.

Among the 1927 bodies was a folding-head saloon on a Crossley chassis, which followed on from a similar body on a Packard in 1926. Surviving photographs of the folding head under construction bear witness to the special interest that the company took in this body. It is likely, but unfortunately not certain, that this folding-head body was the one displayed on the

Olympia Show stand.

Perhaps the highlight of the 1927 output was that Freestone & Webb built their first grand and expensive "de ville" bodies, a reflection no doubt of the esteem in which they were now held. There were four of these: a coupé de ville on the Bentley 6½-litre chassis, a second on a Voisin, and two sedanca de ville bodies on Hispano-Suiza chassis. The company had every right to be proud of these, and displayed the Bentley on its Olympia Show stand. It was of this Voisin that *The Autocar* of 3 June 1927 reported it "bears the stamp of being a production of a firm accustomed to turning

A Weymann six-light saloon body (27/10) is seen here on a Rolls-Royce Twenty chassis, delivered to RW Paul in February 1927. This was presumably the pioneer cinematographer Robert W Paul. Unpainted bonnet panels were a fashion in the mid-1920s.

Freestone & Webb were pushing the boundaries with this remarkable four-light saloon body in spring 1927. The metal panels clearly allowed more adventurous shapes than were possible with Weymann fabric construction, and the huge double trunk is a notable feature. Body number (27/16) was on a Bentley 6½-litre chassis with the 130-inch wheelbase and was built for the pioneer aviator Marcel Desoutter.

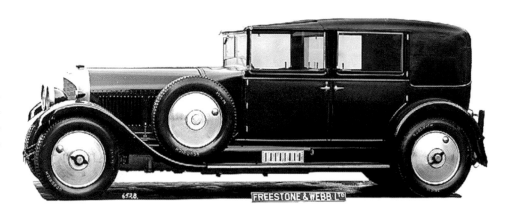

With confidence came even grander coachwork: this coupé de ville body (27/18) was on another Bentley 6½-litre chassis. This is likely to have been the 1927 Olympia Show car, although the identity of the 6½-litre on the Freestone & Webb stand is disputed.

By 1927, the Bentley 3-litre was getting old, and this example looks distinctly old-fashioned with its exposed wire wheels. Body number (27/20) is a fairly conventional four-light Weymann saloon with dummy landau irons – but note that the door tops do not have the usual polished "tôle souple" finish.

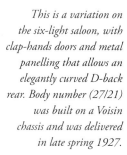

This is a variation on the six-light saloon, with clap-hands doors and metal panelling that allows an elegantly curved D-back rear. Body number (27/21) was built on a Voisin chassis and was delivered in late spring 1927.

out really good work". The two Hispanos were for celebrities of the day, one going to the businessman and socialite Harry Oakes (later Sir Harry) and the other probably to the band leader and impresario Jack Hylton. Attracting orders from such prominent figures could only have been good for the business in general.

As for the chassis that Freestone & Webb bodied in 1927, the majority were again of Bentley manufacture. There were 13 of the 6½-litres, 11 of the older 3-litres (one being a rebody of a Bentley experimental chassis), and two on their new 4½-litre replacement. Rolls-Royce provided seven chassis, of which four were Phantoms and three were Twentys. Crossley and Voisin provided three each; there were two from Hispano-Suiza, and single examples came from Delage, Minerva, and Sunbeam, the last-named being one of the rare 35hp eight-cylinder chassis.

More top-quality work went into this metal-panelled coupé de ville body on a Voisin chassis, with disc-type wheels that make it look much more modern than the six-light saloon pictured opposite. Body number (27/25) incorporated a landaulette-style folding rear roof.

In June 1927, this folding-head body (27/27) on a Crossley chassis was pictured under construction. Note how the rear of the roof was formed as a separate, solid piece. This may have become the 1927 Olympia Show car, listed here with body number (27/35), although Show reports make no mention of a folding head.

This is almost certainly the saloon body (27/26) built on a Rolls-Royce Phantom chassis for Reggie Beaumont-Thomas in summer 1927. Note how the roof peak has now gone from above the windscreen. The side-mounted spare is missing in the picture. Beaumont-Thomas would later play an important part in the Freestone & Webb business.

The six-light fabric-panelled saloon still looked elegant, although its basic design with a peak over the windscreen was now beginning to date. Here it is on a Delage chassis. Body number (27/29) was completed in summer 1927.

*Further evidence of Freestone &
Webb's ability to challenge the
best was this Sedanca de Ville
body (27/33) built on a Hispano
Suiza chassis and delivered to the
American-born businessman and
philanthropist Harry Oakes (later
Sir Harry Oakes)*

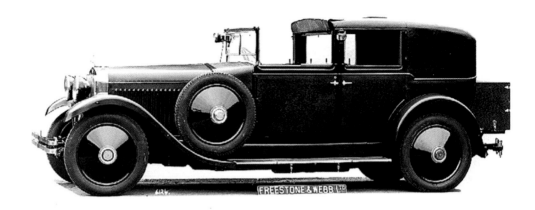

*The artillery-type wheels on this Crossley chassis did the
car no favours, but this neat Weymann saloon (27/35) was
displayed at the 1927 Olympia Show. Dummy landau
irons were quite common on the closed bodies by this time.*

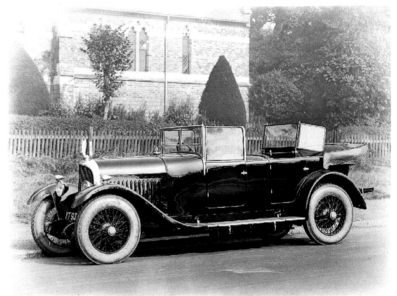

*This dual-cowl phaeton body (27/34) is a distant relative
of the barrel-sided tourer that Freestone & Webb had been
making for several years. It was built on a Voisin chassis
and was completed in October 1927.*

*Only the second body on a Sunbeam
chassis from Freestone & Webb was this
four-light fabric-panelled saloon (27/36)
completed in October 1927. The low-
slung chassis required the spare wheel to
protrude above the bonnet-line.*

*Contemporary with the Sunbeam was
this four-light saloon (27/37) on a Rolls-
Royce Phantom chassis. The design is quite
different, with deeper windows, and the
waistline has been carefully aligned with the
higher bonnet line of this chassis. The plain
rear panels make clear that this is a formal
body, while the dummy landau irons on the
Sunbeam give it a deliberately sporting air.*

THE 1927 BODY LIST

No body numbers are known for 1927. The bodies are therefore listed in order of their month of delivery, in so far as this is known. Dates for Bentley chassis have been deduced from the date of the chassis guarantee that was issued after the completed car had been tested with its body in place. The "ID no" (Identity number) in the first column is a reference guide for research purposes only and does not reflect any numbering system used by Freestone & Webb. It is therefore shown within brackets. This list has been compiled on the basis of surviving evidence and is the most complete available, but it should not be regarded as definitive..

ID no	Type	Date	Chassis type	Chassis no
(27/1)	Saloon	1927, Jan	Bentley 3-litre	TN1555
(27/2)	Weymann saloon	1927, Jan	Bentley 6½-litre	FW2625
(27/3)	Weymann saloon	1927, Jan	Bentley 6½-litre	WK2660
(27/4)	Weymann saloon	1927, Feb	Crossley, probably 20.9	Not known
(27/5)	Weymann saloon	1927, Feb	Bentley 3-litre	TN1561
(27/6)	Weymann saloon	1927, Feb	Bentley 3-litre	TN1565
(27/7)	Weymann saloon	1927, Feb	Bentley 3-litre	TN1575
(27/8)	Weymann saloon	1927, Feb	Bentley 6½-litre	WK2675
(27/9)	Weymann saloon	1927, Feb	Bentley 6½-litre	TW2712
(27/10)	Weymann six-light saloon	1927, Feb	Rolls-Royce Twenty	GMJ7
(27/11)	Two-seat drophead coupé	1927, Mar	Bentley 3-litre	TN1568
(27/12)	Saloon	1927, Mar	Bentley 3-litre	BL1609
(27/13)	Weymann saloon	1927, Mar	Bentley 6½-litre	TW2719
(27/14)	Weymann saloon	1927, Mar	Bentley 6½-litre	FW2606
(27/15)	Weymann saloon	1927, Apr	Bentley 3-litre Speed model	AX1655
(27/16)	Saloon	1927, Apr	Bentley 6½-litre	TW2705
(27/17)	Weymann saloon	1927, Apr	Bentley 6½-litre	BX2402
(27/18)	Coupé de ville	1927, Apr	Bentley 6½-litre	BX2403
(27/19)	Weymann saloon	1927, Apr	Bentley 6½-litre	BX2425
(27/20)	Weymann four-light saloon	1927, May	Bentley 3-litre	AX1666
(27/21)	Panelled saloon	1927, May	Voisin	Not known
(27/22)	Weymann saloon	1927, May	Bentley 6½-litre	TW2720
(27/23)	Weymann saloon	1927, May	Bentley 6½-litre	BX2415
(27/24)	Weymann saloon	1927, May	Bentley 6½-litre	DH2208
(27/25)	Coupé de ville	1927, May	Voisin	Not known
(27/26)	Saloon	1927, Jun	Rolls-Royce Phantom	9LF
(27/27)	Folding-head saloon	1927, Jun	Crossley 18/50 or 20.9	Not known
(27/28)	Weymann saloon	1927, Jun	Bentley 3-litre	AX1659
(27/29)	Six-light saloon	1927, Jun	Delage	Not known
(27/30)	Saloon	1927, July	Rolls-Royce Phantom	68LF
(27/31)	Saloon	1927, Aug	Rolls-Royce Phantom	77LF
(27/32)	Weymann saloon	1927, Sep	Bentley 3-litre	HT1634
(27/33)	Sedanca de ville	1927, Sep	Hispano-Suiza	Not known
(27/34)	Dual cowl phaeton	1927, Oct	Voisin C14	Not known
(27/35)	Weymann saloon	1927, Oct	Crossley 20.9hp	Not known
(27/36)	Saloon	1927, Oct	Sunbeam 35hp	Not known
(27/37)	Saloon	1927, Oct	Rolls-Royce Phantom	5RF
(27/38)	Sedanca de Ville	1927, Oct	Hispano-Suiza	Not known
(27/39)	Weymann saloon	1927, Nov	Bentley 4½-litre	SL3052
(27/40)	Weymann saloon	1927, Nov	Bentley 4½-litre	SL3058
(27/41)	Tourer	1927, Nov	Minerva	Not known
(27/42)	Weymann saloon	1927, Nov?	Rolls-Royce Twenty	GUJ25
(27/43)	Coupé	1927, xxx	Rolls-Royce Twenty	GUJ60
(27/44)	Weymann four-light saloon	1927, xxx	Bentley 3-litre	EXP4

Notes

(**27/18**) There is no agreement on the identity of the Bentley 6½-litre that became the 1927 Olympia Show car. It seems likely to have been this one, although early Bentley historian Michael Hay has identified the Show car as on chassis PR2307, which is numbered as (28/24) in these lists. If Hay's hypothesis is correct, body (28/24) should be deducted from the 1928 list of Freestone & Webb bodies and added to the 1927 list.
(**27/27**) This body is known from photographs of it under construction, and may be the same as the one listed here as number (27/35).
(**27/34**) The body appears from a photograph to be conventionally panelled. The date has been estimated from the registration number.
(**27/35**) This car was displayed on the Freestone & Webb stand at the Olympia Show in 1927.
(**27/43**) Also described as a "three-quarter coupé", ie with four-light construction.
(**27/44**) EXP4 was an experimental 3-litre chassis built in 1922. It was originally fitted with a tourer body but was rebodied in 1927, probably by Freestone & Webb and certainly with a body that looks like their latest style of four-light Weymann saloon. A picture can be found in Nick Walker's book, *Coachwork on Vintage Bentleys*.

This sedanca de ville body (27/38) on a Hispano-Suiza chassis for bandleader Jack Hylton may have been built as one of a pair, its near-twin being the Harry Oakes car numbered as (27/33). There are subtle differences between the two, especially in the area of the running-boards, and of course, this car does not have the projecting luggage trunk.

Photographed in late November 1927, this tourer body (27/41) was on a Minerva chassis. The design has moved on from the barrel-sided type favoured earlier.

Although described as a Weymann saloon, this four-light body (27/42) looks very much as if it has a de ville-style removable front roof, and perhaps even a folding head at the rear. The curved scuttle, clap-hands doors and dropped rear waistline add interest. It was built on a Rolls-Royce Twenty chassis and delivered in November 1927.

1928

Freestone & Webb's output was maintained during 1928, when 43 bodies appear to have left the Brentfield Road works. Not surprisingly, more than half of these were on the latest Bentley 4½-litre chassis, of which there were 23. Next most numerous were 6½-litre Bentleys, with six chassis, and there were three of the older 3-litres as well. Mercedes-Benz provided six more chassis, and Crossley, Delage, La Salle, Minerva and Rolls-Royce were responsible for one chassis each.

The orders for the Mercedes-Benz bodies were clearly the fruit of the relationship established earlier with the British importer. At least four of the chassis were the latest supercharged Type S, which was marketed in Britain as a 36/220 model (although one would not be completed until January 1929 and is recorded here as body (29/1)). The Type S was something of a motoring sensation at the time, offering enormous performance when fully extended, even though owners were warned not to use the supercharger except for short bursts of acceleration. So to be asked to body a group of them was a major coup for Freestone & Webb, and one that they advertised by displaying one of the cars on their stand at Olympia.

As witness to the significance of the Mercedes-Benz patronage, Freestone & Webb had three of these Type S chassis wheeled out of the workshops at Brentfield Road in early October and lined up for a photograph. The Show car, a saloon numbered (28/34) in the lists below, was very nearly finished; the drophead coupé (28/33) was panelled but had no fabric over its hood frame; and the third body was a sports tourer that was still at the body framing stage and became (29/1) in the present lists. (See picture, p14.)

The fourth Type S chassis had actually been completed before these three, in the summer of 1928. Listed here as number (28/20), it was a roadster ordered by a Captain Morton, and had some unusual features that were probably to the customer's own design. The distinctive body had a vee screen and a third seat at the rear in a heart-shaped enclosure. Quite spectacular for the time, with twin side-mounted spare wheels that broke the lines of the running-boards and tool boxes formed as part of the running-boards themselves, this body remained unique but was a clear demonstration of Freestone & Webb's skills as well as the company's

Grand and yet sporting at the same time: this is a four-light Weymann saloon (28/1) on a Bentley 6½-litre chassis, completed in January 1928. It is pleasing to record that this car still survives in superb condition, with its original Freestone & Webb body intact.

There are clear similarities between this body (28/11) on a Mercedes-Benz chassis and the four-light Weymann sports saloon on Bentley chassis pictured bottom left on page 32. The larger wheels of the German chassis do it no favours in this view.

This is one of three bodies built on Bentley 4½-litre chassis in May 1928, here numbered (28/15) to (28/17). The sleek two-door lines would qualify it for the description of coupé.

The proportions are very American, even if the body was built in Britain. This four-light saloon is on a La Salle chassis, which appears to have been the only one ever to be bodied by Freestone & Webb. This body is catalogued as number (28/19).

This variation on the two-door Weymann design for a Bentley 4½-litre chassis is probably the body catalogued here as number (28/23). The more curved rear quarters were probably more difficult to create, but do not improve the design.

willingness to build to special order.

Nevertheless, most of the Freestone & Webb bodies delivered during 1928 were, as usual, saloon types. There were 32 of them, including one described as a coachbuilt type, which was for the Olympia Show Mercedes-Benz. So although Weymann construction remained predominant, the company was clearly keen to show what it could do with more durable metal panelling. Brentfield Road would certainly continue to build fabric-panelled Weymann saloons for a few more years, but it looks as if the company had recognised that the fashion for these was on the wane and that it

would have to turn to traditional metal panelling if it was to have a long-term future.

Tourers were not quite dead yet, and six bodies built in 1928 answered to this description or to the "four-seater" name that indicated a similar body. The other bodies included single examples of roadster, drophead coupé, and coupé types but, perhaps more importantly, there were also two more grand and formal de ville bodies. One was a cabriolet de ville, on a Bentley 6½-litre chassis (there is some debate about whether this had actually been the 1927 Olympia Show car). The other was a landaulette de ville, this time on the sole Rolls-Royce Phantom chassis to pass through Brentfield Road in 1928. These two bodies confirmed that Freestone & Webb had indeed gained a place among the most trusted British coachbuilders, because those who commissioned them must have expected the very highest quality that could be had.

The heart-shaped rear seat, vee-windscreen and long bonnet made this roadster body (28/20) on a supercharged Mercedes-Benz S chassis quite a remarkable creation. It was built for a Captain Morton.

FREESTONE & WEBB Lt

Looking suitably grand is this six-light body on a Bentley 6½-litre chassis. This is most probably body number (28/24), photographed in April 1928 but not delivered until July that year. It is clearly fitted with a removable de ville section at the front of the roof.

The height of this Rolls-Royce Phantom makes its landaulette de ville body (28/28) seem curiously old-fashioned, despite the modern wheel discs.

Freestone & Webb made the most of the Mercedes-Benz Type S supercharged chassis here, creating an eye-catching four-door sports saloon body (28/34) for their stand at Olympia in October 1928.

Pictured when new in September 1928, this four-light Weymann sports saloon body (28/32) on a Bentley 4½-litre chassis has a properly sporting demeanour from which the heavy-looking trunk at the rear does not detract.

This four-light sports saloon (28/37) on the Bentley 6½-litre chassis dispenses with the traditional toolbox on the running-board, and looks all the sleeker for it. It is otherwise very similar to the four-light Weymann body number (28/32) on the shorter 4½-litre chassis pictured above left.

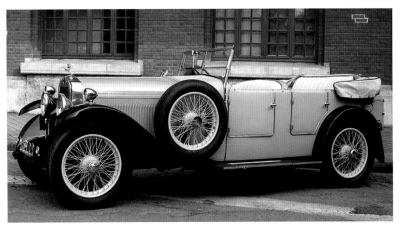

Probably delivered new to South Africa, this Tourer body (28/43) with fabric panels was built on a Delage DMS chassis. (Copyright unknown)

THE 1928 BODY LIST

No body numbers are known for 1928. The bodies are therefore listed in order of their month of delivery, in so far as this is known. Dates for Bentley chassis have been deduced from the date of the chassis guarantee that was issued after the completed car had been tested with its body in place. The "ID no" (Identity number) in the first column is a reference guide for research purposes only and does not reflect any numbering system used by Freestone & Webb. It is therefore shown within brackets. This list has been compiled on the basis of surviving evidence and is the most complete available, but it should not be regarded as definitive..

ID no	Type	Date	Chassis type	Chassis no
(28/1)	Weymann saloon	1928, Jan	Bentley 6½-litre	BR2353
(28/2)	Saloon	1928, Jan	Mercedes-Benz	Not known
(28/3)	Tourer	1928, Jan	Bentley 4½-litre	RN3039
(28/4)	Weymann saloon	1928, Jan	Bentley 4½-litre	NT3130
(28/5)	Weymann saloon	1928, Jan	Bentley 4½-litre	NT3144
(28/6)	Tourer	1928, Feb	Bentley 3-litre	HT1639
(28/7)	Tourer	1928, Feb	Bentley 3-litre	HT1640
(28/8)	Weymann saloon	1928, Feb	Bentley 4½-litre	NT3143
(28/9)	Weymann saloon	1928, Mar	Bentley 6½-litre	MD2452
(28/10)	Weymann saloon	1928, Mar	Bentley 4½-litre	XL3110
(28/11)	Weymann saloon	1928, Apr	Mercedes-Benz	Not known
(28/12)	Weymann saloon	1928, Apr	Crossley Super Six	Not known
(28/13)	Weymann saloon	1928, Apr	Bentley 6½-litre	MD2454
(28/14)	Weymann saloon	1928, Apr	Bentley 4½-litre	XL3120
(28/15)	Weymann two-door saloon	1928, May	Bentley 4½-litre	XL3105
(28/16)	Weymann two-door saloon	1928, May	Bentley 4½-litre	XL3116
(28/17)	Weymann two-door saloon	1928, May	Bentley 4½-litre	KM3078
(28/18)	Weymann saloon	1928, May	Bentley 4½-litre	MF3156
(28/19)	Saloon	1928, May	La Salle	Not known
(28/20)	Roadster	1928, Jun	Mercedes-Benz Type S	Not known
(28/21)	Tourer	1928, Jun	Mercedes-Benz	Not known
(28/22)	Weymann saloon	1928, Jun	Bentley 3-litre	HT1647
(28/23)	Weymann two-door saloon	1928, Jun	Bentley 4½-litre	KM3084
(28/24)	Coupé de ville	1928, July	Bentley 6½-litre	PR2307
(28/25)	Weymann saloon	1928, July	Bentley 4½-litre	TX3243
(28/26)	Weymann saloon	1928, July	Bentley 4½-litre	PM3256
(28/27)	Weymann saloon	1928, July	Bentley 4½-litre	FT3213
(28/28)	Landaulette de ville	1928, July	Rolls-Royce Phantom	35AL
(28/29)	Weymann saloon	1928, Aug	Bentley 4½-litre	FT3214
(28/30)	Weymann saloon	1928, Aug	Bentley 4½-litre	FT3220
(28/31)	Tourer	1928, Aug	Bentley 4½-litre	FT3211
(28/32)	Weymann saloon	1928, Sep	Bentley 4½-litre	PM3257
(28/33)	Drophead coupé	1928, xxx	Mercedes-Benz 36/220	Not known
(28/34)	Saloon	1928, Oct	Mercedes-Benz 36/220	Not known
(28/35)	Six-light saloon	1928, Oct	Minerva	Not known
(28/36)	Weymann saloon	1928, Oct	Bentley 4½-litre	XR3327
(28/37)	Weymann saloon	1928, Nov	Bentley 6½-litre	WT2267
(28/38)	Weymann saloon	1928, Nov	Bentley 4½-litre	UK3296
(28/39)	Weymann saloon	1928, Nov	Bentley 4½-litre	AB3351
(28/40)	Weymann saloon	1928, Dec	Bentley 6½-litre	KF2376
(28/41)	Weymann saloon	1928, Dec	Bentley 4½-litre	XR3333
(28/42)	Coupé	1928, Dec	Bentley 4½-litre	AB3363
(28/43)	Tourer	1928	Delage DMS	26707

Notes
(**28/12**) The date shown here is deduced from the appearance of a picture of this car in *The Motor* for 17 April 1928.
(**28/24**) Michael Hay has proposed this as the 1927 Olympia Show car. See the note for body (27/18), above.
(**28/33**) 36/220 was the UK name for the Type S Mercedes-Benz.
(**28/34**) This car was displayed on the Freestone & Webb stand at Olympia in 1928. A photograph shows it under construction alongside two other bodies on Mercedes-Benz chassis, numbers (28/20) and (28/33).
(**28/43**) The French describe this body as a Torpedo.

Once again, Freestone & Webb made the most of the chassis dimensions on this supercharged Mercedes-Benz sports tourer (29/1). The long, low lines of the body perfectly reflect what such a car was intended to do.

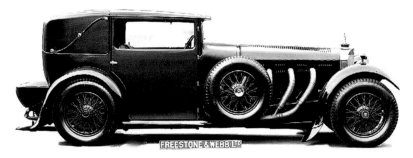

Built at the same time as the body pictured above, number (29/6) had similar proportions but was a closed "sportsman's coupé" for Lord Portarlington, with Weymann fabric construction. It was reviewed briefly in The Autocar *of 12 April 1929, which explained that the headlining had been omitted at the rear to give more headroom! The chassis was a Mercedes-Benz SSK with the 7.1-litre supercharged engine.*

The company's long-serving six-light Weymann saloon design was the basis of this March 1929 body (29/9) on a Bentley 6½-litre chassis, which appears to have a removable roof section above the rear seats. It was delivered to VE Gluckstein, whose initials are painted on the waist rail of the rear door.

1929

Freestone & Webb had a very good year in 1929, building a total of 53 bodies – better than one for every week of the year. The business was clearly in good health, although it is worth pointing out that this total had been achieved with the aid of an order for a dozen delivery vans on the Austin Twenty chassis. These were for the *Evening World* magazine, and were photographed lined up outside the Brentfield Road works on 19 April. They must have been metal-panelled, and (as Chapter 1 suggests) were perhaps built partly as an exercise to get the workforce more used to this type of body construction. They were also the only commercial bodies that the company would ever build.

Saloon bodies were in the majority again, of course, and as many as five may have had metal panels rather than the fabric panels associated with Weymann bodies. There were four tourers, although two of these (on Mercedes-Benz chassis) were quite unlike the sort of bodies that Freestone & Webb had built for Bentley chassis in earlier times. Described as sports tourers, they were sleek and rakish bodies designed to look as fast as the chassis on which they were mounted, and to complement the long bonnets of the supercharged Mercedes-Benz models. They also featured helmet-type front wings, a new fashion that was seen on some other Freestone & Webb bodies this year.

Among the saloons, sporting bodies, and delivery vans, the grand designs continued to appear. There were just two this year, the earlier a Weymann landaulette on a Bentley 6½-litre chassis and the other a limousine on a Lanchester chassis. But there was also a striking new sports coupé for the Bentley Speed Six chassis, which appeared in April with the name of the Grafton Coupé. The choice of the Grafton name remains unexplained (Grafton is a small village near Faringdon in Oxfordshire), but at least three examples of this fabric-panelled sporting design were built, the second on a standard 6½-litre chassis and the last in early 1930. The thinking behind them was clearly related to the two sports tourer bodies on supercharged Mercedes-Benz chassis, but these were taller bodies that incorporated a very distinctive triangular rear side window, accentuated by a dummy landau iron. A similar feature was used on a pair of coupé bodies for the smaller Rolls-Royce Twenty chassis, although these were apparently not known as Grafton Coupés.

Despite the move towards metal panelling, Weymann construction clearly still held sway at Freestone & Webb. Not only were the new Grafton Coupés fabric-panelled, but so was another new sporting coupé design that appeared on a Mercedes-Benz Type SS chassis on the importer's stand at Olympia. The overall design was very much in line with other closed sporting bodies from Brentfield Road this year, with the body set right at the back of the chassis to emphasise the length of the bonnet, but in this case there was a narrow triangular window at each end of the windscreen.

Bentley chassis once again dominated Freestone & Webb's output in 1929. Of the 53 bodies known to have left the workshops that year, no fewer than 31 were for products of the Cricklewood company. There were 18 bodies on the 4½-litre chassis, 12 on the 6½-litre (and Speed Six), and one each on the now superseded 3-litre and the supercharged 4½-litre. Both exhibits on Freestone & Webb's Olympia Show stand in October were Bentleys, one a Grafton coupé on the supercharged chassis, and the other an interesting four-light Weymann saloon with division, on a six-cylinder chassis. Perhaps the ultimate accolade for the company's coachwork however came at the Paris Salon, where Bentley Motors took a stand for the first time. The car they displayed there was a 6½-litre with a Weymann saloon body built by Freestone & Webb.

Other chassis were very much in the minority during 1929. In addition to the 12 Austin Twenty chassis bodied as delivery vans, there were five Mercedes-Benz, continuing the coachbuilder's strong relationship with the British importer; three Rolls-Royce Twenty chassis, and a single Lanchester.

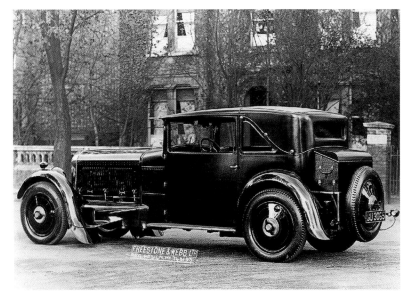

Freestone & Webb made advertising capital out of their Grafton Coupé design on Bentley Speed Six chassis. This one, catalogued as number (29/12), was pictured in April 1929. The triangular quarter-window was interesting, allowing rear-seat passengers to see out while retaining a degree of privacy, but the intricate front wing valance was clearly a key element in the design.

The artillery-type wheels make this Mercedes saloon (29/27) look strangely old-fashioned. The chassis is a 460 Nürburg type, with a naturally-aspirated straight-eight engine.

Cycle wings were very much the fashion in 1929, and here they are again on another Mercedes-Benz with sports coupé bodywork (29/14) that was delivered in April 1929.

... and now for something completely different: this fleet of a dozen delivery vans for the Evening World *was built on Austin Twenty chassis and was pictured in April 1929 outside Unity Works. Their bodies are catalogued with numbers (29/15) to (29/26).*

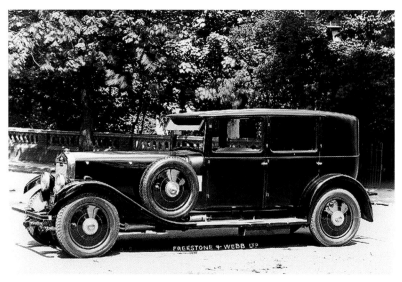

The triangular rear side window appeared again on this Weymann coupé body (29/34) for a Rolls-Royce Twenty chassis. The longer door and resulting shorter rear quarters are less successful than the solution seen on the rebodied car, (29/30), picture right.

1929's fashionable triangular rear window is seen here on a rather smaller body than the Grafton Coupé that seems to have pioneered it. The chassis is actually a 1926 Rolls-Royce Twenty, which was rebodied with this Weymann Coupé (29/30) in 1929.

The overall lines of this four-light body, apparently a limousine, were very familiar by the time it was completed in July 1929. The chassis was a Lanchester.

A Grafton Coupé appeared on Freestone & Webb's 1929 motor show stand, on the latest supercharged Bentley 4½-litre chassis. It seems likely that, at the time of the show, the engine was only mocked-up to look like a supercharged type, as these were in short supply! This body is listed as number (29/43).

This rather neat and very obviously fabric-panelled four-door saloon (29/36) was photographed in July 1929. The chassis was a Rolls-Royce Twenty.

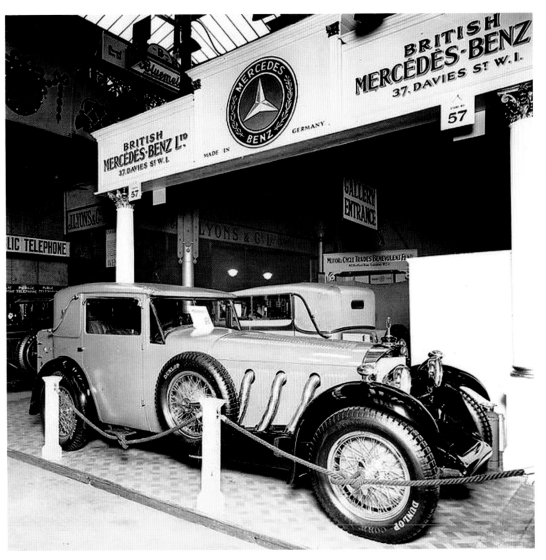

Freestone & Webb's successful association with British Mercedes-Benz continued with this sportsman's saloon (29/42) on the supercharged SS chassis. It was pictured on the importer's stand at Olympia in 1929, and the picture clearly shows the triangular glasses alongside the windscreen that must have improved the driver's view at junctions.

By the end of 1929, when this picture was taken, four-light fabric-bodied saloons were beginning to look old-fashioned. The two-tone effect seen here is nevertheless interesting. This is one of three bodies built, possibly all to the same specification, on Bentley 4½-litre chassis and catalogued here as numbers (29/51) to (29/53).

THE 1929 BODY LIST

No body numbers are known for 1929. The bodies are therefore listed in order of their month of delivery, in so far as this is known. Dates for Bentley chassis have been deduced from the date of the chassis guarantee that was issued after the completed car had been tested with its body in place. The "ID no" (Identity number) in the first column is a reference guide for research purposes only and does not reflect any numbering system used by Freestone & Webb. It is therefore shown within brackets. This list has been compiled on the basis of surviving evidence and is the most complete available, but it should not be regarded as definitive.

ID no	Type	Date	Chassis type	Chassis no
(29/1)	Sports tourer	1929, Jan	Mercedes-Benz Type S	Not known
(29/2)	Weymann saloon	1929, Jan	Bentley 4½-litre	AB3368
(29/3)	Tourer	1929, Jan	Bentley 4½-litre	FB3307
(29/4)	Weymann saloon	1929, Jan	Bentley 4½-litre	FB3308
(29/5)	Weymann saloon	1929, Jan	Bentley 4½-litre	FB3324
(29/6)	Sports tourer	1929, Jan	Mercedes-Benz 38/250 (ie SSK)	Not known
(29/7)	Tourer	1929, Feb	Bentley 3-litre	DN1736
(29/8)	Weymann saloon	1929, Feb	Bentley 4½-litre	RL3441
(29/9)	Weymann landaulette	1929, Mar	Bentley 6½-litre	LB2345
(29/10)	Drophead coupé	1929, Mar	Bentley 4½-litre	RL3432
(29/11)	Weymann saloon	1929, Mar	Bentley 4½-litre	MR3381
(29/12)	Grafton Coupé	1929, Apr	Bentley Speed Six	BA2591
(29/13)	Weymann saloon	1929, Apr	Bentley 4½-litre	MR3396
(29/14)	Sports coupé	1929, Apr	Mercedes-Benz	Not known
(29/15) to (29/26)	Delivery van (batch of 12)	1929. Apr	Austin Twenty	Not known
(29/27)	Six-light saloon	1929, Apr	Mercedes-Benz 460 Nürburg	Not known
(29/28)	Weymann saloon	1929, May	Bentley 6½-litre	BA2593
(29/29)	Weymann saloon	1929, May	Bentley 4½-litre	HB3423
(29/30)	Weymann coupé	1929, Jun	Rolls-Royce Twenty	GYK82
(29/31)	Grafton Coupé	1929, Jun	Bentley Speed Six	FR2630
(29/32)	Saloon	1929, Jun	Bentley 4½-litre	PL3481
(29/33)	Two-door saloon; possibly a Grafton Coupé	1929, July	Bentley Speed Six	FR2631
(29/34)	Weymann coupé	1929, July	Rolls-Royce Twenty	GEN75
(29/35)	Limousine?	1929, July	Lanchester	Not known
(29/36)	Weymann four-door saloon	1929, July	Rolls-Royce Twenty	GEN74
(29/37)	Weymann saloon	1929, July	Bentley 6½-litre	FR2644
(29/38)	Weymann saloon	1929, Aug	Bentley 6½-litre	FR2649
(29/39)	Drophead coupé	1929, Aug	Bentley 6½-litre	FR2650
(29/40)	Weymann saloon	1929, Aug	Bentley 4½-litre	DS3553
(29/41)	Weymann saloon	1929, Sep	Bentley 6½-litre	KR2683
(29/42)	Weymann sportsman's saloon	1929, Sep	Mercedes-Benz Type SS	Not known
(29/43)	Grafton Coupé	1929, Oct	Bentley 4½-litre supercharged	SM3902
(29/44)	Weymann sports saloon with division	1929, Oct	Bentley 6½-litre	KR2700
(29/45)	Weymann saloon	1929, Oct	Bentley 6½-litre	SB2763
(29/46)	Weymann saloon	1929, Oct	Bentley 4½-litre	XF3512
(29/47)	Weymann saloon	1929, Oct	Bentley 4½-litre	XF3513
(29/48)	Weymann saloon	1929, Nov	Bentley 6½-litre	SB2765
(29/49)	Weymann saloon	1929, Nov	Bentley 4½-litre	XF3515
(29/50)	Saloon	1929, Nov	Bentley 4½-litre	KL3580
(29/51)	Saloon	1929, Dec	Bentley 4½-litre	KL3587
(29/52)	Saloon	1929, Dec	Bentley 4½-litre	KL3594
(29/53)	Saloon	1929, Dec	Bentley 4½-litre	PB3539

Notes

(**29/7**) This was the last Bentley 3-litre to receive a Freestone & Webb body.

(**29/9**) The identification of this body as a landaulette depends on photographs that show catches on the roof, suggesting that there may have been a removable or folding section above the rear seat.

(**29/30**) This was a 1926 chassis and was a rebody.

(**29/33**) This car was rebuilt on a new frame in May 1931 after an accident. Some sources claim it was originally built as a Grafton Coupé. A photograph of it dating from the 1950s shows it with a full-size rear side window, which could perhaps have replaced the original triangular window during the rebuild.

(**29/43**) This car was on the coachbuilder's stand at Olympia in October 1929. Although it was a genuine supercharged example, there is some suggestion that the engine fitted during the show was a standard 4½-litre dummied up to resemble the supercharged type.

(**29/44**) This car was on the coachbuilder's stand at Olympia in October 1929.

Chapter Three

THE GOLDEN YEARS 1930-1939

Fear of the longer-term consequences of the Depression very definitely led the two partners of Freestone & Webb to take a thoughtful look at their future. John de Campi (writing in *The Flying Lady* for January-February 2001) notes that AJ Webb considered closing the company as early as 1929. To add to the general gloom, VE Freestone actually left the business during 1930, and never returned.

What appears to have kept Brentfield Road going was an injection of cash from Reggie Beaumont-Thomas, the heir to a great steel fortune and a Freestone & Webb customer since 1927. It appears, says John de Campi, that the Brooklands racer and car dealer Gordon Watney had recommended him to the company on the grounds that their bodies were light in weight and so restricted performance less than those from Barker or Hooper. Beaumont-Thomas had ordered a saloon body on a Rolls-Royce Phantom chassis, and was sufficiently pleased with it to persuade his mother to order a Freestone & Webb limousine de ville for her Phantom II in 1930.

He had also struck up a friendship with AJ Webb, which must have caused onlookers some amusement because Beaumont-Thomas was very tall (at 6ft 7in) while Webb was a very small man. Nevertheless, sympathetic to Webb's concerns over the future of the company, he agreed to invest in it and to become its Managing Director. This arrangement lasted only until 1935; Beaumont-Thomas had remarried in 1934, and his new wife's passion for travel was incompatible with a business life tied to Stonebridge Park. Nevertheless, he had supported the company through its darkest hours and left it in a much healthier state than when he had joined. He remained an investor in the company and a life-long friend of the Webb family.

The early 1930s certainly had been a bad time to be in the bespoke coachwork business. For Freestone & Webb, the effects of the Depression were clearly felt most during 1931 and 1932, when their total output of coachwork was much lower than it had been. The whole issue was no doubt compounded by the collapse of Bentley Motors, which had been a major source of work for Brentfield Road. Nevertheless, the output of bodies increased again in 1933, and remained healthy for the rest of the decade as Freestone & Webb brought some strong-selling new designs to market. There was a minor blip in 1936, and of course the 1939 totals

---

FREESTONE & WEBB ANNUAL PRODUCTION TOTALS, 1930-1939

The annual figures shown here should not be considered definitive, because in some cases it is not clear whether a body was completed in (for example) late 1931 or early 1932. However, they do indicate the annual trends fairly accurately. In all cases, figures relate to calendar year.

1930	42
1931	23
1932	23
1933	49
1934	60
1935	53
1936	38
1937	49
1938	47
1939	26

The overall total for the decade was therefore 410 bodies.

24 THE AUTOCAR.   ADVERTISEMENTS.   OCTOBER 16TH, 1931.

FREESTONE & WEBB LTD.

ON STAND No. 120

People of discrimination will find in Freestone & Webb coachwork an individuality of design and refinement of taste that are unique in these days of mass production. Those who wish to possess a motor carriage which expresses their own personality and in which they can take a pride over many years will find their tastes studied in the minutest detail in Freestone & Webb coachwork.

COACH CRAFT

UNITY WORKS, BRENTFIELD ROAD, STONEBRIDGE PARK, N.W.10

This design for the Bentley 8-litre chassis was displayed at Olympia in 1931, and would later be adapted very successfully for the much smaller Bentley 3½-litre as well. The moulding around the windows flows into a "shoulder" beside the boot, and was a Freestone & Webb characteristic of the time.

were down when coachbuilding work ended three or four months short of the full year because of the outbreak of war.

Nevertheless, the 1930s became golden years for Freestone & Webb, when the company cemented its reputation among the top British coachbuilders. From the time its fortunes began to revive in 1933 to the time it was obliged to close for the duration of the war in 1939, the company built an average of 46 bodies every year – which was very healthy indeed.

The departure of VE Freestone

Meanwhile, the early 1930s saw a rather confusing set of events, as VE Freestone struck out on his own. It is not clear when he formally left the company, but he was certainly working for Thrupp & Maberly during 1930. Whatever the truth of the matter, his name would remain firmly attached to the company he had founded in 1923.

He may well have been persuaded to join Thrupp & Maberly by an old colleague, RI Musselwhite, who, like Freestone, had been a boy apprentice at the Arthur Mulliner coachworks in Northampton. Musselwhite had already had quite a colourful career. Between 1914 and 1923, he had been the Managing Director of the Cunard Motor and Carriage Co, another London coachbuilder. Cunard had been closely associated with Napier, and closed in 1925 when that company stopped building motor car chassis; its premises were sold to Weymann's Motor Bodies (1925) Ltd. In the mean time, Musselwhite had embarked on a series of career moves, first going to Windovers and then to

Barker, and then from about 1926 becoming Works Director at Thrupp & Maberly.

The upshot of all this was that Musselwhite and Freestone decided the time was right to revive the old Cunard business, and The Motor reported in its issue of 14 October 1930 that they had now become joint directors of a new Cunard company, based at Chase Road in Acton. Nick Walker notes (in *A-Z British Coachbuilders 1919-1960*) that Freestone was to take charge of the factory layout and of production. However, no sooner had the new company begun building car bodies than it was taken over by Stewart & Ardern, the London agents for Morris cars. The Cunard company survived a little longer, but VE Freestone took his leave of it during 1931. What he did for the next four years remains unclear, but by early 1935 he was back in business with yet another coachbuilding company.

This new company had the name of Freestone Endura, and according to the London Gazette, its Registered Office was at Endura Works, Abbey Road, Park Royal, London NW10. However, this new company appears not to have been a great success. Only four Freestone Endura bodies are known for certain – although there could of course have been others. Two were large limousines on Daimler chassis, one was a very stylish drophead coupé on a Minerva, and the fourth was a drophead coupé on a Bentley 3½-litre that was delivered in October 1935. It was not particularly distinguished, although its concealed-head feature was interesting.

That apart, all that is known of Freestone Endura is contained in three entries in the *London Gazette*. On 11 August 1939, that publication recorded that a liquidator had been appointed for the Freestone Endura Company Ltd, and that the liquidator was CH Barclay of 103 Cannon Street, London EC4. A Committee of Inspection had also been appointed. Thanks no doubt to the intervention of war less than month later, further proceedings seem to have been delayed, and the *London Gazette* did not record the dissolution of Freestone Endura until its issue of 21 August 1945. The disposal of the Freestone Endura Works was meanwhile recorded in the London Gazette for 31 May 1940, when a company called Leopold Behrman Ltd applied for land to be registered in their name at the Freestone Endura Works in West Twyford, Middlesex – which was actually at Park Royal. The Behrman company – if it was the same one – was a timber merchant and a maker of domestic flooring by the time of its liquidation in 1978.

As for VE Freestone himself, it is not clear what he did either during or after the 1939-1945 war,

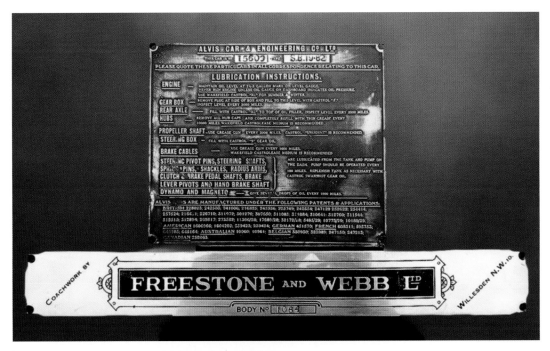

It is not clear when
Freestone & Webb began
to use body numbers, but
the earliest example known
for certain dates from
1930. This picture shows
the mortal remains of a
1933 Alvis that carried a
pillarless body numbered
1064. The body number
can be seen stamped into
the coachbuilder's plate
that would have been
screwed to the body sill.
(John Fox)

Not all body plates were
the same, and this one is
from a 1935 body, number
1174. The plate spent
many years misleadingly
screwed to a 1938 Riley
Lynx Sprite, which at the
time of writing survived
in New Zealand.
(Kevin Naylor)

BODY NUMBERS

Body numbers first seem to have appeared during 1930. An exact start date is not clear, but the earliest known example is on the Bentley 8-litre that was on the 1930 Olympia Show stand. This carried number 965, stamped into a section of the coachbuilder's sill plate that was specially reserved for the number.

Perhaps more important is to understand why body numbers began to appear at all. It may have been that there were now enough Freestone & Webb bodies in existence to make some kind of numbering system valuable in case a customer returned to Brentfield Road with a request for repairs or modifications. However, it seems equally likely that the numbering began as a way of impressing potential clients with the quantity of bodies that Freestone & Webb had built. In 1930, at a time when economic conditions were worsening, this would have been a reassuring move.

One way or another, it seems clear that the choice of the number 965 was made to impress rather than to give an accurate indication of the company's output. Freestone & Webb had clearly not built 965 bodies – or anything like that number – by the time of the Olympia Show in 1930. The calculated total up to the end of 1929 is just 264, and even adding all 41 bodies thought to have been built during 1930 gives a figure well short of 965!

Once the practice had begun, however, it seems to have been fairly consistent. With a stretch of the imagination, it is just about possible to account for the right number of bodies having been built between number 965 in 1930 and body number 1024 that opens the surviving order book in 1933. The 59 numbers between them could have been taken up by the 23 known bodies in 1931, the 24 known bodies in 1932, four in early 1933 and perhaps some of the later 1930 bodies. There could also of course have been some bodies not discovered in the research for this book that would contribute further to the total in the relevant period!

As far as it is possible to tell, body numbers were allocated on the placement of orders, and as a result they do not reflect the order in which bodies were built or completed. In some cases, bodies were never built, and the body number had nothing entered against it in the order book. (See the note on the "No Entries", on page 47.)

Showtime again, and this was the 1932 Freestone & Webb stand at Olympia. The two cars on display illustrate the more curvaceous lines that the company now favoured. In the foreground is a most attractive coupé on Delage D8S chassis (catalogue number (32/18), and behind it is the neat saloon on a Talbot 95 chassis (32/19). Both had metal-panelled bodies.
(Tom Clarke)

but records show that he died in the London district of Brent (which includes Stonebridge Park, where Freestone & Webb were located) in 1966 at the age of 84.

A firm footing, 1933-1939

After that slightly shaky start to the new decade, the management at Freestone & Webb quite clearly decided that the business had to be set on a firm footing. They achieved this in several ways. First, they seem to have deliberately targeted buyers of the "small" Rolls-Royce 20/25 chassis, and in that they were very successful. Second, they developed a small number of highly attractive designs that they built in small series, so streamlining the manufacturing process. And third, they forged links with several of the upper-crust British car makers – notably Alvis, Daimler and Lagonda – to ensure that they were not wholly dependent on chassis from Rolls-Royce and Bentley.

None of this affected the company's traditional willingness to build coachwork to individual order, and throughout the 1930s Freestone & Webb continued to build some low-volume designs that were ordered in only penny numbers. However, the backbone of their business was that small number of

highly popular designs that remained available for several years. Besides reducing complication in the workshops, the idea also appealed to the major dealers, who seem to have welcomed the opportunity to order small batches of bodies to the same design which they could then sell on quite quickly, each one probably attracting a customer for the next.

The first of these volume-built designs was the Continental saloon, which was built for the Rolls-Royce 20/25 chassis between early 1933 and autumn 1934. The basic idea of the Continental saloon had come from Park Ward and was copied by several coachbuilders; it was essentially a four-light sports saloon with an with an integral boot large enough to carry the luggage needed on a trip to the European continent; its appeal lay not only in its well-balanced lines but also in the aspirations it suggested.

Freestone & Webb's interpretation of the theme started out as design 1275 (of which two were made), then became 1275/A, which attracted five orders; version 1275/B was built on seven chassis in 1933 and continued into 1934, and version 1275/C accounted for three more in 1933 and again continued into 1934. In 1933, no fewer than 17 of the bodies that Brentfield Road built for the 20/25 chassis were variants of the

Continental saloon, in 1934 there were another five, and the final example seems to have been mounted to a chassis in 1935.

By the standards of bespoke coachbuilding in the early 1930s, this was success indeed. It also reflected that presumed decision by Freestone & Webb to target the buyers of the latest "small" Rolls-Royce. The 20/25 had been introduced in 1929, but the only one that passed through Brentfield Road before 1932 was bodied as a cabriolet de ville in 1931. So it certainly looks as if the new focus on that chassis was the result of a deliberate policy. The idea must surely have come from AJ Webb, who by this stage running the business without help from VE Freestone – or perhaps it came from Reggie Beaumont-Thomas, who was now acting as Managing Director. One way or another, the new strategy certainly worked, and both the 20/25 and its 25/30 successor would go on to account for a sizeable proportion of Freestone & Webb's business in the 1930s.

A second series-built design appeared at Olympia in 1934, and this was a sports saloon for the Bentley 3½-litre chassis. It immediately began to attract orders. The dealer Car Mart took a first batch of three in spring 1935, each one described in the Freestone & Webb order book as a "Show model replica". Five more swiftly followed, one built specifically for stock although it rapidly found a buyer. There were then four more before the end of 1935, including one of variant 1507/C which had an extra two inches of length in the body. Twelve bodies to the same design in as many months was another success by bespoke coachbuilding standards, closely emulating the 23 examples of the Continental saloon in two years (which averaged just over 11 examples each year).

By early 1935, it was clear that Freestone & Webb had the bit between their teeth. The company followed its Continental saloon for the Rolls-Royce 20/25 chassis with another successful saloon, this time numbered 1567 but lacking any memorable name. Not that it needed one. Production began with a batch of eight for the London dealer Jack Barlcay in early 1935, and by the autumn there were orders for two more.

This saloon design was followed almost immediately by number 1569 for a coupé on the 20/25 chassis, and Jack Barclay immediately ordered a batch of four – presumably as an exclusive design because no others were built. This alliance between dealer and coachbuilder was certainly not unique to Freestone & Webb, but it did illustrate how the two elements of the high-class motor trade could get together for mutual benefit, and it was undeniably valuable to

Sports Fixed Head Close Coupled Coupe on 3½-litre Bentley.

COACHCRAFT

COACHWORK of DISTINCTION
and Quality on the new Bentley Chassis
• • • • • • •

Designs and Specifications to clients' own requirements gladly submitted on request.

OUR COACHWORK MAY BE INSPECTED ON STAND No. 29 at the forthcoming Olympia Show.

FREESTONE & WEBB LTD.
Unity Works, Brentfield Road, Willesden,
LONDON, N.W.10.
Telephone: Willesden 4017-8-9.

Brentfield Road.

However, the design that might realistically be described as Freestone & Webb's blockbuster also appeared in 1935, and it was so successful that it was still being built (in updated form) by the time war broke out in 1939 and its key characteristics had been incorporated into designs for chassis other than the Bentley 3½-litre on which it first appeared. This design had a marked influence on designs from other British coachbuilders in the later 1930s, and some of its elements persisted right through until the early 1950s.

The basic features of the design appeared in 1933, as elements in a unique and flamboyant coupé body on a Rolls-Royce Phantom II for the wealthy mill-owner and politician (and serial Phantom owner) Sir John Leigh. This was a long way from the eventual sports saloon design, but the chiselled lines of its roof and the contrasting curved rear quarter-panels made an indelible impression. Probably uncertain about how much of this highly distinctive style could be transferred to a more everyday sports saloon, Brentfield Road cautiously tried out the chiselled roof edges on a sports saloon for the Bentley 3½-litre in early 1935, finishing the full-size drawing for design 1598 in March and completing a first body in July.

It must have been immediately obvious that this was the way to go. Design 1598 was modified to incorporate the curved rear quarter-panels of the coupé for Sir John Leigh and became design number 1617, better known as the Brougham saloon. It was shown to the public on the coachbuilder's stand at Olympia in October, and the orders started pouring in.

This October 1933 advertisement promotes Freestone & Webb's work for the latest Bentley 3½-litre chassis. The design shown, which looks very French in inspiration, is probably meant to be generally representative rather than to promote any particular style.

THE BROUGHAM DESIGNS

The basic Brougham saloon design was developed in 1935 and remained available on Bentley chassis right through to 1939, the last example actually being delivered at the start of 1940. There were six major variants of the design.

Design 1598
1 example built in 1935.

Design 1617
Revised rear pillars, giving "Top Hat" effect.
2 examples built in 1935 (including the first of 4 for Dex Garages)
6 examples built in 1936 (including the remaining 3 for Dex Garages)
1 example built in 1937

Design 1617/A
Revised rear roof line and chrome window frames, for 4¼-litre chassis. The boot still opened at the top.
3 examples built in 1936

Design 1755
This was a revised 1617/A, with a longer side to the rear quarters and a rearward-opening boot lid. The 1937 bodies are all shown in the order book as having design 1755 (1617/A).
2 examples built in 1936
6 examples built in 1937 (all for Dex Garages; some delivered in 1938)

Design 1785/A
This was very similar to design 1755, but with a side-mounted fuel filler, rolled edges to the wings and running-boards, and faired-in sidelights.
1 example built in 1937

Design 1880
This final version of the design had the spare wheel mounted alongside the bonnet instead of on the tail, and a modified rear wing line. It also featured chamfered edges, which softened the razor-edge features a little. For 1939, the corners were chamfered as well.
1 example built in 1937
6 examples built in 1938
3 examples built in 1939 (of which the last was delivered in 1940)

The original Brougham design for the Bentley 3½-litre was adapted to provide no fewer than 11 designs for other chassis, beginning in 1936.

Design 1632/A
This was essentially a version of design 1617/A for the Rolls-Royce 20/25 chassis.
3 examples built in 1936

Design 1753
This was an adaptation of the Brougham saloon design for the Lagonda LG45 chassis.
1 example built in 1936

Design 1775
This was a two-seat Brougham coupé for the Frazer-Nash BMW 326 chassis.
1 example built in 1937

Design 1779
This was a four-seat coupé derivative of Design 1617/A for the Bentley 4¼-litre chassis.
1 example built in 1937

Design 1806
This adapted the Brougham features to a Sedanca de Ville for the Bentley 4¼-litre chassis.
1 example built in 1937

Design 1813
This was an adaptation of the Brougham saloon design for the Daimler Light Straight-Eight chassis.
1 example built in 1937

Design 1910
This adapted the Brougham features to a Limousine for the Packard Eight chassis.
2 examples built in 1938

Design 1919
This was an adaptation of the Brougham saloon design for the SS Jaguar 3½-litre chassis.
1 example built in 1938

Design 1928
This adapted the Brougham features to a very upright and formal Limousine for the Mercedes-Benz 540K chassis.
1 example built in 1938

Design 1947
This was an adaptation of the Brougham saloon design for the Lagonda V12 chassis.
1 example built in 1938

Design 1963
This adapted the Brougham features to a Touring Limousine for the Mercedes-Benz 540K chassis.
1 example built in 1938

The name Brougham (although not new to car bodies) was probably chosen because the curved rear quarter-panels echoed a feature of the special carriages built during the 19th century for the statesman Lord Brougham, while the lower edges of the front doors were swept forward in a further echo of their design. The sharp edges used for the roof and some other panels quickly acquired the snappy description of "razor-edge". And those curved quarter-panels formed a distinctive shape where they met the horizontal top surface of the boot, reminding some motor traders of the way the top and brim sections of a top hat met. So another name that quickly became attached to this style was the "Top Hat". Over the years, the use of these different terms has become rather loose, the Top Hat name for example being given to the original design 1598 as well as the later types.

Pillarless designs

Just as the early 1930s saw the first of Freestone & Webb's successful new series-built designs (the Continental saloon for the Rolls-Royce 20/25), so they also saw the company experimenting with a new method of construction that had been brought in from the European continent. The trend towards close-coupled saloon bodies, particularly sports saloons, meant that door openings were not as wide as they had once been, and this particularly affected entry and exit for the rear seat passengers. An answer lay in "pillarless" bodies.

New methods of construction, with metal body frames instead of traditional wooden ones, had made it possible to dispense with the central door pillar so that the two doors on each side closed against one another. When both were open, there was a virtually unimpeded access to the passenger compartment, and Freestone & Webb built their first body to this pillarless design on a Bugatti T46 chassis in 1930, although there were none during the difficult years of 1931 and 1932, and the next one was built in 1933 on an Alvis chassis. In Britain at least, Freestone & Webb were ahead of the game here: only later would Rolls-Royce import a pillarless body built by Vanvooren in Paris and show it to selected coachbuilders as an example of what could be achieved.

However, the pillarless bodies did not have a long-term future at Freestone & Webb. In 1934, three more were built on Alvis chassis, one on a Daimler, and one on a Bentley. All were saloons except the Bentley, which was a two-door saloon coupé. The following year brought five more pillarless saloons, four on Alvis chassis and one on a Bentley, but that was effectively the end of the experiment. After building those 12

bodies between 1930 and 1935, Freestone & Webb made only more pillarless type, and this 1937 example was to an earlier design.

Sir John Leigh's Phantoms

Freestone & Webb's association with Sir John Leigh during the 1930s resulted in a remarkable series of bodies that demonstrated the company's skills to the full. Sir John, who had made his fortune in the Lancashire cotton industry and subsequently bought the *Pall Mall Gazette* and entered politics, ordered no fewer than nine bodies, all of them on Rolls-Royce Phantom chassis; in only one case was a design repeated. Two dated from 1931, there was one in each year from 1933 to 1936, two more followed in 1937, and the last one was built in 1939.

The earliest of these bodies was a drophead coupé in summer 1931 on the second production Phantom II Continental chassis. This body is numbered (31/12) in this book. Two more open bodies followed later. In

---

THE "NO ENTRIES"

In the surviving order book, there are ten order numbers between 1932 and 1939 against which there is no entry. These are:

1044 and 1045	1932 or 1933
1125	1934
1181	1935
1203	1936
1347 to 1351	1939

The reason for an absence of entries against the last five is obvious. They are the last five numbers before Freestone & Webb suspended coachbuilding activities for the 1939-1945 war, and had probably been written into the book in anticipation of orders which never came when war was declared in autumn 1939.

However, the others need more explanation. Most probably, they represent anticipated orders that did not materialise; perhaps an order number (or body number) was allocated and the details were kept separately until the order was confirmed. By the time it was clear that there would be no firm order, the body numbers had moved on and there was no reason to go back and re-allocate "unused" numbers. The quantity (five in seven years) is probably about right for this explanation to make sense.

Bernard King has suggested that 1044 might have been allocated to a body built to design 1283 on Rolls-Royce 20/25 GYZ2. However, there is no indication of this in the Freestone & Webb records.

This exquisite interior detailing is in body number 1184, on a Rolls-Royce 20/25 chassis. It was delivered to Elsie and Doris Waters, "Gert and Daisy" of BBC Radio fame, and the trays in the back of the division were fitted out with a variety of ladies' perquisites. (Joanne Goldman)

The Brougham saloon design was a major success for Freestone & Webb. Here it is in a November 1935 advertisement from the Society Journal, the car shown being Bentley 3½-litre B6EF with body number 1165.

1934, Sir John took delivery of a drophead coupé with dickey seat (1094), again on a Phantom II Continental chassis, and then in May 1937 a cabriolet (1238) was completed for him on the new V12-engined Phantom III chassis.

Sir John's second Freestone & Webb body was delivered soon after the first, in autumn 1931, and was a distinctive sedanca de ville with sharp-edged lines (31/19) that to a degree anticipated the razor-edge lines that the company would adopt a few years later. This was on a standard Phantom II chassis. There were two limousine bodies, the first being a four-light style on a

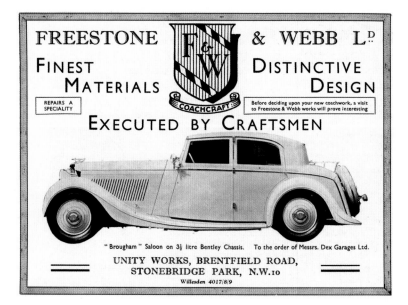

FREESTONE & WEBB L.D
FINEST MATERIALS
DISTINCTIVE DESIGN
REPAIRS A SPECIALITY
Before deciding upon your new coachwork, a visit to Freestone & Webb works will prove interesting
EXECUTED BY CRAFTSMEN

"Brougham" Saloon on 3½ litre Bentley Chassis. To the order of Messrs. Dex Garages Ltd.
UNITY WORKS, BRENTFIELD ROAD, STONEBRIDGE PARK, N.W.10
Willesden 4017/8/9

Towards the end of the decade, Daimler had become a customer and was advertising a Freestone & Webb design as an option for its 4-litre Light Straight Eight chassis.

Daimler
LIGHT STRAIGHT EIGHT

COACHWORK BY FREESTONE & WEBB LTD.
A saloon in which good taste and dignity are preserved in a less orthodox style

Phantom II Continental (1124) that was delivered in early 1935. The second (1334) was on a Phantom III chassis and was the last of Sir John's Freestone & Webb bodies, being delivered in summer 1939.

The only body style duplicated was design number 1700, a six-light saloon for the Phantom III chassis. The first example (1199) was delivered in summer 1936 and the second (1253) in summer 1937. All of these were distinctive and tasteful designs, but perhaps the crowning glory was the magnificent fixed-head coupé (1063) on Phantom II Continental chassis delivered in December 1933. As explained above, this hugely imposing body pioneered the Brougham style of blind rear panels and razor-edge roof lines that Freestone & Webb would use to such good effect on their saloon bodies from 1935.

FREESTONE & WEBB L^{D.}
UNITY WORKS, BRENTFIELD ROAD,
STONEBRIDGE PARK, N.W. 10
Willesden 4017/8/9

Four Door "Brougham" Saloon mounted on 4½ Litre Bentley Chassis

FINEST MATERIALS
DISTINCTIVE DESIGN
EXECUTED BY CRAFTSMEN

REPAIRS, RENOVATIONS and ALTERATIONS A SPECIALITY

The importers

Throughout the decade, Brentfield Road continued to cultivate relationships with the importers of foreign chassis, and during the 1930s the company built coachwork on chassis by Alfa Romeo, Ansaldo, Bugatti, Buick, Cord, Darracq, Delage, Frazer-Nash BMW, Hispano-Suiza, Hudson, Mercedes-Benz, Packard and Talbot. Most of these were singletons, but that relationship with the London-based importers earned a large batch order for bodies on Delage chassis that accounted for around half of Freestone & Webb's body output in 1938.

There is more about the Delage contract in Chapter 4, but it will suffice here to say that it was most unusual and appears to have been a direct transfer of orders from the coachbuilder Coachcraft, which was running into financial difficulties at the time. Whether Freestone & Webb actually completed all the bodies during 1938 or continued building them into 1939 is by no means clear.

The copies

It was not at all uncommon in the 1930s for customers to ask even a leading coachbuilder like Freestone & Webb to build a copy of another coachbuilder's design. There were several reasons for this, not the least of them being that the customer hoped to get the body made more cheaply than by the originator of the design! In some cases, the customer simply wanted a new example of an older and much-liked body; in others, the originator of a popular design may have been swamped with requests for it and was unable to offer an acceptable delivery date, so the customer turned elsewhere.

The Freestone & Webb order book reveals three instances of this occurring during the 1930s. The earliest one was in 1937, when a customer wanted a drophead coupé for his Rolls-Royce 25/30 chassis: the order book clearly states that the body was to be "similar to customer's (John Charles) body". In 1938, the body for a Rolls-Royce Wraith was to be "on lines Arthur Mulliner job", and then in 1939 there were four touring saloons on the Wraith chassis which were to be "as HJM 1938 Show exhibit". HJM was of course HJ Mulliner, and the bodies were faithful copies of a design that coachbuilder showed at Olympia in 1938, complete with wheel spats that were quite unlike anything Freestone & Webb were offering at the time.

Freestone & Webb kept the Brougham saloon design fresh through regular changes. This advertisement from approximately 1936 shows a later version (design 1617/A) on a Bentley 4¼-litre chassis.

SOURCES
As already explained, the lists of bodies built by Freestone & Webb between 1923 and 1932 have been compiled from a variety of contemporary records, in the absence of any documentation from the company itself. From early 1933, however, a much more definitive listing of bodies is possible thanks to the survival of an order book. This order book was among the documents collected by Lawrie Dalton in the 1960s and 1970s, and it is to him that we owe its survival. It now belongs to the Science Museum at Wroughton, where it has accession number MS/2109/1.

This handwritten book covers bodies numbered from 1024 to 1833, although there are many blanks and many cancellations (especially in the post-war years), with the result that there were actually far fewer bodies than the 810 that the body numbers might lead us to expect. See the separate note on Body Numbers.

Chapter Four

THE COACHWORK 1930-1939

1930

The effects of the Depression were probably not being felt too badly at Freestone & Webb in 1930. Research suggests that 41 bodies were delivered that year, a figure that may have been down on the record years of 1929 and 1925 but was broadly similar to the annual outputs for 1927 and 1928. If business was not increasing, it was at least holding up.

Saloons of one type or the other accounted for 30

The huge swathe of brightwork on the waistline of this fixed-head coupé (30/7) was a new feature for Freestone & Webb when the body was completed in early 1930. The chassis is a supercharged Mercedes-Benz SS, and the car was displayed later that year on the coachbuilder's stand at Olympia.

Many years later, perhaps in the 1950s, the body from that 1930 Show Mercedes was transferred to a Hispano-Suiza H6B chassis. An extra window was inserted in each rear quarter but the body remains very recognisable, and still survives on the Hispano chassis.(Bart van Mol/Dutch Wikipedia)

of those 41 bodies, and the other 11 consisted of two drophead coupés, two fixed-head coupés and a sports coupé, two tourers and four sedancas de ville. The latter were all on the latest Rolls-Royce Phantom II chassis and represented the year's quota of "grand" bodies – twice as many as in 1929.

It seems clear that metal-panelled bodies were gaining ground at Brentfield Road during this year. In fact, 1930 may have been the tipping point when metal-panelled types outnumbered those with fabric panels, although the Weymann patents for body framing were used for both types. The metal-panelled body on Freestone & Webb's first 8-litre Bentley (number (30/36) in the table below) was an example that incorporated the Weymann patents. Also notable was that Bentley Motors ordered a metal-panelled four-door saloon as a demonstrator on the 4½-litre chassis, and this has number (30/1) in the table.

Some of the 1930 saloons appear to have been "semi-Weymann" types, with metal lower panels and fabric roof panels, the latter typically enamelled to give a gloss finish comparable to that on the painted metal panels. Fabric panels remained in favour for sporting bodies, where lighter weight was required, and there were notable examples on a Hispano-Suiza H6B (number (30/17)) and on a Mercedes-Benz SS (number (30/37)).

As for chassis types, the majority were again Bentleys.

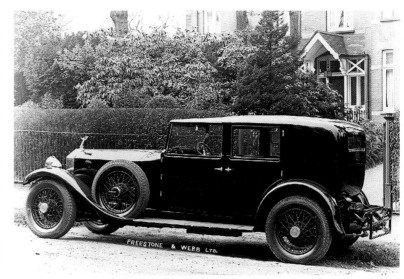

There were 18 bodies on the 4½-litre, eight on the 6½-litre (including one Speed Six), and one each on the supercharged 4½-litre and the latest 8-litre. Most numerous among the others was the Rolls-Royce Phantom II, with five bodies. Five Mercedes-Benz continued the coachbuilder's successful relationship with the British importer of that marque, all of them on the latest supercharged SS chassis. The others were single examples from Bugatti, Delage, Hispano-Suiza and Invicta.

This very elegant Sedanca de Ville body is catalogued here as (30/9) and was pictured when new in March 1930. It was on a Rolls-Royce Phantom II chassis.

Quite clearly fabric-panelled was this four-light saloon on a Delage chassis. Its squarish lines looked back to the 1920s rather than forward to the new decade.

The letterbox-like windscreen on this fabric-bodied Sportsman's Coupé (30/17) can not have made life easy for the driver, but was a characteristic of many low-slung, sporting machines at the time. There are some similarities between this April 1930 body on a Hispano H6B chassis and the one on a Mercedes SS (29/42) shown at Olympia some six months earlier.

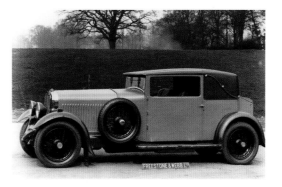

The size of the Rolls-Royce Phantom II chassis gave coachbuilders ample scope to create elegant bodies, and this one, numbered (30/16) was a Sedanca de Ville that was photographed in May 1930.

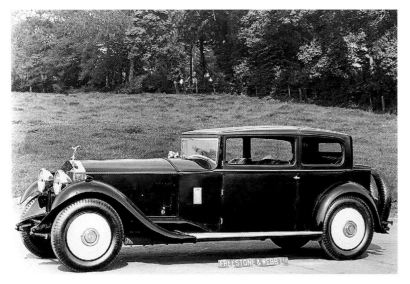

Another Phantom II chassis, this time clothed with a Sedanca de Ville body (30/22) for Reggie Beaumont-Thomas. This was delivered in May 1930 and is said to have won several concours events. The silverware in this picture with (presumably) Mrs Beaumont-Thomas taken in September the same year seems to confirm that story.

Despite the size of the Rolls-Royce Phantom II chassis, excellent proportions ensured that this two-door body (30/21) worked very well indeed.

This unusual view of body number (30/27) on a Bentley 4½-litre chassis shows how the fabric panelling was put together around the roof and rear quarters. The roof ventilator just visible here was a common feature at the time. (Thesupermat/WikiMedia Commons)

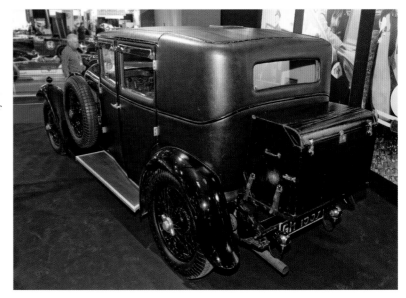

The wide bright metal waist moulding here was clearly from the same school of thought as that on the 1930 Olympia Show Mercedes (30/7), although this body on a Bentley Speed Six chassis with the 152½-inch wheelbase was completed some months after that car, in July 1930. This Weymann saloon body (30/28) is interesting but not altogether happy: the pontoon-type running-boards appear to have contained stowage space but unbalance the styling.

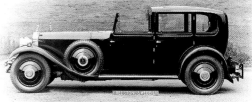

This was another car for the Beaumont-Thomases, and was a Limousine de Ville (30/29) on Rolls-Royce Phantom II chassis. Reggie's wife ordered it with specially woven blue Bedford Cord in the rear compartment, figured walnut wood, silver plated fittings and real tortoiseshell back plates for the window winders and door handles. The body also featured sideways-facing occasional seats, a dropping division, and a cocktail cabinet.

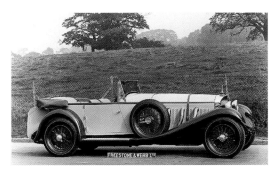

The Mercedes-Benz SS continued to provide opportunities for Freestone & Webb to demonstrate their skill, and this October 1930 Tourer (30/35) incorporates the angled glasses alongside the windscreen that had been seen on some other bodies.

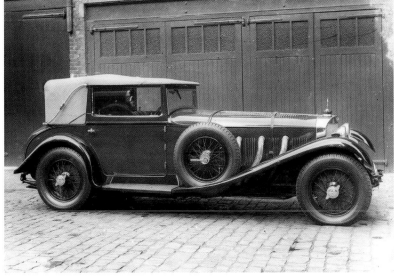

Freestone & Webb could rightly have been proud of this one, which was the first Bentley 8-litre they were commissioned to body. It appeared on the 1930 Olympia Show stand, and still survives in a museum in Sweden. It is numbered (30/36) here, but also carried the body number 965.

Yet another Mercedes-Benz SS, and opinions differ about whether this body (30/37) was a fixed-head or drophead coupé; from this picture, a drophead coupé seems more likely.

The sole Invicta chassis bodied by Freestone & Webb was number S68. Body number (30/41) survives, but is now on chassis S86. (Andrew Crisford)

The four-light body (30/40) on this Bugatti Type 46 looks conventional enough, but is actually pillarless. The body commission came through a dealer in Paris.

THE 1930 BODY LIST

Some of the 1930 bodies did carry numbers, but the only one so far known for certain is number 965. The bodies for this year are therefore listed in order of their month of delivery, in so far as this is known. The "ID no" (Identity number) in the first column is a reference guide for research purposes only and does not reflect any numbering system used by Freestone & Webb. For that reason it is shown within brackets.

The list has been compiled on the basis of surviving evidence and is the most complete available, but it should not be regarded as definitive.

ID no	Type	Date	Chassis type	Chassis no
(30/1)	Weymann saloon	1930, Jan	Bentley 4½-litre	XF3510
(30/2)	Saloon	1930, Jan	Bentley 4½-litre	PB3531
(30/3)	Grafton Coupé	1930, Feb	Bentley 6½-litre	SB2770
(30/4)	Saloon	1930, Feb	Bentley 4½-litre	KL3583
(30/5)	Saloon	1930, Feb	Bentley 4½-litre	KL3585
(30/6)	Saloon	1930, Feb	Bentley 4½-litre	PB3537
(30/7)	Fixed-head coupé	1930, Feb	Mercedes-Benz Type SS	Not known
(30/8)	Saloon	1930, Mar	Bentley 4½-litre	PB3543
(30/9)	Sedanca de ville	1930, Mar	Rolls-Royce Phantom II	150XJ
(30/10)	Fabric saloon	1930, Mar	Delage	Not known
(30/11)	Weymann saloon	1930, Apr	Bentley 6½-litre	NH2736
(30/12)	Weymann saloon	1930, Apr	Bentley 6½-litre	NH2746
(30/13)	Saloon	1930, Apr	Bentley 6½-litre	LR2799
(30/14)	Saloon	1930, Apr	Bentley 4½-litre	PB3530
(30/15)	Saloon	1930, Apr	Bentley 4½-litre	AD3656
(30/16)	Sedanca de ville	1930, Apr	Rolls-Royce Phantom II	28GN
(30/17)	Weymann sports coupé	1930, Apr?	Hispano-Suiza H6B	Not known
(30/18)	Weymann saloon	1930, May	Bentley 6½-litre	LR2792
(30/19)	Saloon	1930, May	Bentley 4½-litre	AD3660
(30/20)	Saloon	1930, May	Bentley 4½-litre	AD3669
(30/21)	Saloon	1930, May	Rolls-Royce Phantom II	18GN
(30/22)	Sedanca de ville	1930, May	Rolls-Royce Phantom II	63GN
(30/23)	Weymann saloon	1930, Jun	Bentley Speed Six	KR2695
(30/24)	Weymann saloon	1930, Jun	Bentley 6½-litre	SB2762
(30/25)	Weymann saloon	1930, Jun	Bentley 4½-litre	AD3670
(30/26)	Weymann saloon	1930, Jun	Bentley 4½-litre	FS3605
(30/27)	Weymann saloon	1930, July	Bentley 4½-litre	FS3615
(30/28)	Weymann saloon	1930, July	Bentley Speed Six	LR2790
(30/29)	Sedanca de ville	1930, July	Rolls-Royce Phantom II	167GN
(30/30)	Weymann saloon	1930, July	Bentley 4½-litre	AD3671
(30/31)	Two-seat tourer	1930, July	Bentley 4½-litre	FS3603
(30/32)	Weymann saloon	1930, July	Bentley 4½-litre	FS3609
(30/33)	Weymann saloon	1930, July	Bentley 4½-litre	FS3624
(30/34)	Saloon	1930, Oct	Bentley 4½-litre	FS3614
(30/35)	Tourer	1930, Oct	Mercedes-Benz Type SS	Not known
(30/36) 965	Weymann saloon	1930, Oct	Bentley 8-litre	YF5009
(30/37)	Fixed-head coupé	1930, Oct	Mercedes-Benz Type SS	Not known
(30/38)	Drophead coupé	1930, Dec	Mercedes-Benz Type SS	Not known
(30/39)	Drophead coupé	1930	Mercedes-Benz Type SS	77642
(30/40)	Weymann pillarless saloon	1930	Bugatti Type 46	46209
(30/41)	Drophead coupé	1930	Invicta S Type	S68

Notes
(**30/1**) Despite being described as a Weymann saloon, this had metal panels and was ordered as a demonstrator for Bentley Motors.
(**30/7**) Photographs by Charles K Bowers dated February 1930 show that this body was completed many months before the car became an exhibit on the F&W stand at Olympia in 1930. It originally had blind rear quarters, but was later transferred to a 1925 Hispano-Suiza H6C chassis, when additional side windows were let into the rear of the roof. It is not clear who transferred the body and made the alterations, or when this was done, but it had certainly been done by the 1950s. The body still survives today on the Hispano chassis.
(**30/36**) This body is known to have the Freestone & Webb body number 965. The car was displayed on the Freestone & Webb stand at Olympia in 1930 and was also on the stand of J Buchanan & Co at that year's Scottish Show.
(**30/37**) This car was pictured in *The Autocar* dated 17 October 1930, and the delivery date is an assumption based on this. It is not beyond the bounds of possibility that the car is the same as the one recorded here as (30/39).
(**30/39**) See note for (30/37) above.
(**30/40**) The delivery date of this car is not known.
(**30/41**) This body now survives on Invicta chassis S86.

1931

The totals for 1931 show that the Depression had begun to affect the Freestone & Webb business quite dramatically. That year, the company appears to have turned out no more than 23 bodies, which was just over half the previous year's total.

Even so, there were some interesting ones among them. One was a special two-door touring saloon, designed largely by the customer and mounted on a left-hand-drive Cord chassis, an advanced American type that would always be uncommon in Britain. The customer apparently wanted to use it for continental touring with his family and therefore thought the left-hand steering would be more appropriate. This extraordinary car, with room for six in three-abreast seating and a vast luggage boot at the rear, merited a page of photographs in *The Motor* of 17 February 1931 and has number (31/2) in the table below.

Also worth noting is the body listed here as number (31/22), not least because it was on an Italian-built Ansaldo chassis – a very rare marque in Britain. The four-door saloon was pictured in *The Autocar* magazine report on the 1931 Olympia Show and was notably long and low like many of that year's Freestone & Webb bodies. Nevertheless, there seem to have been no repeat orders; perhaps the British Ansaldo importers did not weather the Recession.

The traditional Freestone & Webb stand at Olympia in October once again focussed on imported chassis. Its two exhibits were a low-slung drophead coupé on Mercedes-Benz 370S chassis – a much less expensive type than the supercharged models that were still available and perhaps chosen for that reason – and a four-light saloon with metal centre pillars on a Sunbeam 20hp chassis. The Ansaldo, meanwhile, was displayed on the importer's stand at the show.

Despite the Recession, Freestone & Webb fulfilled orders for no fewer than four limousine bodies in 1931, all on the 8-litre Bentley chassis. There were two grand sedanca de ville types on the Rolls-Royce Phantom II, but as usual, most bodies were saloons. Fabric panels had now mostly been replaced by metal panels, and only three saloons seem to have had the older style, which was by now losing popularity fast. The total was then made up by three drophead coupés (one described as a coupé cabriolet) and a pair of two closed coupés.

As usual, most of the chassis that Freestone & Webb bodied during 1931 were of Bentley origin. Even though the Cricklewood maker had collapsed and been purchased by Rolls-Royce that year, there were still chassis to be had. So Brentfield Road bodied no fewer than nine 8-litres, accompanied by four of the recently-introduced 4-litres, a pair of supercharged 4½-litres and one unsupercharged 4½-litre. The remaining seven chassis consisted of three Rolls-Royce Phantom II types (of which one was a Continental), and one each by Ansaldo, Cord, Mercedes-Benz and Sunbeam.

The future probably looked bleak at Brentfield Road as 1931 drew to a close, but the year was notable in

This four-light Saloon (31/3) on a Bentley 8-litre chassis represented the height of sophistication in 1931. It was delivered in March that year and, as was increasingly the case with Freestone & Webb bodies, was fully panelled. The helmet-type front wings are an interesting feature on a grand car like this one.

Freestone & Webb came up with a real stunner in this four-light saloon body (31/5), on an 8-litre Bentley chassis from April 1931. The lines of the roof and the integral boot are supremely assured, and the contrast paint around the windows is a master-stroke.

This quite remarkable two-door Touring Saloon body was built on a left-hand-drive Cord chassis and was delivered in February 1931. The customer did much of the design himself, and it featured two rows of three-abreast seating and an enormous luggage boot. The car was intended for continental touring. This body is catalogued as number (31/1).

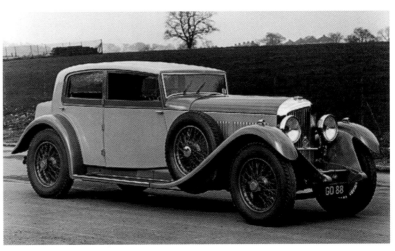

retrospect for an order of coachwork for the cotton magnate and politician Sir John Leigh. The glamorous drophead coupé for his Phantom II Continental (listed here as number (31/12)) was the first of several bodies he would order from Freestone & Webb over the next few years, several of them spectacular enough to be invaluable advertisements for the company's skills. It was also probably during 1931 that the plan was conceived to develop bodies for the buyers of the small Rolls-Royce, the 20/25 model.

Another vast limousine (31/7) on an 8-litre Bentley chassis, for Bentley's Chairman Woolf Barnato. The car has enormous presence, which is exactly what was required of it. It was delivered in May 1931.

Freestone & Webb's 1931 bodies on Bentley 8-litre chassis emphasised the car's length and were deliberately low-slung. This magnificent coupé (31/10) from June that year even had twin rear-mounted spare wheels to increase its visual length.

Textile magnate Sir John Leigh was a serial owner of the Rolls-Royce Phantom II, and a serial customer of Freestone & Webb. This powerful-looking drophead coupé (31/12) was on the Continental chassis and, like the 8-litre coupé (31/10) illustrated above, used twin rear-mounted spare wheels to add to the impression of length.

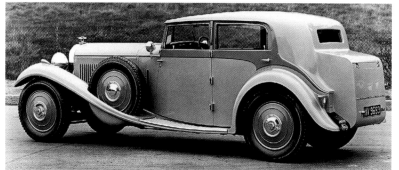

With contrast paint around the windows and a similarly contrasting waist moulding that trails stylishly over the rear wing, this September 1931 body (31/15) on an 8-litre Bentley was in most respects another triumph for Freestone & Webb. The boot does appear rather bulbous in this view, which also shows the distinctive "shoulders" between boot and rear wing. This design would later be scaled down to suit the Bentley 3½-litre chassis.

Another Phantom II for Sir John Leigh, this time on the standard chassis as befits a Sedanca de Ville. This body is catalogued as number (31/19) and was new in September 1931.

The Italian-built Ansaldo chassis was never common in Britain, but Freestone & Webb secured the contract to build this body (31/22) on one. It is noticeably low-slung in their 1931 idiom, while the treatment of wings and running-boards is interesting. The car was illustrated in The Autocar report on the 1931 Olympia Show.

A shaped waist moulding was used to advantage again here on a pert Drophead Coupé built on a Mercedes-Benz 370S chassis. This car, catalogued here as number (31/20), represented Freestone & Webb at the 1931 Olympia Show.

THE 1931 BODY LIST

The 1931 bodies presumably did carry numbers, although none have so far come to light. They are therefore listed in order of their month of delivery, in so far as this is known. The "ID no" (Identity number) in the first column is a reference guide for research purposes only and does not reflect any numbering system used by Freestone & Webb. For that reason it is shown within brackets. This list has been compiled on the basis of surviving evidence and is the most complete available, but it should not be regarded as definitive

ID no	Type	Date	Chassis type	Chassis no
(31/1)	Weymann saloon	1931, Jan	Bentley 4½-litre	FS3619
(31/2)	Two-door touring saloon	1931, Feb	Cord (front-wheel drive, LHD)	Not known
(31/3)	Sedanca de ville	1931, Feb	Rolls-Royce Phantom II	179GY
(31/4)	Saloon	1931, Mar	Bentley 8-litre	YF5025
(31/5)	Coupé	1931, Apr	Bentley 8-litre	YR5081
(31/6)	Saloon	1931, Apr	Bentley 8-litre	YR5091
(31/7)	Limousine	1931, May	Bentley 8-litre	YF5010
(31/8)	Weymann saloon	1931, Jun	Bentley 4½-litre Supercharged	SM3921
(31/9)	Weymann saloon	1931, Jun	Bentley 4½-litre Supercharged	SM3925
(31/10)	Coupé	1931, Jun	Bentley 8-litre	YF5021
(31/11)	Limousine	1931, Jun	Bentley 8-litre	YM5032
(31/12)	Drophead coupé	1931, Jun	Rolls-Royce Phantom II Continental	6GX
(31/13)	Limousine	1931, Aug	Bentley 8-litre	YM5028
(31/14)	Saloon	1931, Aug	Bentley 4-litre	VF4012
(31/15)	Saloon	1931, Sep	Bentley 8-litre	YR5089
(31/16)	Limousine	1931, Sep	Bentley 8-litre	YM5042
(31/17)	Saloon	1931, Sep	Bentley 4-litre	VF4011
(31/18)	Coupé cabriolet	1931, Sep	Bentley 4-litre	VF4020
(31/19)	Sedanca de ville	1931, Sep	Rolls-Royce Phantom II	14GX
(31/20)	Drophead coupé	1931, See note	Mercedes-Benz 15-75 (ie 370S Mannheim)	Not known
(31/21)	See note	1931, See note	Sunbeam 20hp	Not known
(31/22)	Four-light saloon	1931, Oct	Ansaldo	Not known
(31/23)	Saloon	1931, Dec	Bentley 4-litre	VF4007

Notes
(**31/3**) This car was ordered by "Bentley Boy" Lt Commander Glen Kidston as a replacement for his earlier Park Ward-bodied Phantom II that had been damaged in an accident. The Freestone & Webb body was very similar to the earlier Park Ward body and was painted in the same colours of Ivory and Black.
(**31/20**) This car was displayed on the Freestone & Webb stand at Olympia in 1931. The body was probably therefore completed in September or October that year.
(**31/21**) This car was displayed on the Freestone & Webb stand at Olympia in 1931. The body was probably therefore completed in September or October that year. However, very little information is available about it, except that it was a panelled type (ie not a Weymann fabric body) and that it was finished in Light Champagne with Heron mouldings and Fawn hide upholstery. It was most probably a saloon.
(**31/22**) This car was displayed on the importer's stand at Olympia in 1931. This was stand number 11; the importer was LC Rawlence & Co Ltd, of 39 Sackville St, London W1. The coachbuilder's record photographs are dated 7 October 1931, and the body must therefore have been completed in September or October that year.

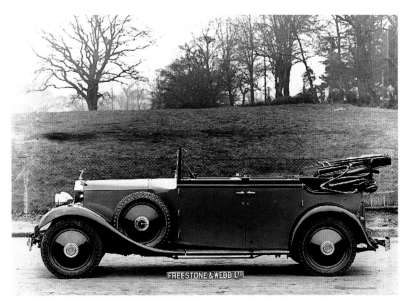

1932

The two years 1931 and 1932 were the worst for Freestone & Webb. In 1932, a further 23 bodies left the Brentfield Road works – a total that was exactly the same as the low one of the previous year.

Bentley Motors had gone, although the chassis it had produced were still the most numerous to receive Freestone & Webb coachwork. There were six bodies for 4-litre chassis and three for the 8-litre type. Two Rolls-Royce Phantom II chassis were bodied, one a standard type and the other one a Continental, but a saviour was the small 20/25 chassis, for which Brentfield Road attracted no fewer than eight orders for 1932 delivery. This is the main evidence for believing that the coachbuilder had begun to target 20/25 owners as a deliberate policy, because the chassis had been introduced in 1929 but there were no known Freestone & Webb bodies on it before 1932, except for a single cabriolet de ville in 1931. The 20/25 would later account for a sizeable proportion of Freestone & Webb's business.

There was one body for a Buick chassis and one for a Lanchester, although in each case they were the small chassis of the day – doubtless reflecting the economic conditions of the time – and the only other chassis to pass through the works were both displayed on the company's stand at Olympia in October. One was a most attractive coupé for a French-built Delage D8S, and the other was a saloon on a Talbot 95 chassis.

Unsurprisingly, the range of body styles in 1932 was a restricted one. Saloons predominated; there were 16 of them, including a four-light sports saloon on a Phantom II Continental chassis, and all seem to have been metal-panelled types and not to have used any of the Weymann patents. The Buick and Lanchester were both bodied as drophead coupés, and there were fixed-

The first body completed in 1932 (32/1) was built on a Rolls-Royce 20/25 chassis. It was either an All-weather or a Cabriolet de Ville, depending on who was describing it. One way or another, converting it from fully closed to fully open must have involved quite a lot of work – and there was a lot of top hamper to accommodate behind the rear seats.

The influence of the great French coachbuilders was never too far away, and four-light body (32/3) on a Bentley 4-litre chassis has distinct echoes of Kellner's work. The use of a contrasting colour lifted the whole design.

This drophead coupé body (32/9) for a Buick chassis gave a very English appearance to the American original. It is neat and pleasing, but not particularly distinguished.

On the other hand, the fixed-head coupé body (32/14) on this Rolls-Royce 20/25 from July 1925 is delightfully proportioned and a real credit to the coachbuilder. It was new to the Countess Rothermere, wife of the British newspaper proprietor.

This rather pert boot shape – which did not allow a very great capacity – would appear on several Freestone & Webb designs in the early 1930s. This July 1932 photograph probably shows body (32/15), on a Rolls-Royce 20/25 chassis.

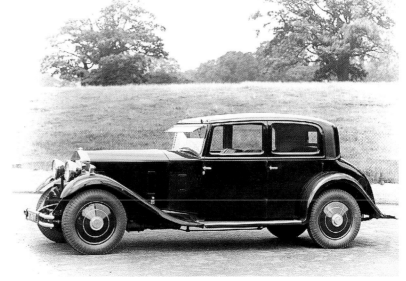

head coupés for Rolls-Royce 20/25 and Delage chassis. Two bodies were sedanca de ville types, and there was one cabriolet de ville, but not all of these were the grand bodies that Freestone & Webb had been used to building. One certainly was, for an 8-litre Bentley; but the others were on smaller chassis. One was on a Bentley 4-litre and the cabriolet de ville was on the "small" Rolls-Royce 20/25, which was surely evidence of customers cutting costs down to the bone.

The 3-litre Talbot 95 was introduced in 1932, and Freestone & Webb were commissioned to build the body for this one. It was clearly from the same school of thought as other four-light saloons that Brentfield Road produced at the time, being both neat and very well-proportioned. This one is catalogued as number (32/19), and was displayed on the coachbuilder's stand at Olympia.

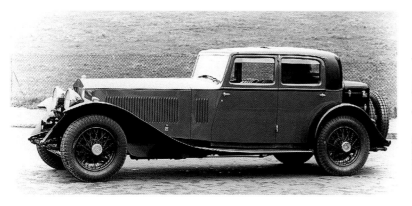

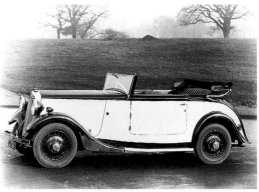

The long bonnet, short body and stubby trunk combine to give this four-light saloon a look of effortless power. Body (32/20) was ordered by Lord Londesborough on a Rolls-Royce Phantom II chassis.

The new "small" Lanchester chassis was the basis for this neat drophead coupé, for which the body is here numbered (32/23).

THE 1932 BODY LIST

The 1932 bodies presumably did carry numbers, although only one has so far been found, and is problematical (see the Notes below). They are therefore listed in order of their month of delivery, in so far as this is known. The "ID no" (Identity number) in the first column is a reference guide for research purposes only and does not reflect any numbering system used by Freestone & Webb. For that reason it is shown within brackets. This list has been compiled on the basis of surviving evidence and is the most complete available, but it should not be regarded as definitive.

ID no	Type	Date	Chassis type	Chassis no
(32/1)	Cabriolet de ville	1932, Feb	Rolls-Royce 20/25	GFT29
(32/2)	Saloon	1932, Mar	Bentley 4-litre	VF4005
(32/3)	Saloon	1932, Apr	Bentley 4-litre	VA4084
(32/4)	Saloon	1932, May	Bentley 8-litre	YM5045
(32/5)	Sedanca de Ville	1932, May	Bentley 8-litre See notes	YX5109
(32/6)	Saloon	1932, May	Bentley 4-litre	VA4080
(32/7)	Saloon	1932, Aug	Rolls-Royce 20/25	GAU10
(32/8)	Saloon	1932, Jun	Bentley 4-litre	VA4093
(32/9)	Drophead Coupé	1932, Jun	Buick	Not known
(32/10)	Saloon	1932, Oct	Rolls-Royce 20/25	GAU62
(32/11)	Saloon	1932, Oct	Rolls-Royce 20/25	GAU61
(32/12)	Saloon	1932, July	Bentley 8-litre	YM5049
(32/13)	Saloon	1932, July	Bentley 4-litre	VA4092
(32/14)	Fixed-head Coupé	1932, July	Rolls-Royce 20/25	GKT29
(32/15)	Saloon	1932, Oct	Rolls-Royce 20/25	GMU37
(32/16)	Saloon	1932, Nov	Rolls-Royce 20/25	GMU66
(32/17)	Saloon	1932, Sep	Rolls-Royce 20/25	GMU59
(32/18)	Coupé	1932, Oct	Delage 29.4hp (ie D8S)	36211
(32/19)	Saloon	1932, Oct	Talbot 95	Not known
(32/20)	Saloon	1932, Oct	Rolls-Royce Phantom II	74MS
(32/21)	Saloon	1932, Nov	Rolls-Royce Phantom II Continental	86MS
(32/22)	Sedanca	1932, Dec	Bentley 4-litre	VA4099
(32/23)	Drophead coupé	1932, Dec	Lanchester	Not known

Notes
(32/1) This was the first Rolls-Royce 20/25 chassis to be bodied by Freestone & Webb.
(32/5) The probability is that the body from this car survives on a Rolls-Royce Phantom II chassis (115TA). The Bentley chassis survives, but without its original coachwork, and the sedanca de ville body on the Phantom II is known to have been a replacement for the original Hooper saloon that it had when new in 1935. Bentley 8-litre YX5109 is known to have been sold through Jack Barclay, and there is a Jack Barclay plate on the body that survives on the Phantom II chassis. The coachbuilder's plate on this body shows the body number as 1001; working back from the known date of body 1024 (see the 1933 lists), body 1001 would probably have been built in early 1932 – roughly when Bentley YX5109 received its body at Freestone & Webb.
(32/18) This car was displayed on the Freestone & Webb stand at Olympia in 1932. The body has metal rather than fabric panels.
(32/19) This car was displayed on the Freestone & Webb stand at Olympia in 1932. The body was described as "coachbuilt panelled" (ie with metal rather than fabric panels) in *The Motor* magazine.
A sports cabriolet built in 1932 on a Mercedes-Benz Type SS chassis has also sometimes been attributed to Freestone & Webb, but was most probably actually built by Corsica.

1933

Freestone & Webb bounced back in 1933 with a total of 49 bodies delivered by the end of the year. More than twice the 1932 figures, this was not only an indication that the business remained viable but was also a vindication of the policy of focussing on buyers of the Rolls-Royce 20/25 chassis.

A very large proportion of the bodies from Brentfield Road this year were for the 20/25. There are a few question marks over the exact figure, as the notes to the table below reveal, but it could be as high as 35. By any reckoning, that is a very high number: it is well over one and a half times as many as the total number of bodies on all chassis that Freestone & Webb had turned out in 1932. That high total of 20/25 chassis stands out, and so does the fact that no fewer than 17 of the bodies on the 20/25 chassis that year – that is, nearly half of them – were of the new Continental saloon design, number 1275 and its variants.

As a business tactic, designing a special body for the 20/25 that could be made in quantity made very good sense: building multiple bodies to the same design (albeit with minor variations) simplified production and lowered costs. At the same time, the more bodies that the company built on this new chassis, the more other potential customers might be tempted to approach them for coachwork. In practice, 1933 would see the fulfilment of orders for several other body designs on the 20/25 chassis – but that, of course, was all to the good. Otherwise, the number of Rolls-Royce chassis bodied by Freestone & Webb during 1933 was much as might have been expected, with three bodies for Phantom II Continental chassis and one for the standard Phantom II.

The other eight bodies from Brentfield Road that year were on a variety of chassis. Two were on the Bentley 4-litre, which was by this stage being sold off to get rid of remaining stocks. Unique among the 1933 crop was a Bugatti, which was specially bodied for Victor Rothschild of the well-known family; other imported chassis were from Alfa Romeo and Delage, who provided one each; and Freestone & Webb had clearly made an effort to attract custom from some of the grander British chassis manufacturers.

Alvis was certainly aiming to take over from where Bentley had left off, and Lagonda was aiming to position its larger chassis in the same area of the market. Each of them put a single chassis through the Freestone & Webb workshops that year. Perhaps the links with these two chassis makers were fostered in order to keep the Freestone & Webb name associated with upmarket sporting chassis, and perhaps that was

Pictured at an enthusiasts' event in 1990, this Bentley 4-litre carries a smart drophead coupé body (33/3). (Klaus-Josef Rossfeldt)

a deliberate tactic when the company discovered that it would not be granted one of the new Bentley 3½-litre chassis in time to produce a body for Olympia in October.

The Freestone & Webb stand at Olympia in 1933 nevertheless showed a fine selection of modern designs. The three cars displayed were a pillarless saloon on Alvis chassis (which would have seemed very avant-garde at the time), a coupé de ville on Lagonda chassis, and a particularly elegant two-door saloon on a Delage D8S. Freestone & Webb clearly intended to let the buying public know that it was very much still in business.

The coachbuilder's surviving records begin in 1933, so we know that this Rolls-Royce 20/25 had body number 1026 to design 1272. It was the only one built with this "swept-tail" design, which incorporates what appear to be flashing turn signals below the number-plate.

By this stage, Freestone & Webb were focussing on designs suitable for quantity production, and their Continental Saloon for the Rolls-Royce 20/25 was an early success. This one has an attractive two-tone colour scheme, and is body number 1030, completed in June 1933.

The coachbuilder's own photograph hardly does justice to this magnificent creation for Victor Rothschild. The lines of the sports saloon body work supremely well with the curvaceous wings on this Bugatti Type 46 chassis. This was body number 1035; it still survives today, having been restored to an extremely high standard.

Early 1930s Freestone & Webb style at its best: this Saloon Coupé had body number 1037 and was on a Rolls-Royce 20/25 chassis. The car belonged to pianist Vladimir Horowitz, who used it at his home in Switzerland.

It is hard to credit that this car has the same wheelbase as the Continental Saloon pictured above. Body number 1031 was a six-light D-back saloon with division on a 20/25 chassis.

Ordered in 1932 but not completed until spring 1933, this All-weather body was number 1034 and was on a Talbot 95 chassis. The rear-seat passengers had their own aero screen. It was hard to make an All-weather body look stylish, and this Freestone & Webb effort was no more than averagely successful.

Freestone & Webb had to match the achievements of the leading Italian coachbuilders with this roadster body on an Alfa Romeo chassis. This magnificent car – with body number 1053 – has some very English touches about it but is nevertheless wholly in the spirit of the Italian chassis. It still survives, in top-class condition.

Pictured on a dull day at the end of November 1933 was this close-coupled saloon on a Delage D8 chassis. Once again, the coachbuilder's record photograph does not do justice to the sheer magnificence of body number 1061, which had been displayed on the Freestone & Webb stand at Olympia in October. This outstanding car still survives, and has been restored to the highest standards.

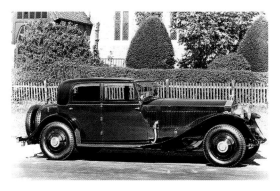

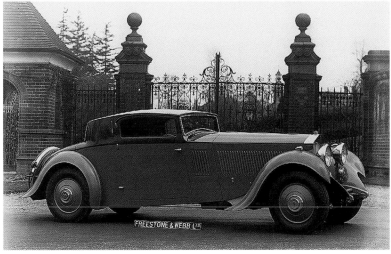

Characteristically Freestone & Webb in shape was this sports saloon body for a Rolls-Royce Phantom II Continental chassis. Body number 1060 was photographed when new in October 1933.

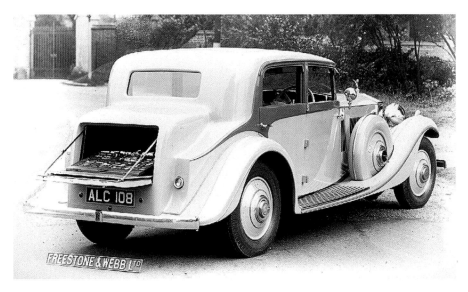

Positively oozing confidence by the coachbuilder is body 1063, a fixed-head coupé on a Rolls-Royce Phantom II Continental chassis. This was another car for regular customer Sir John Leigh, and in the rear panels above the waistline can be seen an early iteration of the shape that would mature into the Brougham saloon style. Once again, a dull day for the coachbuilder's photograph did this spectacular car no favours.

The records reveal that the body first seen on a Bentley 8-litre in 1931 was now known as design 1306. The tail had been redesigned (very much for the better) for this body on a Phantom II Continental chassis in June 1933. This one had body number 1041.

THE 1933 BODY LIST

The 1933 bodies presumably all carried numbers, but a few of them were numbered before the surviving order book was opened. In the lists that follow, the four not recorded in that book have been given ID numbers of the same kind as those used for the pre-1933 bodies. These are reference numbers for research purposes only and do not reflect any numbering system used by Freestone & Webb. For that reason they are shown within brackets.

All the subsequent bodies built in 1933 are identified in the list by the order number allocated by Freestone & Webb. The list has been compiled on the basis of surviving evidence and is the most complete available, but the possibility of new or more accurate information emerging should not be discounted. The order book also allows this table to show body design numbers, of which a full list appears in Appendix C.

Note that in some cases, completion dates are problematical; some of the bodies catalogued here as 1933 deliveries may actually have been delivered in 1932.

ID no	Type	Date	Chassis type	Chassis no
(33/1)	Saloon	1933, Jan	Bentley 4-litre	VA4095
(33/2)	Saloon coupé	1933, Jan See note	Rolls-Royce 20/25	GZU23
(33/3)	Drophead coupé	1933, Jun	Bentley 4-litre	VA4100
(33/4)	Coupé	1933, Sep See note	Rolls-Royce 20/25	GSY42
1024	1275 Continental saloon	1933, Mar? See note	Rolls-Royce 20/25	GRW54
1025	1275 Continental saloon	1933, Jan See note	Rolls-Royce 20/25	GHW47
1026	1272 Four-light saloon	1933, Jan See note	Rolls-Royce 20/25	GHW4
1027	1200/A Two-light fixed-head coupé	1933, May See note	Rolls-Royce 20/25	GEX4
1028	1200/A Two-light fixed-head coupé	1933, Jun See note	Rolls-Royce 20/25	GWX19
1029	1275/A Continental saloon	1933, Jun See note	Rolls-Royce 20/25	GWX29
1030	1275/A Continental saloon	1933, Jun	Rolls-Royce 20/25	GWX80
1031	1283 Six-light saloon with division	1933, Mar See note	Rolls-Royce 20/25	GRW26
1032	1286 Limousine	1933, Mar See note	Rolls-Royce 20/25	GRW60
1033	1200/A Coupé	1933 See note	Rolls-Royce 20/25	GFT43
1034	1225 All-weather	1933, May	Talbot 95	35022
1035	1299/A Sports saloon	1932, Feb	Bugatti "5-litre" (Type 46)	46533
1036	1296 Saloon	1933, Mar See note	Rolls-Royce 20/25	GRW62
1037	1281 Saloon coupé	1933, Apr	Rolls-Royce 20/25	GEX44
1038	1275/A Continental saloon	1933, Apr	Rolls-Royce 20/25	GAW35
1039	1275/A Continental saloon	1933, Apr See note	Rolls-Royce 20/25	GAW34
1040	1275/A Continental saloon	1933, Jun See note	Rolls-Royce 20/25	GWX57
1041	1306 Saloon with division?	1933, Jun	Rolls-Royce Phantom II Continental	82MY
1042	1307 Saloon	1933, Mar	Rolls-Royce 20/25	GAW40
1043	1283 Six-light saloon with division	1933, Aug See note	Rolls-Royce 20/25	GSY12
1044	NO ENTRY			
1045	NO ENTRY			
1046	1275/B Continental saloon	1933, July See note	Rolls-Royce 20/25	GDX2
1047	1275/B Continental saloon	1933, Aug See note	Rolls-Royce 20/25	GSY65
1048	1281 Four-light saloon coupé	1933, Sep See note	Rolls-Royce 20/25	GLZ7
1049	1275/B Continental saloon	1933, Sep See note	Rolls-Royce 20/25	GLZ27
1050	1275/B Continental saloon	1933 See note	Rolls-Royce 20/25	See note.
1051	1275/B Continental saloon	1933, Sep See note	Rolls-Royce 20/25	GLZ18
1052	1275/C Continental saloon	1933, Sep See note	Rolls-Royce 20/25	GSY94
1053	1318 Two-seat sports	1933, July	Alfa Romeo 1750SS	See note.
1054	1324 Two-door fixed-head sedanca coupé	1933 See note	Rolls-Royce 20/25	GLZ42
1055	1281 Four-light saloon coupé	1933, Oct See note	Rolls-Royce 20/25	GLZ71
1056	1275/B Continental saloon	1933, Dec See note	Rolls-Royce 20/25	GBA53
1057	1275/B Continental saloon	1934, Mar See note	Rolls-Royce 20/25	GXB23
1058	1281 Four-light fixed-head saloon coupé	1934, Jan See note	Rolls-Royce 20/25	GGA2
1059	1338 Coupé de ville	1933, Sep See note	Lagonda 3-litre LWB	Not known
1060	1247/A Sports saloon	1933, Sep	Rolls-Royce Phantom II Continental	99MW
1061	3786A Two-door close-coupled four-light saloon	1933, Sep See note	Delage D8S	38220
1062	1324 Two-door fixed-head sedanca coupé	1934, Jan See note	Rolls-Royce 20/25	GBA64
1063	1369 Fixed-head coupé	1933, Oct See note	Rolls-Royce Phantom II Continental	42PY
1064	1372 Four-light pillarless saloon	1933, Sep	Alvis Speed 20 SB	10864
1065	1281/A Four-light fixed-head saloon coupé	1933, Sep See note	Rolls-Royce 20/25	GED81
1066	1275/C Continental saloon	1933, Aug See note	Rolls-Royce 20/25	GKC18
1067	1275/C Continental saloon	1933, Dec See note	Rolls-Royce 20/25	GBA51
1068	1306 Saloon	1933, Dec	Rolls-Royce Phantom II	126PY

THE 1933 BODY LIST

Notes

(33/2) & (33/4) The date shown for each of these cars is the date off test in Rolls-Royce records.

1024 This is the first body recorded in the surviving order book.

1024 to 1029 & 1031 to 1032 The date shown for each of these cars is the date off test in Rolls-Royce records.

1033 This was a rebody of a 1931 chassis that originally carried a Corsica saloon body. The completion date is an estimate.

1035 A photograph and comments appeared in *The Motor* during March 1933.

1036, 1039 to 1040 & 1043 The date shown for each of these cars is the date off test in Rolls-Royce records.

1044 & 1045 There are no entries against these two numbers in the order book. Bernard King has suggested 1044 might have been a 1283 design on Rolls-Royce 20/25 number GYZ2.

1046 to 1049 The date shown for each of these cars is the date off test in Rolls-Royce records.

1050 No chassis number is recorded in the order book. GSY42 has been suggested, and Bernard King has suggested GYZ38. The date is an assumption.

1051 & 1052 The date shown for each of these cars is the date off test in Rolls-Royce records.

1053 No model type is recorded in the order book, which simply notes that this was a "6-cylinder Alfa Romeo". It appears to have been a 1750SS model. The order was placed through the dealer Fuggle, and the car appears to have been at the 1933 Olympia Show, although it was not on the Freestone & Webb stand.

1055 to 1058 The date shown for each of these cars is the date off test in Rolls-Royce records.

1057 Bernard King has suggested that the chassis was actually GRC46.

1058 The order book shows the chassis number as GGA2. A pencil annotation, possibly by Lawrie Dalton, reads "GEX4?" but this chassis had body number 1027.

1059 Ordered via Jack Barclay. This car was on the Freestone & Webb stand at the 1933 Olympia Show and was described in *The Motor* as an enclosed limousine. The date shown is an assumption based on the car's appearance at Olympia.

1061 The design number shown in the order book is out of sequence and appears to have been mis-recorded. This car was on the Freestone & Webb stand at Olympia in 1933. A completion date of September has therefore been suggested here.

1062 The date shown for this car is the date off test in Rolls-Royce records.

1063 Delivery date December 1933; for Sir John Leigh.

1064 The chassis number was not recorded in the order book and has been supplied by the Alvis Owner Club. The car was ordered by dealer Charles Follett and was on the Freestone & Webb stand at Olympia in 1933. It had Alvis car number 15609.

1065 to 1067 The date shown for each of these cars is the date off test in Rolls-Royce records.

The Leigh Continental, body 1063, still survives today and has been the subject of a concours-quality restoration. This close-up of the rear quarters shows their intricate and innovative shape.

Pictured after it had fallen on hard times, this particularly interesting car combines Freestone & Webb's first known work for Alvis (it is a Speed 20) with a pillarless body numbered 1064. It was displayed on the Freestone & Webb stand at Olympia in 1933. (Alvis Owner Club, via John Fox)

Another example of design 1306 was completed in December 1933 for Arthur Sainsbury of the grocery (latterly supermarket) family. It was on a Rolls-Royce Phantom II chassis.

1934

The Freestone & Webb workshops must have been positively buzzing during 1934. The order book lists no fewer than 60 bodies for that year, beginning with number 1069 and ending with number 1129 (a range which includes a single number against which no details have been entered). Very noticeable in the order book are annotations to show that some bodies were being built "for stock": Brentfield Road had quite clearly begun to batch-produce the more popular designs, building against anticipated orders

Design 1403 for a four-light saloon is seen here on a Rolls-Royce 20/25 chassis. The boot was becoming an important feature, and Freestone & Webb made sure that their solution for this body was properly recorded by the cameraman. This was body number 1069, pictured in late January 1934. Note the decorative flashes that echo the side mouldings.

This is body 1081 again, this time showing the design of the boot. A neat partition (right) divides the main luggage area from the section relegated to tools and the filler cap.

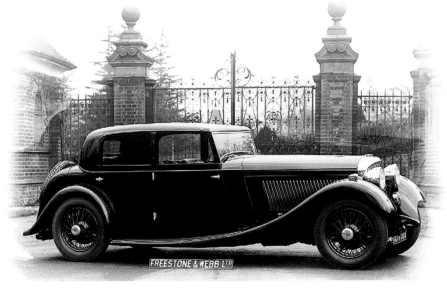

Freestone & Webb pulled out all the stops for the new Bentley 3½-litre, and came up with sports saloon design 1436. This lovely design was pictured here on the first 3½-litre to pass through the Brentfield Road workshops. The body was number 1081.

rather than only against firm ones. This was certainly a sign that confidence had returned to the business.

The strong 1934 performance was undoubtedly influenced by wider economic factors, but good management had also played its part: the focus on the Rolls-Royce 20/25 chassis had been a wise one, and the strong display at the 1933 Olympia Show was probably an important factor in the flood of orders for 1934. That total of 60 was the largest number of bodies the company had ever built in a single year, and it would never be bettered.

The largest number of chassis were by Rolls-Royce, with 19 of the 20/25 type and six Phantom IIs, of which four were Continentals. The new Bentley 3½-litre accounted for 14 of the total, and was closely followed by 12 bodies on the rival 4½-litre Lagonda chassis. There were three bodies on Alvis chassis, and two bodies on different types of Daimler chassis marked the first known appearance of that marque in the Freestone & Webb story. Imported marques continued to figure, with one each from Buick, Packard and Hispano-Suiza. And a real surprise was a solitary Ford 8hp, a small family car that was bodied as an "open four-seater sports" on behalf of a dealer.

There was a great variety of coachwork on those 60 chassis, too. Although there were no surprises on the Rolls-Royce 20/25, which continued to take saloon bodies of various types, including the latest versions of the Continental design, there were several different bodies for the Bentley 3½-litre. These included drophead coupés and a few different sports saloon types as Freestone & Webb groped their way towards a design that would sell as well as their Continental design on the Rolls-Royce 20/25 chassis.

They were not there yet, although the one that they showed at Olympia in October was certainly a most

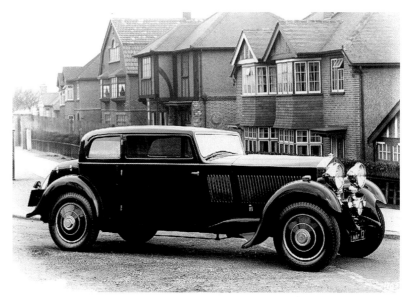

Saloon Coupé design 1281/A made its bow on this Rolls-Royce 20/25 chassis in April 1934. There are deliberate echoes of the grand Phantom II Continental coupé for Sir John Leigh, but this is a less flamboyant design on a smaller chassis. Body number 1084 simply works well.

Pushing the boundaries again... but the result was no thing of beauty. This four-light Saloon was on an Alvis Speed 20 chassis and was built to pillarless design number 1404. It is one of two made, both completed in early 1934. It was either number 1071 or number 1072.

Lagonda dealers ordered several bodies for the 4½-litre chassis during 1934. Freestone & Webb rose to the challenge with this foursome drophead coupé for London dealer Warwick Wright; the one pictured is probably body 1085. There was a fixed-head variant for dealer Gaffkin Wilkinson as well.

Saloon design 1403 for the Rolls-Royce 20/25 chassis was greatly enhanced by the two-colour paintwork on this example, which had body number 1092.

Very little information is available about this seven-seat Limousine on a Buick Master 8 chassis. The tall passenger cabin may have been designed to accommodate formal headgear, and the roof rack may well have been intended to carry flowers if, as seems likely, body 1088 was ordered by a funeral director.

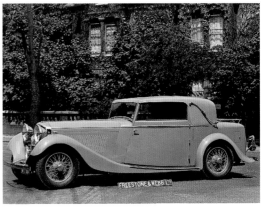

Big boots were certainly in demand, and the one on this Bentley 3½-litre was clearly designed to accommodate enough luggage for a touring holiday. This saloon coupé body has number 1093.

attractive design; numbered 1507, it was actually a scaled-down version of a body that had appeared earlier on the Bentley 8-litre chassis, and did its job of attracting a few orders for copies for the following season. Perhaps even more important in business terms was that December 1934 saw the completion of the first of a batch of six bodies to design 1441/A. It looks as if Freestone & Webb were now confident enough in the market to build bodies for stock against anticipated orders.

There were more pillarless saloon designs on Alvis and Daimler chassis, and among the two-door saloon bodies (some described as saloon coupés) was also one that was pillarless, for a Bentley chassis. Of de ville designs there were only two, a sedanca and a coupé on the Phantom II chassis. For the American chassis, limousine bodies were a natural choice, but limousines were not confined to cars of this size; alongside the Bentley sports saloon with design 1507 on the coachbuilder's stand at Olympia in October, there was a saloon-limousine design on the latest straight-eight Daimler chassis. The key feature of this was a removable division, which allowed the car to be used as both an owner-driver saloon and as a formal limousine according to need. It was a concept that would feature in many later bodies from Freestone & Webb.

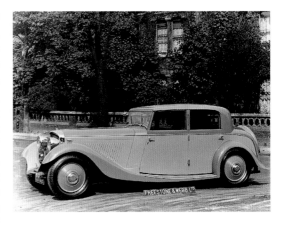

Another long-term success was this sports saloon for the Bentley 3½-litre chassis. Design 1441/A is pictured here in August 1934, the body having number 1093.

*Fixed-head Coupé design
1281/B evolved from
1281/A and incorporated
blind rear quarters, which
gave it a quite different
appearance. Here it is on
a 1934 Rolls-Royce 20/25;
the body has number
1106.
(Via Tom Clarke)*

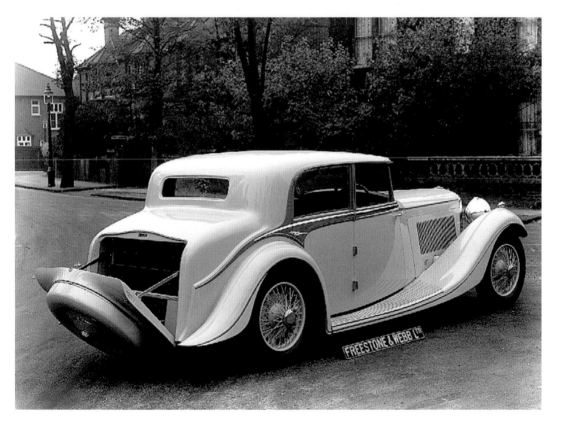

*The 1934-season sports saloon design for the Bentley chassis was previewed at Olympia in 1934. This was the Show car,
with body 1113, and once again a record photograph was taken of the boot arrangement. This body design, number 1507,
had been very successfully scaled down from number 1306, designed for large chassis like the Bentley 8-litre and Rolls-Royce
Phantom II. It would be another success for Freestone & Webb.*

THE 1934 BODY LIST

All the 1934 bodies are identified in this list by the order number allocated by Freestone & Webb. The order book also allows this table to show body design numbers, of which a full list appears in Appendix C.

ID no	Type	Date	Chassis type	Chassis no
1069	1403 Saloon	1934, Jan	Rolls-Royce 20/25	GHA11
1070	1399 Four-door, four-light pillarless saloon	1934, See note	Daimler 20hp LQ2	Not known
1071	1404 Four-door, four-light pillarless saloon	1934, See note	Alvis Speed 20	11189
1072	1404 Four-door, four-light pillarless saloon	1934, Feb	Alvis Speed 20 SB	11270 (car no 16140)
1073	1423 Foursome drophead coupé	1934, See note	Lagonda 4½-litre	Z10578
1074	1423 Foursome drophead coupé	1934, See note	Lagonda 4½-litre	Z10579
1075	1423 Foursome drophead coupé	1934, See note	Lagonda 4½-litre	Z10652
1076	1372 Four-door, four-light pillarless saloon	1934, Apr	Alvis Speed 20 SB	11265 (car no 16177)
1077	1275/B Continental saloon	1934, May See note	Rolls-Royce 20/25	GUB27
1078	1275/B Continental saloon	1934, Aug See note	Rolls-Royce 20/25	GKC9
1079	1446 Open four-seater sports	1934, See note	Ford 8hp	Not known
1080	1423 Foursome drophead coupé	1934, See note	Lagonda 4½-litre	Z10581
1081	1436 Sports saloon	1934, Feb	Bentley 3½-litre	B89AE
1082	1441 Sports saloon	1934, Apr	Bentley 3½-litre	B8AH
1083	1381 Saloon	1934, May See note	Rolls-Royce 20/25	GUB3
1084	1281/A Four-light saloon coupé	1934, Apr	Rolls-Royce 20/25	GXB58
1085	1423 Foursome drophead coupé	1934, Apr	Lagonda 4½-litre	Z10747
1086	1422 Three-position drophead coupé	1934, May	Bentley 3½-litre	B34AH
1087	1478 Saloon	1934, Jun See note	Rolls-Royce 20/25	GNC6
1088	1461 Seven-seat limousine	1934, See note	Buick Master 8	A-67
1089	1424A Four-light fixed-head coupé	1934, See note	Lagonda 4½-litre	Z10702
1090	1460 Pillarless saloon coupé	1934, Jun	Bentley 3½-litre	B32AH
1091	1424B Four-light fixed-head coupé	1934, See note	Lagonda 4½-litre	Z10788
1092	1403 Saloon	1934, July	Rolls-Royce 20/25	GRC61
1093	1470 Two-light saloon coupé	1934, July	Bentley 3½-litre	B136AH
1094	1463 Drophead coupé with dickey	1934, Jun	Rolls-Royce Phantom II Continental	47RY
1095	1423 Foursome drophead coupé	1934, See note	Lagonda 4½-litre	Z10866
1096	1423 Foursome drophead coupé	1934, See note	Lagonda 4½-litre	Z10867
1097	1423 Foursome drophead coupé	1934, See note	Lagonda 4½-litre	Not recorded
1098	1462 Saloon with division	1934, July See note	Rolls-Royce 20/25	GNC75
1099	1423/A Foursome drophead coupé	1934, See note	Lagonda 4½-litre	Z10871
1100	1441/A Sports saloon	1934, July	Bentley 3½-litre	B188AH
1101	1441/A Sports saloon	1934, Aug	Bentley 3½-litre	B11BL
1102	1424/C Two-light fixed-head coupé	1934, See note	Lagonda 4½-litre	Z10934
1103	1306 Sedanca de ville	1934, Aug See note	Rolls-Royce Phantom II Continental	185RY
1104	1281/B Two-light fixed-head coupé	1934, Sep See note	Rolls-Royce 20/25	GED17
1105	1281/B Two-light fixed-head coupé	1934, Sep See note	Rolls-Royce 20/25	GYD44
1106	1281/B Two-light fixed-head coupé	1934, Oct See note	Rolls-Royce 20/25	GYD56
1107	1275/C Continental saloon	1934, Aug See note	Rolls-Royce 20/25	GYD42
1108	1275/C Continental saloon	1934, Aug	Rolls-Royce 20/25	GYD20
1109	1436/A Sports Saloon	1934, Aug	Bentley 3½-litre	B65BL
1110	1499 Drophead coupé	1934, Aug	Rolls-Royce Phantom II Continental	203RY
1111	1501 Four-light touring limousine	1934, See note	Packard 8	378997
1112	1275/C Continental saloon	1934, Dec See note	Rolls-Royce 20/25	GWE25
1113	1507 Sports saloon	1934, Oct	Bentley 3½-litre	B80BN
1114	1518 Four-light saloon limousine	1934, Sep	Daimler 25hp Straight 8	38299
1115	1512 Coupé de ville	1934, Oct	Rolls-Royce Phantom II	134SK
1116	1521 Two-door close-coupled Silentbloc saloon	1934, Sep	Hispano-Suiza 30hp short chassis	Not known
1117	1441/A Sports saloon	1934	Bentley 3½-litre	Not known
1118	1520 Three-position drophead coupé	1934, Oct	Bentley 3½-litre	B25BN
1119	1441/A Sports saloon	1934, Nov	Bentley 3½-litre	B56CR
1120	1403 Saloon	1935, Aug See note	Rolls-Royce 20/25	GYH46
1121	1403 Saloon	1935, Sep See note	Rolls-Royce 20/25	GOH58
1122	1528 Six-light limousine	1934, Dec See note	Rolls-Royce 20/25	GWE39
1123	1536 Saloon with division	1935, Feb See note	Rolls-Royce 20/25	GFE31
1124	1535 Four-light limousine	1935, Feb	Rolls-Royce Phantom II Continental	170SK
1125	NO ENTRY			
1126	1377/A Four-light saloon coupé	1935, Jan See note	Rolls-Royce 20/25	GWE80
1127	1512 Coupé de ville	1934, Dec	Rolls-Royce Phantom II	114SK
1128	1540 Three-position drophead coupé	1934, Dec	Bentley 3½-litre	B78CR
1129	1441/A Sports saloon	1934, Dec	Bentley 3½-litre	B68CR

THE 1934 BODY LIST

Notes

1070 & 1071 The completion dates shown are an assumption.

1072 This body had a hatchback arrangement, with the rear window and boot lid incorporated in a single panel.

1073 to 1075 The completion dates shown are an assumption.

1077 & 1078 The date shown for each of these cars is the date off test in Rolls-Royce records.

1079 & 1080 The completion dates shown are an assumption.

1081 This was the first Bentley 3½-litre to be bodied by Freestone & Webb.

1083 The date shown for this car is the date off test in Rolls-Royce records.

1087 The date shown for this car is the date off test in Rolls-Royce records.

1088 & 1089 The completion dates shown are an assumption.

1091 The completion date shown is an assumption.

1095 to 1097 The completion dates shown are an assumption.

1098 The date shown for this car is the date off test in Rolls-Royce records.

1099 The completion date shown is an assumption.

1102 The completion date shown is an assumption.

1103 to 1107 The date shown for each of these cars is the date off test in Rolls-Royce records.

1111 The completion date shown is an assumption.

1112 The date shown for this car is the date off test in Rolls-Royce records.

1113 This car was displayed on the Freestone & Webb stand at Olympia in 1934.

1114 This car was displayed on the Freestone & Webb stand at Olympia in 1934. Its completion date of September 1934 has been estimated from this.

1116 This car was displayed at Olympia on the stand of J Smith & Co (Motor Agents) Ltd, the sole Hispano concessionaires in the UK. Its completion date of September 1934 has been estimated from this.

1117 This body is recorded in the order book as having been built for Freestone & Webb stock. Its completion date is an estimate only, and its eventual fate is not known.

1118 This body was built as a drophead coupé but was returned to Freestone & Webb and modified to a fixed-head coupé in October 1935.

1120 to 1123 The date shown for each of these cars is the date off test in Rolls-Royce records.

1121 This body was built for stock, but clearly found a buyer quite quickly.

1126 The date shown for this car is the date off test in Rolls-Royce records.

Body number 1116 was also at Olympia in 1934, although it was displayed on the stand of the Hispano Suiza concessionaires, J Smith & Co. It was a two-door close-coupled Silentbloc saloon on the short-chassis K6 model. This picture shows it after rediscovery many years later. (Via Nelson Thorpe)

This three-position drophead coupé had body number 1118 and was new in October 1934 on a Bentley 3½-litre chassis. However, it clearly did not meet its owner's needs, and Freestone & Webb turned it into a fixed-head coupé a year later.

Body 1123 was a saloon with division on Rolls-Royce 20/25 chassis. It had design number 1536 and was clearly derived from sports saloon 1507 for the Bentley chassis and ultimately from the much larger design 1306 first seen in 1931.

FREESTONE ENDURA

After leaving Freestone & Webb, VE Freestone established another company called Freestone Endura. Not much is known about the company's activities, but it did build at least two large Limousine bodies on Daimler chassis. This is one of them, pictured in February 1935. The arrangement of the door hinges (four at the front and three at the rear, arguably overkill) may have been requested by Daimler Hire, which was quite possibly the customer for these cars.

Quite different was this drophead coupé on a Minerva chassis, pictured in October 1935 when it was presumably new.

The most notable feature of this drophead coupé on Bentley 3½-litre chassis was a fully disappearing top. The windscreen arrangement was interesting, too. The car was delivered in October 1935.

1935

The 1935 calendar-year was again a busy one for Freestone & Webb, and the records suggest that a total of 53 bodies were built, numbered between 1130 and 1183 (there was one blank number, 1181). As usual, it is impossible to be certain of the exact figure, thanks in some cases to late deliveries and in others to the unavailability of a completion or delivery date; however, this total is the most accurate that can be established for the moment.

What is clear, however, is that batch-building was now very much part of everyday life at Brentfield Road, and that dealers were taking every advantage of it to order cars for stock. This is particularly clear in batches of eight saloon bodies to design 1567 and four coupés to design 1569 on the Rolls-Royce 20/25 chassis for London dealer Jack Barclay. There were also smaller batches, such as three sports saloons to design 1507 on the Bentley 3½-litre for Car Mart, and the Freestone & Webb order book has the annotation "stock body" against several body numbers, notably for the successful design 1507 on Bentley chassis. Such bodies would sometimes remain in stock until they were finally mounted on a chassis a year or more after being built, and the delivery dates of these chassis do complicate attempts to calculate the coachbuilder's annual output.

The selection of chassis for which the 1935 bodies were built was much as before. The majority (22) were for the Bentley 3½-litre, and that total was closely followed by 18 for the Rolls-Royce 20/25. Alvis and Lagonda chassis accounted for four bodies each, and there was a single Hispano-Suiza. Two bodies built for stock in 1935 were later mounted on the Bentley 4¼-litre chassis which replaced the 3½-litre during 1936 and shared its dimensions.

The body types from Brentfield Road in 1935 brought few surprises. Saloons and sports saloons were in the majority and were accompanied by five pillarless saloons, of which four were on Alvis chassis and the fifth on a Bentley. There were coupés and fixed-head coupés, a small number of drophead coupés, a limousine and a single sedanca. More unusual were a coupé de ville with dickey seat and an all-weather tourer, both on Bentley chassis and both destined to remain unique.

At the Olympia Show in October, the Freestone & Webb stand had three cars. As always, the company tried to show its versatility by displaying a variety of chassis, and there were bodies on Alvis (a pillarless saloon), Talbot (a two-door saloon) and Bentley (a sports saloon). The Talbot was one of four chassis on which Rootes had commissioned special coachwork to draw attention to the launch of the new 110 model; the other bodies were by Gurney Nutting, Offord and Vanden Plas. It was, however, the Bentley exhibit that was the highlight – and indeed one of the highlights of the whole show. It was the first public showing of Brougham saloon design 1617, which, with later evolutions, would form a staple of the Freestone & Webb repertoire until the outbreak of war in 1939. It would also be very influential on other coachbuilders in the later 1930s, and some aspects of its design would still be fashionable in the immediate post-war years.

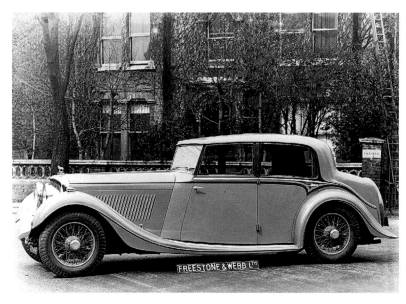

Design 1507 was a hit at the 1934 Olympia Show, and early 1935 saw Brentfield Road turning out several "Show model replicas", as the surviving records call them. Body 1135 was typical, and this picture shows how good this sports saloon looked on the Bentley 3½-litre chassis.

The customer for body number 1160 clearly wanted a Sedanca Coupé along the lines of the "Owen" sedancas built by Gurney Nutting, and that was what he got. To Freestone & Webb, this was design 1568, and the company built only this one.

Elements of other contemporary Freestone & Webb designs made their way into this one, an All-weather Tourer that had body number 1140. Just one example was built, on a Bentley 3½-litre chassis.

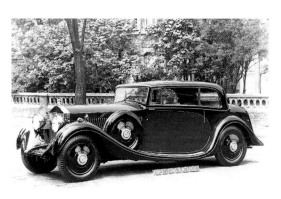

Jack Barclay also ordered four of these Fixed-head Coupés to design 1569. The use of a scalloped side feature is very apparent here, where it forms the boundary between the two colours. This is the first of the four, with body number 1153.

London dealer Jack Barclay ordered eight of these saloon bodies to design 1567 on Rolls-Royce 20/25 chassis. This one was the first, numbered 1145. Note the scallop on the trailing edge of the rear door panel; this Art Deco feature would be seen more and more on Freestone & Webb bodies, and would often mark the boundary between two paint colours.

Design 1617 was an immediate success, and the Newcastle dealer Dex Garages placed an order for four bodies to the show design, whose construction was under way before the end of the year. Freestone & Webb had finally developed a distinctive and attractive sports saloon body for the Bentley 3½-litre chassis, after trying out elements of it on a single body (design 1598) that was built in the early summer of 1935. Its attraction lay not just in the harmonious balance of lines but also in its pioneering use of razor-edge styling, which was new to British coachbuilding and quickly gained its followers (as well as its copyists). This is explained in more detail in Chapter 3.

Body number 1162 was another one-off, a pillarless saloon on the Bentley 3½-litre chassis. The overall outline resembles other Freestone & Webb bodies of the time.

The company was riding a wave of success in 1935 when it came up with another stunning new design for the Bentley chassis. The Brougham saloon drew on shapes explored on the 1933 Phantom II coupé for Sir John Leigh. This one, body number 1165 to design 1598, was the pilot example, and only one was built before it was modified to become the hugely influential design 1617.

Not a lot was altered, but immediately obvious is that a front bumper was added and the wings lost their rather fussy swage line. This was body 1169, which introduced razor-edge styling to the world at the Olympia Show in October 1935. The basic Brougham saloon design would remain in production until the outbreak of war, with periodic minor updates.

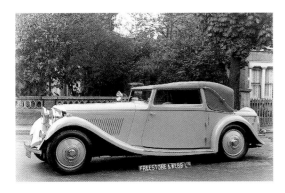

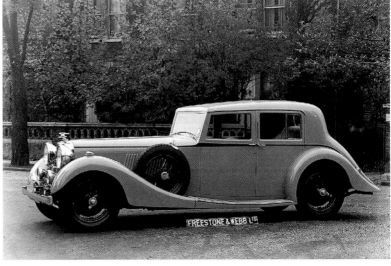

Work on Bentley and Rolls-Royce chassis was taking up an increasingly large proportion of Freestone & Webb's time by the mid-1930s. Body 1171 was a three-position drophead coupé to design 1614 – with some echoes of the Owen design from Gurney Nutting. Just the one was built.

Pillarless designs were still in the Freestone & Webb repertoire, and this Saloon is one of four built on Alvis 3 ½-litre chassis to design 1609. The swept tail design recalls Freestone & Webb designs from earlier in the decade and looked attractive but cannot have offered much room for luggage. This is the second of the four, with body number 1173. It became an exhibit on the coachbuilder's stand at Olympia in 1935.

To highlight the launch of their new 3 ½-litre 110 model, Talbot ordered a body from each of four different coachbuilders. Freestone & Webb's contribution was this close-coupled fixed-head coupé, with body number 1176, and it became another exhibit on their Olympia stand in October 1935.

The big luggage boot on this four-light coupé detracts from its grace, but was no doubt welcomed by the customer. This is body 1183, on a Rolls-Royce 20/25 chassis and the only one built to design 1624.

This four-light fixed-head coupé (1182) was created for a Hispano-Suiza K6 chassis, and had most attractive lines. It was pictured in 1959, having survived the intervening years very well indeed. (Via Nelson Thorpe)

THE 1935 BODY LIST

As in other calendar-year lists, there are some problems caused by both early and late delivery dates. However, the list that follows gives a fair indication of the Freestone & Webb output during 1935.

ID no	Type	Date	Chassis type	Chassis no
1130	1507 Sports saloon	1935, July	Bentley 3½-litre	B34EF
1131	1507 Sports saloon	1935, Apr	Bentley 3½-litre	B180DG
1132	1507 Sports saloon	1935, Jun	Bentley 3½-litre	B77DK
1133	1275/C Continental saloon	1935 See note	Rolls-Royce 20/25	Not known
1134	1507 Sports saloon	1935, Jan	Bentley 3½-litre	B29CW
1135	1507 Sports saloon	1935, Feb	Bentley 3½-litre	B183CW
1136	1507 Sports saloon	1935, July	Bentley 3½-litre	B182DG
1137	1441/A Sports saloon	1935, Mar	Bentley 3½-litre	B32DG
1138	1507 Sports saloon	1935 See note	Bentley 3½-litre	Not known
1139	1507 Sports saloon	1935 See note	Bentley 3½-litre	See note
1140	1586 All-weather tourer	1935, Apr	Bentley 3½-litre	B198CR
1141	1592 Fixed-head coupé	1935, May See note	Rolls-Royce 20/25	GLG18
1142	1555 Foursome drophead coupé	1935 See note	Lagonda 4½-litre	See note
1143	1555 Foursome drophead coupé	1935 See note	Lagonda 4½-litre	Z11149
1144	1555 Foursome drophead coupé	1935 See note	Lagonda 4½-litre	Z11374
1145	1567 Saloon	1935, Mar See note	Rolls-Royce 20/25	GSF54
1146	1567 Saloon	1935, Apr See note	Rolls-Royce 20/25	GRF24
1147	1567 Saloon	1935, Jun See note	Rolls-Royce 20/25	GLG69
1148	1567 Saloon	1935, Jun See note	Rolls-Royce 20/25	GPG26
1149	1567 Saloon with division	1935, Aug See note	Rolls-Royce 20/25	GYH20
1150	1567 Saloon	1935, Oct See note	Rolls-Royce 20/25	GEH24
1151	1567 Saloon	1935, Aug See note	Rolls-Royce 20/25	GYH58
1152	1567 Saloon	1935, Oct See note	Rolls-Royce 20/25	GEH3
1153	1569 Fixed-head coupé	1935, May See note	Rolls-Royce 20/25	GLG53
1154	1569 Fixed-head coupé	1935, Sep See note	Rolls-Royce 20/25	GYH44
1155	1569 Fixed-head coupé	1935, Sep See note	Rolls-Royce 20/25	GOH8
1156	1569 Fixed-head coupé	1935, Oct See note	Rolls-Royce 20/25	GOH72
1157	1560 Two-door, four-light close-coupled saloon	1935 See note	Lagonda 4½-litre	Z11193
1158	1507 Sports saloon	1935, Mar	Bentley 3½-litre	B200CR
1159	1507/C Sports saloon	1935, Apr	Bentley 3½-litre	B154DG
1160	1568 Sedanca coupé	1935, May	Rolls-Royce 20/25	GPG2
1161	1577 Fixed-head coupé	1935, Apr	Bentley 3½-litre	B84DG
1162	1579 Pillarless saloon	1935, Apr	Bentley 3½-litre	B48DG
1163	1441 Sports saloon	1935, May	Bentley 3½-litre	B190DG
1164	1567 Saloon	1935, Aug See note	Rolls-Royce 20/25	GHG30
1165	1598 Brougham saloon	1935, July	Bentley 3½-litre	B6EF
1166	1507 Sports saloon	1935 See note	Bentley 3½-litre	See note
1167	1567 Saloon	1935, Dec See note	Rolls-Royce 20/25	GLJ5
1168	1615 Limousine	1937, Apr	Rolls-Royce 25/30	GHO12
1169	1617 Brougham saloon	1935, Oct	Bentley 3½-litre	B125EJ
1170	1619 Coupé de ville with dickey	1935, Nov	Bentley 3½-litre	B97EJ
1171	1614 Three-position drophead coupé	1935, Sep	Bentley 3½-litre	B156EF
1172	1609 Four-door, four-light pillarless saloon	1935, Oct	Alvis 3½-litre SA25.63	13086 (car no 17685)
1173	1609 Four-door, four-light pillarless saloon	1935, Oct	Alvis 3½-litre SA25.63	13093 (car no 17891)
1174	1609 Four-door, four-light pillarless saloon	1935, Nov	Alvis 3½-litre SA25.63	13106 (car no 17780)
1175	1609 Four-door, four-light pillarless saloon	1935, Nov See note	Alvis 3½-litre SA25.63	13138 (car no 18331)
1176	1601A Two-door, four-light saloon	1935, Oct	Talbot 110	4502
1177	1617 Brougham saloon	1935, Nov	Bentley 3½-litre	B185EJ
1178	1617 Brougham saloon	1936, Aug	Bentley 3½-litre	B66FB
1179	1617 Brougham saloon	1936, July	Bentley 4¼-litre	B7GP
1180	1617 Brougham saloon	1936, Sep	Bentley 4¼-litre	B187GP
1181	NO ENTRY			
1182	1629 Four-light fixed-head coupé	1935 See note	Hispano-Suiza 30hp	16041
1183	1624 Four-light fixed-head coupé	1935, Nov	Rolls-Royce 20/25	GBJ15

THE 1935 BODY LIST

Notes

1130-1133 & 1134-1136 These six bodies are all described in the order book as "Show model replica". The last of them, number 1136, was built for stock.

1133 This body may have been mounted on chassis GRC46. The completion date shown for the body is an assumption.

1138 The completion date shown for the body is an assumption.

1138 & 1139 One of these bodies may have been mounted on chassis B28CR.

1141 The date shown for this car is the date off test in Rolls-Royce records.

1142 The Lagonda Club believes this body is likely to have been on chassis number Z11077. The completion date shown for the body is an assumption.

1143 & 1144 The completion dates shown for these bodies are an assumption.

1145-1152 This batch of eight bodies to design 1567 was ordered by Jack Barclay. The dates shown for 1146-1152 are the dates off test in Rolls-Royce records.

1153-1156 This batch of four bodies to design 1569 was ordered by Jack Barclay. The date shown for each of these cars except 1153 is the date off test in Rolls-Royce records.

1157 The completion date shown for the body is an assumption.

1158 This car was completed in March 1935 but not delivered until December. It appears that the original customer did not take delivery and that another had to be found.

1164 The date shown for this car is the date off test in Rolls-Royce records.

1166 This body may have been mounted initially on chassis number B166EF. If so, it was later transferred to B52HK. Another possible candidate is B81FC, delivered in December 1936. The completion date shown for the body is an assumption.

1167 The date shown for this car is the date off test in Rolls-Royce records.

1169 This car displayed on the Freestone & Webb stand at Olympia in 1935. It was delivered in December that year.

1173 This car was displayed on the Freestone & Webb stand at Olympia in 1935.

1175 The date of completion shown is an estimate. The date of despatch from Alvis was August 1936.

1176 This car was displayed on the Freestone & Webb stand at Olympia in 1935. Its date of completion has been deduced from this.

1179 This was the first Bentley 4¼-litre chassis to receive a body by Freestone & Webb.

1179 & 1180 These two bodies were built for stock, which doubtless explains the late delivery dates. They also formed part of a batch of four to design 1617 that were built for Dex Garage.

1182 The completion date shown for the body is an assumption.

1936

Freestone & Webb's total of 38 bodies during 1936 was notably lower than its total for 1935. Every one of them was a closed body, although there was no lack of variety.

Sports saloon types were dominated by the Brougham style, of which there were now derivatives for Rolls-Royce and Lagonda chassis as well as the Bentley, and to keep the design fresh it was given a makeover at the Olympia Show in October. The construction of a six-light sports saloon body was an interesting development, sports saloons traditionally having a four-light design at the time, and there was a single "Airline saloon coupé", which was essentially a two-door swept-tail saloon that was heavily influenced by aerodynamic experiments in coachbuilding on the European continent.

There were also other types of saloon body, saloon limousines, a touring limousine and a limousine de ville, a sedanca de ville and of course some fixed-head coupés. What Freestone & Webb meant by the description "touring limousine" seems to have been a limousine body with a large boot which had the space to accommodate the luggage of the car's occupants when they were touring. Over the next year or so, the "touring" designation would be added to several saloon body types as well, when it again seems to have been associated with an enlarged boot.

The majority of the 1936 bodies were on Rolls-Royce chassis: seven were on the 20/25, nine on its 25/30 successor, and five on the new Phantom III.

Aerodynamic designs were briefly popular in the mid-1930s, and Freestone & Webb called this one an Airline Saloon Coupé. It was their design number 1645 and was a one-off with body number 1190, on a Bentley 3½-litre chassis in February 1936. The influence of the streamlined Autobahnkurier bodies on Mercedes-Benz chassis of the time is unmistakable. (SHRMF)

Just 11 Bentleys were bodied this year, four with the outgoing 3½-litre chassis and seven with its 4¼-litre replacement (the latter not including a pair of 4¼-litres which received stock bodies built in 1935). Talbot contributed two chassis, and Alvis, Daimler, Hudson and Lagonda just one each.

This seems to have been the first year when a Freestone & Webb body incorporated rear-wheel spats, initially full spats as an aerodynamic aid on the Airline body but then as a cosmetic feature on a sedanca de ville for a Rolls-Royce 25/30 chassis.

This six-light Saloon body has design number 1283/C and is a descendant of design 1283 that was first seen in 1932. By 1936 it still looked very formal, if a little old-fashioned, but there were no repeat orders. The body had number 1193, and the chassis was a Rolls-Royce 20/25, number GBK12. (Real Car Co)

It should come as no surprise that a demand arose for the Brougham saloon body on the small Rolls-Royce chassis, and Freestone & Webb obliged with design number 1632/A. Although body number 1194, seen here, is very similar indeed to the Bentley version, design 1617, evolution has brought a quarter-light window to the rear door.

There was only ever one of these Fixed-head Coupé bodies to design 1722, on a Bentley 4¼-litre chassis. The boot has lines characteristic of Freestone & Webb, and the two-colour scheme harks back to some of the company's earlier designs. The car was delivered in September 1936, with body number 1211.

The quarter-light was added to the Bentley bodies, too. This is body number 1197, built in summer 1936 and of course on the latest Bentley 4¼-litre chassis. With the shortened waist moulding and a slightly altered rear roof line, it had become design 1617/A.

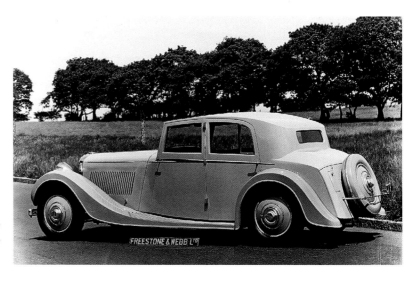

Sir John Leigh switched his allegiance from the Rolls-Royce Phantom II to the latest V12-engined Phantom III, but he did not waver from his devotion to Freestone & Webb coachwork. Suitably grand, and very modern-looking for August 1936, this is body number 1199 to design 1700. Sir John would order a second one like it a year later, but there were no others. (Klaus-Josef Rossfeldt)

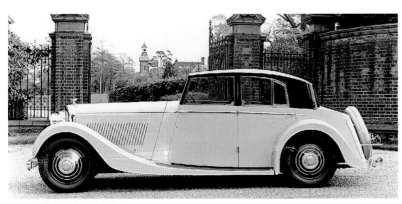

The Brougham saloon design was revised yet again for the 1937 season, becoming number 1755 when fitted to a Bentley 4¼-litre chassis. The two-colour paintwork gives a new dimension to the familiar lines on the 1936 Olympia Show car, which had body number 1214.

The razor-edge Brougham saloon design was adapted again as number 1753 for this Lagonda LG45 chassis. With body number 1215, this was another 1936 Olympia Show car, but there were no repeat orders. The car survives today in fine condition. (Coys Auctioneers)

The lines drawn up for Sir John Leigh's two Phantom III saloons adapted quite well to the smaller Rolls-Royce 25/30 chassis. This was design 1743, of which just the one example (numbered 1218) was built. (Via Tom Clarke)

This most unusual Sedanca de Ville had body number 1219 and was built for the dance-band leader Geraldo. The shape of the body at the rear is particularly interesting, and the spats helped make the car distinctive if a little austere.

This was the first of three bodies to design 1760 on the Rolls-Royce Phantom III chassis. It was designed as a Touring Limousine, and had body number 1222.

THE 1936 BODY LIST

As in other calendar-year lists, there are some problems caused by both early and late delivery dates. However, the list that follows gives a fair indication of the Freestone & Webb output during 1936.

ID no	Type	Date	Chassis type	Chassis no
1184	1628/A Saloon	1936, Jan see note	Rolls-Royce 20/25	GLJ54
1185	1617 Brougham saloon	1936, Jan	Bentley 3½-litre	B76FB
1186	1632/A Brougham saloon	1936, Jan	Rolls-Royce 20/25	GCJ39
1187	1643 Saloon	1936, Feb See note	Rolls-Royce 20/25	GCJ41
1188	1617 Brougham saloon	1936, Feb	Bentley 3½-litre	B9FC
1189	1617 Brougham saloon	1937, Apr	Bentley 4¼-litre	B33JY
1190	1645 'Airline' Saloon Coupé	1936, Feb	Bentley 3½-litre	B11FC
1191	1617 Brougham saloon	1936, Feb	Bentley 3½-litre	B35FC
1192	1628/A Saloon	1936, Feb See note	Rolls-Royce 20/25	GLJ73
1193	1283/C Six-light saloon	1936, Apr See note	Rolls-Royce 20/25	GBK12
1194	1632/A Brougham saloon	1936, Apr See note	Rolls-Royce 20/25	GBK63
1195	1632/A Brougham saloon	1936, May	Rolls-Royce 25/30	GUL39
1196	1617/A Brougham saloon	1936, May	Bentley 4¼-litre	B134GA
1197	1617/A Brougham saloon	1936, July	Bentley 4¼-litre	B252GA
1198	1628/A Saloon	1936, May	Rolls-Royce 25/30	GUL68
1199	1700 Saloon	1936, Aug	Rolls-Royce Phantom III	3AZ68
1200	1763 Saloon limousine	1937, Feb	Rolls-Royce Phantom III	3AX131
1201	1691 Limousine de ville	1936, Dec	Rolls-Royce Phantom III	3AX17
1202	1705 Saloon	1936, Jun	Rolls-Royce 25/30	GTL51
1203	NO ENTRY			
1204	1698 Special light four-door cabriolet	1936, See note	Hudson Terraplane 8	662321
1205	"1708 on 1601A" Four-door Speed Saloon	1936, Apr (approx)	Talbot 3½-litre (ie BG 110)	4521
1206	"1708 on 1601A" Four-door Speed Saloon	1936, Apr (approx)	Talbot 3½-litre (ie BG 110)	4523
1207	1628/A Saloon	1936. Aug	Rolls-Royce 25/30	GRM24
1208	1628/A Saloon	1936, July	Rolls-Royce 25/30	GTL52
1209	1628/A Saloon with division	1936, Sep	Rolls-Royce 25/30	GRM57
1210	1562 Four-light saloon	1936, Sep See note	Rolls-Royce 20/25	GTK46
1211	1722 Fixed-head coupé	1936, Sep	Bentley 4¼-litre	B12HK
1212	1731 Fixed-head coupé	1936, Sep	Bentley 4¼-litre	B14HK
1213	1751 Sedanca de ville	1937, Jan	Rolls-Royce Phantom III	3AX59
1214	1755 Brougham saloon	1937, May	Bentley 4¼-litre	B136HK
1215	1753 Brougham saloon	1936, Oct	Lagonda LG45	12146
1216	1737 Four-light sports saloon	1936, Oct	Daimler 3½-litre	30-581
1217	1765 Four-light saloon	1937, Oct	Alvis 4.3-litre SA	13164 (car no 19023)
1218	1743 Six-light sports saloon	1936, Sep	Rolls-Royce 25/30	GXM29
1219	1761 Sedanca de ville	1936, July	Rolls-Royce 25/30	GTL66
1220	1741 Sedanca de ville	1936, Aug	Rolls-Royce 25/30	GRM20
1221	1755 Brougham saloon	1936, Dec	Bentley 4¼-litre	B9HM
1222	1760 Touring limousine	1936, Nov	Rolls-Royce Phantom III	3AZ186

Notes
1184 The date shown for this car is the date off test in Rolls-Royce records.
1187 The date shown for this car is the date off test in Rolls-Royce records.
1192-1193 The dates shown for these cars are the dates off test in Rolls-Royce records.
1194 This body was built for stock.
1197 This body was built for stock and is assumed to be the one on chassis B252GA.
1204 The order book shows that this body had a special patent head fitting, apparently by J Ingram. The date shown for this car is an assumption.
1205 & 1206 These two bodies appear to have been four-door variants of the two-door 1935 Olympia Show car, which had body number 1176.
1210 The date shown for this car is the date off test in Rolls-Royce records.
1214 This car was displayed on the Freestone & Webb stand at Olympia in 1936.
1215 This car was displayed on the Freestone & Webb stand at Olympia in 1936. Its date of completion has been assumed from this.
1216 This car was displayed on the Freestone & Webb stand at Olympia in 1936. Its completion date has been estimated from that.
1217 Although this chassis was delivered to Freestone & Webb in September 1936, and work on its body began then, the completed car was not delivered until October 1937. It was displayed at Olympia on the Freestone & Webb stand in 1937.
1219 This body had purely cosmetic spats on the rear wheels.

This most attractive Limousine body was a one-off to design number 1641 for a Rolls-Royce Phantom III chassis. The rear details of body number 1223 are especially interesting, combining a vertical rear panel with swept wings not unlike those seen on earlier Freestone & Webb bodies for Alvis chassis.

Yet another variation on the Brougham design, this time Freestone & Webb's number 1779 for a Bentley 4¼-litre. The lines worked supremely well on this Coupé body, numbered 1232, and it is surprising and disappointing that no more were made.

1937

The output of bodies from Brentfield Road went back up again in 1937, when the total reached 49. Although there were 50 numbers between 1223 and 1272, one body delivered in 1937 was actually renumbered and therefore figures in the order book as both number 1230 and number 1245. Why this should have happened is far from clear, but it looks as if it had started life as a stock body that had been allocated to a particular Bentley 4¼-litre chassis but was subsequently diverted to another one. Perhaps changing the body number was the tidiest way of keeping the records straight.

The largest number of bodies for any chassis type was 18, for the Rolls-Royce 25/30, although there is an unresolved question here. Bodies 1258 to 1260 were recorded in the order book as saloon limousines to the popular design 1827, but they were for stock and have no chassis numbers allocated to them. Lawrie Dalton annotated the order book that in his opinion the three bodies had never been made. An alternative possibility is that they were made for stock but never found homes on Rolls-Royce chassis; perhaps they were sold off as surplus stock to a specialist such as

Coopers of Putney and were eventually adapted to fit some other type of chassis. If so, this would be a rare but not unique occurrence of Freestone & Webb over-estimating demand for a body to one of their batch-built designs.

In second place numerically came the Bentley 4¼-litre with 13. Six of these carried bodies to design 1755, which was the latest iteration of the Brougham sports saloon. In the Freestone & Webb order book, all the design numbers are shown as "1755 (1617A)", which probably indicates that the master drawing for the body had been made by modifying that for design 1617/A. The two designs certainly were closely related, but by the time of the Olympia Show in October, the company clearly believed that a further modification was needed to keep the design fresh. The result was design 1880, distinguished by what the order book calls chamfered edges; just the one would be built in 1937. There was also a further variation of the Brougham design during 1937, when a single body (to design 1779) was built as a two-door coupé to individual order. It was a most impressive and attractive body, but sadly remained unique.

There were also seven bodies of various types for Rolls-Royce Phantom III chassis, but that number was just exceeded by the eight bodies on Daimler chassis. Daimler was gradually becoming a Freestone & Webb customer, having started in 1934 with orders for two bodies and then taken one more on its new 3½-litre straight-eight chassis during 1936; and now came an order for seven more bodies on that chassis, plus an eighth on the latest 4½-litre straight-eight. There were five different designs, too, one being a version of the ever-popular Brougham saloon, four having a touring saloon design numbered 1879, two others having alternative touring saloon designs (numbered 1869

This is another one-off body, a Saloon Coupé to design number 1554. It is on Bentley 4¼-litre chassis and dates from January 1937. In this case, the scalloped feature at the rear of the door was not emphasised by contrasting paint colours. This is body number 1233.

This rather different take on a saloon limousine was design 1811 for a Hispano-Suiza K6 chassis. The deep windows are a notable feature, but the upward curve of the waist moulding gives body 1241 a slightly strange look from behind. This picture was taken in 1955. (Via Nelson Thorpe)

and 1878) and one being a limousine with removable division.

Single bodies on Frazer-Nash BMW, Hispano-Suiza and Mercedes-Benz chassis made up the total. The BMW was probably a 326 model and the body was built for the importers AFN (who added the Frazer-Nash name and badges to the car). The body, number 1234, is described in the order book as a two-door, two-seater Brougham coupé to design number 1775. It must have been much shorter than that year's Brougham coupé on Bentley 4¼-litre chassis, which was a full four-seater, but the likelihood is that the two bodies were constructed more or less in parallel. However, nothing more is known about it and there are no known photographs. The Hispano was given a saloon limousine body to a new design, number 1811, and the Mercedes-Benz was a 540K model bodied as a touring saloon.

Freestone & Webb advertised their intentions for

Brougham saloon number 1235 was a one-off variant to design 1785/A. The car dates from March 1937 and the chassis is a Bentley 4¼-litre.

the 1938 season with a four-car display at Olympia in October. Two were on Daimler chassis, one a saloon and the other a saloon limousine with an electrically-operated drop glass in its division. The new chamfered-edge Brougham design 1880 on Bentley 4¼-litre chassis was a natural choice, and the fourth car was the Mercedes-Benz 540K touring saloon, which added its supercharged glamour to the proceedings.

Neat design makes body 1244 to design 1782 look smaller than it really is: the chassis is a Rolls-Royce Phantom III. The two-colour paintwork certainly helps to give this car a less heavy look. (Via Tom Clarke)

This saloon limousine was created from design 1760, which could also be a touring limousine. The chassis is a Rolls-Royce Phantom III and the body is number 1240. It was delivered in April 1937.

THE 1937 BODY LIST

As in other calendar-year lists, there are some problems caused by both early and late delivery dates. However, the list that follows gives a fair indication of the Freestone & Webb output during 1937.

ID no	Type	Date	Chassis type	Chassis no
1223	1641 Limousine	1937, Jan	Rolls-Royce Phantom III	3AX51
1224	1628/A Saloon with division	1936, Dec	Rolls-Royce 25/30	GWN1
1225	1774 Drophead coupé	1937, Jan	Rolls-Royce Phantom III	3AZ174
1226	1755 (1617A) Brougham saloon	1937, Mar	Bentley 4¼-litre	B168JD
1227	1755 (1617A) Brougham saloon	1938, May	Bentley 4¼-litre	B126JD
1228	1755 (1617A) Brougham saloon	1937, Mar	Bentley 4¼-litre	B177HM
1229	1755 (1617A) Brougham saloon	1937, Oct	Bentley 4¼-litre	B46KT
1230	1755 (1617A) Brougham saloon	1938, Jan	Bentley 4¼-litre	B162KT
1231	1755 (1617A) Brougham saloon	1938, Oct	Bentley 4¼-litre	B196LS
1232	1779 Two-light Brougham coupé	1937, Jan	Bentley 4¼-litre	B147HM
1233	1554 Four-light saloon coupé	1937, Jan	Bentley 4¼-litre	B36JD
1234	1775 Two-seat Brougham coupé	1937, See note	BMW (Frazer-Nash)	Not known
1235	1785/A Brougham saloon	1937, Mar	Bentley 4¼-litre	B144JD
1236	1805 Saloon with division	1936, Nov	Rolls-Royce 25/30	GGM33
1237	1562 Saloon	1937, Jan	Rolls-Royce 25/30	GWN74
1238	1787 Cabriolet	1937, May	Rolls-Royce Phantom III	3BU136
1239	1809 Saloon with division	1937, Feb	Rolls-Royce 25/30	GRO55
1240	1760 Saloon limousine	1937, Apr	Rolls-Royce Phantom III	3BU58
1241	1811 Four-light saloon limousine	1937, See note	Hispano-Suiza 30/120hp	15123
1242	1798 Two-light drophead Coupé	1937, Jan	Rolls-Royce 25/30	GRO1
1243	1806 "Brougham" de ville	1937, Feb	Rolls-Royce 25/30	GRO19
1244	1782 Saloon	1937, Jun	Rolls-Royce Phantom III	3BT93
1245	1755 (1617A) Brougham saloon	1937, May	Bentley 4¼-litre	B73JY
1246	1813 Brougham saloon	1937, See note	Daimler 3½-litre	43629
1247	1851 Two-light fixed-head sedanca coupé	1937, July	Rolls-Royce 25/30	GRP45
1248	1827 Saloon with division	1937, May	Rolls-Royce 25/30	GHO73
1249	1827 Saloon with division	1937, July	Rolls-Royce 25/30	GRP75
1250	1827 Saloon with division	1938, Feb	Rolls-Royce 25/30	GGR48
1251	1818 Sports saloon	1937, Apr	Bentley 4¼-litre	B170JD
1252	1821 Six-light saloon	1937, Jun	Rolls-Royce 25/30	GMO11
1253	1700 Six-light saloon	1937, July	Rolls-Royce Phantom III	3BT99
1254	1827 Four-light saloon	1937, Oct	Rolls-Royce 25/30	GAR5
1255	1827 Four-light saloon	1937, See note	Rolls-Royce 25/30	Not known
1256	1837 Two-seat drophead coupé	1937, July	Bentley 4¼-litre	B34KT
1257	1760 Saloon with division	1937, Aug	Rolls-Royce Phantom III	3CP2
1258	1827 Saloon limousine	1937, See note	Rolls-Royce 25/30	Not known
1259	1827 Saloon limousine	1937, See note	Rolls-Royce 25/30	Not known
1260	1827 Saloon limousine	1937, See note	Rolls-Royce 25/30	Not known
1261	1867 Limousine	1937, Aug	Rolls-Royce 25/30	GMP42
1262	1867 Limousine	1938, Feb	Rolls-Royce 25/30	GGR42
1263	1869 Touring saloon	1937, See note	Daimler 3½-litre	47768
1264	1874 Touring limousine	1937, Oct	Daimler 4½-litre	44236
1265	1835 Touring saloon	1937, Oct	Mercedes-Benz 540K	256883
1266	1880 Brougham saloon	1937, Oct	Bentley 4¼-litre	B131KU
1267	1879 Touring saloon	1937, Oct	Daimler 3½-litre	43674
1268	1620 Pillarless saloon	1937, Nov	Bentley 4¼-litre	B139KU
1269	1878 Touring saloon	1937, Nov/Dec	Daimler 3½-litre	26790
1270	1879 Touring saloon	1937, Nov/Dec	Daimler 3½-litre	47762
1271	1879 Touring saloon	1937, Nov/Dec	Daimler 3½-litre	47763
1272	1879 Touring saloon	1937, Nov/Dec	Daimler 3½-litre	47801

THE 1937 BODY LIST

Notes

1221 & 1226 - 1231 This was a batch of seven for Dex Garages, which included one (1230) intended to be kept in stock.

1230 There is a mystery associated with this body. It was built for stock and the order book suggests it may have been intended at one point for chassis B37JY. The order book also notes that it was renumbered as 1245 before being mounted on B73JY. (Note the similarity between B37JY and B73JY and the potential for confusion.) However, there is a body to design 1617 or 1617/A mounted on B56HK, an August 1936 delivery. The body number is not known, but the most likely possibility is that it is actually either number 1230 or number 1245.

1234 The date for this body is an assumption.

1241 The date for this body is an assumption.

1242 This body was described in the order book as "similar to customer's (John Charles) body".

1243 This unique derivative of the Brougham design family was built for Dodie Smith, who wrote *101 Dalmatians*.

1245 See the note for body number 1230.

1246 The order book describes this body as "on lines of Bentley Show car 1214". The date for this body is an assumption.

1248-1250 This was a batch of three bodies for Jack Barclay. 1248 and 1249 had sliding roofs, but 1250 did not.

1255 The date for this body is an assumption.

1258-1260 The order book shows that these three bodies were built for stock. None of them has been traced to a chassis, and historian Lawrie Dalton annotated the order book to the effect that he believed they had never been built. The dates for these bodies are an assumption.

1263 The date for this body is an assumption.

1264 This body had an electrically operated glass in its division and was displayed on the Freestone & Webb stand at Earls Court in 1937. Its completion date is an estimate based on this.

1265 This car was displayed on the Freestone & Webb stand at Earls Court in 1937. Its completion date is an estimate based on this.

1266 This car was displayed on the Freestone & Webb stand at Earls Court in 1937. The car was delivered to its first owner in November 1937, and the October completion date is an estimate based on its appearance at Earls Court.

1267 This car was displayed on the Freestone & Webb stand at Earls Court in 1937, and its completion date is an estimate based on this.

1268 This was Freestone & Webb's last pillarless saloon. The design number dates to about 1935 and suggests it was an old design.

1269-1272 These four bodies are described in the order book as being built for Daimler for stock. It is not fully clear that 1269 was included in the "stock" batch, but it was certainly delivered to Daimler. Build dates are estimated.

Those Brougham rear quarters seemed to get everywhere. Here they are on body 1247, a sedanca coupé on the Rolls-Royce 25/30 chassis. This was the only example built.

Most unusual in the Freestone & Webb repertoire was this two-seat drophead coupé, to design 1837. The sleek lines of the lower body are a delight; the two-seater hood less so when erected. Just the one example was built, with body number 1256, on a Bentley 4¼-litre chassis.

This formal limousine makes an interesting comparison with the earlier 1937 limousine pictured on page 82. The extended rear wings prevent the body looking too upright and staid. Just three of these bodies were built, this one having number 1262 and being on a Rolls-Royce 25/30 chassis.

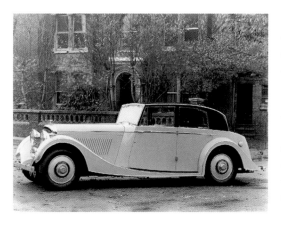

Inevitably, there was a new variation of the Brougham saloon at Olympia in October 1937. This was the Show car, a Bentley 4¼-litre with body number 1266 and design 1880, which introduced the novelty of "chamfered corners" according to the Freestone & Webb order book.

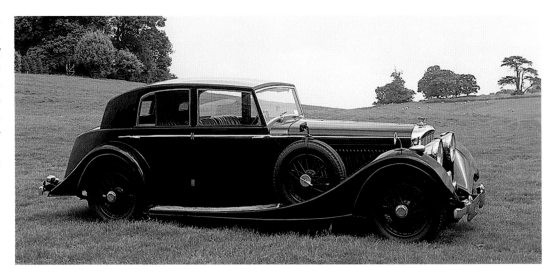

Dating from February 1938, this is Brougham Saloon design 1880, still looking good on a Bentley 4¼-litre chassis. This is body number 1275. The basic design had been introduced in 1935 but remained popular. (Klaus-Josef Rossfeldt)

1938

Output levels were more or less maintained during 1938, with a total of 47 bodies – although it is by no means certain that all of these bodies were actually completed that year. The completion dates of two large batches of bodies on Delage chassis are far from clear, even though the first ones were certainly laid down during 1938.

The Delage contract was an extraordinary one, and the only known contract of its type in Freestone & Webb's history. London dealer University Motors had the Delage franchise for the UK, and had been selling small quantities of D6-70 chassis with bodies that were built in Britain by Coachcraft, who were based at Hanwell in west London. There were two designs, a saloon based on the French original and a drophead coupé which contained rather more input from Coachcraft's own designer, Geoffrey Durtnal. However, during 1938 Coachcraft began to suffer from

financial difficulties, and University Motors clearly took fright. The details are not clear, but it looks as if they approached Freestone & Webb and asked them to take over the coachwork contract.

Estimating from dates in the Freestone & Webb order book, the contract would have been agreed in the early summer of 1938. It covered a total of 24 Delage chassis, of which half were to have saloon bodies and the other half were to be drophead coupés. Brentfield Road drew up its own copies of the Coachcraft designs, allocating them design numbers 1956 and 1964 for saloons and coupés respectively. The bodies were allocated Freestone & Webb numbers in the usual way, and the saloons ran from 1290 to 1301 while the dropheads followed from 1302 to 1313. However, it seems very likely that no Freestone & Webb builder's plates were attached; these were, after all, contract bodies with little input that Brentfield Road would have wished to call its own.

The whole business seems to have been kept under

Not every Brougham saloon was the same, despite the high degree of standardisation that Freestone & Webb had achieved. Whereas body 1275 illustrated above had quarter-lights in its rear doors, body 1277 had them in the front doors instead. This is a Jack Barclay sales picture, taken when the car was no longer new. (Via Tom Clarke)

This was the only body by Freestone & Webb on an SS Jaguar of any kind. It was a razor-edge saloon, clearly a version of the Brougham design and numbered 1281. Here it is after winning a prize for the "Smartest car driven by a lady" at the Ramsgate Concours in July 1938. (LAT)

wraps to some extent, and author John Dyson was not aware of it when he wrote his book on Coachcraft (*Coachcraft: 1930s Coachbuilding Style*); nor did the UK-based Delage club have any idea that this had happened when asked in 2017. Unfortunately, the Freestone & Webb order book contains the chassis numbers of only the first two saloons, and the only other information bearing on the subject seems to be that a Coachcraft-built D6-75 Vita saloon (not a D6-70) was delivered to them in March 1939. In the circumstances, the question of whether all these Delage bodies were actually built inevitably arises.

The Delage contract took up around half of Brentfield Road's capacity during 1938, so there were just 23 bodies on other chassis. Seven of these were on the Bentley 4¼-litre chassis, and six of those were a batch to design 1880, the latest version of the ever-popular Brougham saloon. The seventh was a coupé de ville. There were five bodies on Daimler chassis, as that company followed up on the designs exhibited at Earls

Court in October 1937 and also asked for further new styles. Three Mercedes-Benz 540K passed through the Brentfield Road workshops, including one which was a replica of the 1937 Earls Court Show car and was ordered for the German Embassy in London.

There were just two bodies for the Rolls-Royce 25/30 chassis, one a saloon and the other a coupé de ville. The single body on a Phantom III chassis has been variously described as a cabriolet and an all-weather body with a four-piece windscreen. Then there were some interesting oddities. The Packard importers ordered a pair of razor-edge limousines on their Eight chassis, with minor differences between them. University Motors was behind the order of a single Brougham saloon for the new Lagonda V12 chassis, and would follow up during 1939 with orders for more. The Brougham saloon design was also adapted to meet a single and most unusual order for an SS Jaguar chassis, which did at least win its class in a concours event at Ramsgate for its proud owner in July

There had been a Mercedes-Benz 540K with Freestone & Webb Touring Saloon coachwork at Earls Court in 1937. The German Embassy in London ordered a replica, with body design 1835, and this is it. Apparently not delivered until 1939, it has body number 1280. (Copyright not known)

Described as a Saloon but with the absence of a boot suggesting a Limousine, this was a one-off body on a left-hand-drive Mercedes-Benz 540K chassis. It is hard to imagine anything more stiff-backed and formal, and yet the main body lines are clearly those of a razor-edge Brougham Saloon. This was body number 1282, to design number 1928.

On the coachbuilder's stand at Earls Court in 1938 was this razor-edge touring saloon on a Mercedes-Benz 540K chassis. The body, to design number 1963, looks large, formal and rather heavy from this angle. There were no repeat orders for the design, and body number 1315 remained unique.

Razor-edge styling came together here with the earlier Freestone & Webb predilection for trailing waist mouldings and contrast paint around the windows. This enclosed limousine – the large boot is clearly for touring – was one of two bodies made to design 1910 on Packard eight-cylinder chassis. This one had body number 1283.

1938. There were no repeat orders, however: most SS Jaguar buyers were quite happy with the elegant bodies provided as standard by the Coventry factory.

Finally, AFN came back for another body on the Frazer-Nash BMW 326 chassis. This was described in the order book as a touring saloon, and had a neat design that embodied all the latest Freestone & Webb characteristics, including the latest luggage boot style. However, it took a long time for AFN to sell the car; perhaps there was already a degree of anti-German feeling in Britain by the time it was offered for sale, or perhaps the car was just too expensive. One way or another, it did not find a home until June 1940, when it went to the bandleader Billy Cotton, who was also an amateur racing driver and enthusiastic driver of BMWs. Cotton seems not to have used it much, though. It was laid up during the war and was sold on soon afterwards. Again, its German origins may have had much to do with its fate.

This style of body on the Daimler 4-litre chassis was described as the "round" type. The body is either number 1316, in which case this is the 1938 Earls Court Show car, or number 1319, which was built as a replica of it.

Body number 1317 was a most unusual commission for Freestone & Webb, an all-weather tourer. Just one example of design 1971 was built, on a Rolls-Royce Phantom III chassis. It was delivered in December 1938, but the style of the body makes it look older.

This neat touring saloon was built for AFN Ltd, importers of the BMW 326 chassis on which it was built. In Britain, these chassis were marketed as Frazer-Nash BMW types. There was just one like this, with body number 1318, and the car did not find a new owner until June 1940. (Roy Pollard)

THE 1938 BODY LIST

As in other calendar-year lists, there are some problems caused by both early and late delivery dates. However, the list that follows gives a fair indication of the Freestone & Webb output during 1938.

ID no	Type	Date	Chassis type	Chassis no
1273	1880 Brougham saloon	1938, Mar	Bentley 4¼-litre	B156LS
1274	1880 Brougham saloon	1938, Jan	Bentley 4¼-litre	B96LS
1275	1880 Brougham saloon	1938, Feb	Bentley 4¼-litre	B66LS
1276	1880 Brougham saloon	1938, Apr	Bentley 4¼-litre	B17LE
1277	1880 Brougham saloon	1938, Mar	Bentley 4¼-litre	B158LS
1278	1880 Brougham saloon	1939, Apr	Bentley 4¼-litre	B48MR
1279	1867 Limousine	1938, July	Rolls-Royce 25/30	GZR20
1280	1835 Touring saloon	1938, See note	Mercedes-Benz 540K	189381
1281	1919 Brougham saloon	1938	SS Jaguar 3½-litre	30180
1282	1928 Four-light Saloon	1938, May	Mercedes-Benz 540K	189397
1283	1910 Limousine	1938, See note	Packard 8-cylinder	502281
1284	1910 Limousine	1938, See note	Packard 8-cylinder	502282
1285	1874 Touring limousine	1938	Daimler 4½-litre	44290
1286	1874 Touring limousine	1938	Daimler 4½-litre	44293
1287	1933 Coupé de ville	1938, May	Bentley 4¼-litre	B41LE
1288	1937 Two-door, two-light coupé de ville	1938, Apr	Rolls-Royce 25/30	GZR7
1289	1947 Brougham saloon	1938	Lagonda V12	14033
1290	1956 Four-light saloon	1938	Delage D6-70	51537
1291	1956 Four-light saloon	1938	Delage D6-70	51545
1292	1956 Four-light saloon	1938	Delage D6-70	Not known
1293	1956 Four-light saloon	1938	Delage D6-70	Not known
1294	1956 Four-light saloon	1938	Delage D6-70	Not known
1295	1956 Four-light saloon	1938	Delage D6-70	Not known
1296	1956 Four-light saloon	1938	Delage D6-70	Not known
1297	1956 Four-light saloon	1938	Delage D6-70	Not known
1298	1956 Four-light saloon	1938	Delage D6-70	Not known
1299	1956 Four-light saloon	1938	Delage D6-70	Not known
1300	1956 Four-light saloon	1938	Delage D6-70	Not known
1301	1956 Four-light saloon	1938	Delage D6-70	Not known
1302	1964 Drophead coupé	1938	Delage D6-70	Not known
1303	1964 Drophead coupé	1938	Delage D6-70	Not known
1304	1964 Drophead coupé	1938	Delage D6-70	Not known
1305	1964 Drophead coupé	1938	Delage D6-70	Not known
1306	1964 Drophead coupé	1938	Delage D6-70	Not known
1307	1964 Drophead coupé	1938	Delage D6-70	Not known
1308	1964 Drophead coupé	1938	Delage D6-70	Not known
1309	1964 Drophead coupé	1938	Delage D6-70	Not known
1310	1964 Drophead coupé	1938	Delage D6-70	Not known
1311	1964 Drophead coupé	1938	Delage D6-70	Not known
1312	1964 Drophead coupé	1938	Delage D6-70	Not known
1313	1964 Drophead coupé	1938	Delage D6-70	Not known
1314	1969 Touring limousine	1938	Daimler 4½-litre	48301
1315	1963 Touring saloon	1938	Mercedes-Benz 540K	189385
1316	1974 Touring saloon	1938	Daimler 4-litre	47794
1317	1971 All-weather tourer	1938, Dec	Rolls-Royce Phantom III	3DL94
1318	1968 Touring saloon	1938	Frazer-Nash BMW 326	84120
1319	1974 Touring saloon	1938	Daimler 4-litre	47806

Notes
1280 This car was delivered to the German Embassy in London in 1939. The date of completion is an assumption.
1283 & 1284 Body number 1283 had a spare wheel mounted on the left-hand side next to the bonnet; body number 1284 did not. The completion dates of these two cars are an assumption.
1285 & 1286 The order book notes that "T&M divisions added to drawing". Presumably these were to a Thrupp & Maberly design.
1289 This car was displayed on the Freestone & Webb stand at Earls Court in 1938.
1290-1313 The completion dates shown here are an assumption.
1314 This car was displayed on the Freestone & Webb stand at Earls Court in 1938.
1315 This car was displayed on the Freestone & Webb stand at Earls Court in 1938.
1316 This car was displayed on the Freestone & Webb stand at Earls Court in 1938.
1319 The order book describes this body as a Show Replica, "as 1316".

Just 26 bodies came from the Freestone & Webb works during 1939. Their numbers began at 1320 and ended at 1351, although there were no entries against the five numbers from 1347 to 1351, and number 1346 was to have been the saloon body for the new Bentley. The largest number of bodies was on the new Rolls-Royce Wraith, which had now replaced the 25/30, although the most popular body (design 1998, a touring saloon) was actually a copy of one by HJ Mulliner on that company's stand at the 1938 Earls Court Show. Another (design 1996) was described in the order book as "on lines of A Mulliner job", and two touring limousines to design 2034 were noted as for Arthur Mulliner stock. Presumably, then, Freestone & Webb were a little late in having their own designs for the new Wraith chassis ready.

Demand for bodies on the Bentley 4¼-litre chassis dropped to just three, all for the Brougham saloon to design 1880, which now came with chamfered corners as well as chamfered edges. More numerous were the seven bodies for Daimler chassis, probably all ordered by the Daimler company itself and including one

Unusually on a Darracq T23 chassis, this touring saloon was built to a unique design for Albemarle Motors. The body, number 1323, betrays some characteristic Freestone & Webb features towards the rear.

1939

The year 1939 was of course interrupted by the outbreak of war, which led to the suspension of coachbuilding activities for the duration. Like others in the business, Freestone & Webb had been preparing for the Earls Court Show in October, but the declaration of war in early September led to that show being cancelled.

Among the bodies in preparation over the summer was one intended for Earls Court on the new Bentley Mk V chassis: Freestone & Webb had been promised one of the new chassis but it never arrived at Brentfield Road and was simply not completed at the Rolls-Royce works in Derby. The planned new body design never saw the light of day, although full-size renderings had been prepared during August. Daimlers were to have figured on the Freestone & Webb stand, too, and touring saloon bodies were built on both 4-litre and

Clearly proud of the intricate boot arrangements with fitted suitcases, the coachbuilder had this picture taken of body number 1327.

Freestone & Webb built four of these touring saloons to design number 1998 in 1939. Next to the first one in the order book is the note "as HJM 1938 Show exhibit" – so the design was a copy of an HJ Mulliner original. The rear wheel spat was certainly not a Freestone & Webb feature of the time – although spats would become commonplace after the 1939-1945 war. This is body number 1327, the first of the four.

design (number 2001) that the order book describes as a "semi-touring saloon". Quite what that unusual description covered is not clear! There were three bodies to various designs on Lagonda V12 chassis, and a single limousine for a Rolls-Royce Phantom III. Meanwhile, the usual clutch of imported chassis was represented by just one Darracq, which was bodied as a touring saloon.

Exactly when coachbuilding activity was formally suspended at Brentfield Road is not currently known, but it was probably during September or October 1939. A few bodies already in build were probably completed and delivered, and then the works was turned over to assisting the war effort. It would be six long years before any more coachbuilt bodies came from Freestone & Webb.

This body, number 1341, was a touring saloon with division and was built in late 1939 on Rolls-Royce Wraith WHC 54. The car has a claim to TV fame, as it appeared in a 1974 episode of Dad's Army. *(Real Car Co)*

The test of appearance for coachwork is that it should look good from every angle, and this rear view of body 1334 when new in 1939 passes with flying colours.

The height of elegance, 1939-style – and bodies like this would still be in fashion in the late 1940s. This limousine body was for that inveterate Rolls-Royce Phantom owner, Sir John Leigh, and is on a Phantom III chassis. It was delivered in June 1939 and had body number 1334. (Castillo Olivares via Klaus-Josef Rossfeldt)

THE 1939 BODY LIST

As in other calendar-year lists, there are some problems caused by both early and late delivery dates. However, the list that follows gives a fair indication of the Freestone & Webb output during 1939.

ID no	Type	Date	Chassis type	Chassis no
1320	2009 Sports saloon	1939, May	Bentley 4¼-litre	B184MR
1321	2004 Six-light touring limousine	1939	Daimler 4½-litre	48313
1322	1880 Brougham saloon	1939, Apr	Bentley 4¼-litre	B178MR
1323	2005 Touring saloon	1939 See note	Darracq T23	93612
1324	2007 Touring saloon	1938	Lagonda V12	16053
1325	2033 Six-light saloon	1939, Jun See note	Rolls-Royce Wraith	WLB34
1326	1998 Touring saloon with division	1939, Apr See note	Rolls-Royce Wraith	WMB26
1327	1998 Touring saloon with division	1939, Apr See note	Rolls-Royce Wraith	WMB39
1328	2001 Six-light semi-touring saloon	1939 See note	Daimler 4-litre	47812
1329	2001 Six-light semi-touring saloon	1939 See note	Daimler 4-litre	47818
1330	1996 Saloon	1939, Mar See note	Rolls-Royce Wraith	WRB58
1331	2001 Six-light semi-touring saloon	1939 See note	Daimler 4-litre	47823
1332	1947 Brougham saloon	1939	Lagonda V12	14080
1333	1869 Touring saloon	1939	Daimler 4-litre	47813
1334	2026 Limousine	1939, Jun	Rolls-Royce Phantom III	3DL154
1335	2027 Saloon with division	1939, Aug See note	Rolls-Royce Wraith	WHC4
1336	1880 Brougham saloon	1939, Aug	Bentley 4¼-litre	B111MX
1337	1880 Brougham saloon	1940, Jan	Bentley 4¼-litre	B17MX
1338	2034 Six-light touring limousine	1939, Aug See note	Rolls-Royce Wraith	WHC50
1339	2034 Six-light touring limousine	1939, Oct See note	Rolls-Royce Wraith	WEC29
1340	1998 Touring saloon	1939, Sep See note	Rolls-Royce Wraith	WHC55
1341	1993 Touring saloon with division	1939, Sep See note	Rolls-Royce Wraith	WHC54
1342	2044 Six-light touring limousine	1939, Oct	Daimler 4½-litre	Not known
1343	2045 Six-light touring saloon	1939, Oct	Daimler 4-litre	47821
1344	1998 Touring limousine	1939, Oct	Rolls-Royce Wraith	Not known
1345	2046 Touring saloon	1939, Oct	Lagonda V12	Not known
1346	2049 Saloon	Not built	Bentley Mk V	B54AW
1347	NO ENTRY			
1348	NO ENTRY			
1349	NO ENTRY			
1350	NO ENTRY			
1351	NO ENTRY			

Notes

A Freestone & Webb Sports Saloon body has also been reported on Bentley 4¼-litre chassis B195MX, which dates from August 1939. It is not currently possible to identify the body number, but there is a good chance that this body was transferred from another chassis.

1323 The car appears not to have been registered until 1945.

1325 This was the first Freestone & Webb body for a Rolls-Royce Wraith.

1325-1327 Completion dates shown for these cars are the dates off test in Rolls-Royce records.

1326 & 1327 These two bodies were annotated in the order book, "As HJM 1938 Show exhibit." Despite the excellence of their own designs, Freestone & Webb continued to copy those of other coachbuilders when asked!

1328-1329 Completion dates shown for these cars are an assumption.

1330 This body is annotated in the order book, "On lines of A Mulliner job." The completion date shown is the date off test in Rolls-Royce records.

1331 The completion date shown for this body is an assumption.

1335 The completion date shown is the date off test in Rolls-Royce records.

1338-1341 Completion dates shown for these cars are the dates off test in Rolls-Royce records.

1342 This car was planned for the Freestone & Webb stand at the 1939 Earls Court Show. Its completion date has been estimated from that.

1343 This car was planned for the Freestone & Webb stand at the 1939 Earls Court Show. Its completion date has been estimated from that.

1344 The completion date shown is an estimate only.

1345 This car was planned for the Freestone & Webb stand at the 1939 Earls Court Show.

Chapter Five

AUSTERITY 1940-1949

The first half of the 1940s might just as well not have existed for the traditional coachbuilding trade. Workshops were closed on Government orders well before the end of 1939, and it was not until 1945 that they were able to open once again for business. In the mean time, the nature of that business had changed fundamentally and irrevocably. Social and economic changes that followed the war reduced the demand for high-end luxury goods, while in the motor industry the trend was now away from separate bodies and chassis and towards integral or monocoque construction, which introduced new and more complex requirements into the body manufacturing process.

Freestone & Webb started coachbuilding again as soon as they possibly could, but it took some time for the business to build back up again, and it would be 1947 before the company's future began to look anything like safe. From the Brentfield Road order book, it is clear that there were multiple cancellations of orders in this period, and that there were also multiple delays in delivery. One result of this is that it is impossible to state with any degree of certainty which bodies or even how many were produced in a given year. So the catalogue of Freestone & Webb bodies in the following chapter groups all the 1945-1949 bodies together.

The War Years

There is little detail available about what went on at Brentfield Road between 1939 and 1945. Government policy was to make use of all available skilled men and women to assist the war effort, and companies with a particular expertise were instructed to use that expertise to produce goods with a military value. Many car manufacturing companies were turned over to aircraft

The year 1946 saw Brentfield Road slowly returning to business, and a real life-saver was a batch contract from Daimler to build limousine bodies over the next few years or so. This picture from a Daimler catalogue shows the larger type, on the DE36 chassis. The catalogue offers the style as "close-coupled limousine with partition and folding seats or as a saloon with front and rear seating with a division if required. Upholstery, furnishings and painting to choice."

construction, and the coachbuilding skills of Freestone & Webb were put to good use in the manufacture of wing tips for Supermarine Spitfire fighter aircraft.

The Spitfire, which in the early years of the war was Britain's best fighter aircraft, was built with detachable wing tips. This was mainly so that different configurations for different purposes could be produced using the same basic design; Spitfire variants used in high-level reconnaissance roles needed a different configuration from those used as ground-support fighters or (as in the case of the Seafire variant) aboard aircraft carriers.

Like the coachbuilt bodies that Freestone & Webb had been building before the war, these wing tips were constructed by adding light metal skin panels over a rigid frame, which in the Spitfire's case was of metal rather than wood. Nevertheless, the skills involved in constructing them were much the same as those involved in coachbuilding. So it is probable that a number of Freestone & Webb employees were exempted from military service and were able to remain at Brentfield Road on war work. No doubt many of those men formed the nucleus of the company's workforce when it was finally able to begin coachbuilding again in 1945.

A Cautious Start, 1945-1948

When the war ended in 1945, Freestone & Webb were in a relatively fortunate position. Their premises had been left undamaged by the aerial bombing of London, and they still had a core of skilled employees who had of course been working through the war on aircraft component manufacture. Long-time employee Henry Simmons took over as chief designer, and the company gradually got back on its feet.

However, the picture was certainly not as rosy as this suggests. First of all, the immediate post-war years would be affected by a series of austerity measures imposed by the Government as the country tried to rebuild economically. Second, the number of car manufacturers who were still producing separate chassis that could take coachbuilt bodies had been drastically reduced. The austerity measures ensured that there would be no imported chassis from the likes of Packard, and at home only three makers offered any promise.

These three were Bentley, Daimler and Rolls-Royce. All of them had been Freestone & Webb customers before the war, but the announcement from Rolls-Royce in 1946 that it would produce a range of cars with standardised bodywork for the post-war Bentley chassis was an immediate blow to the hopes of every coachbuilder still in business. By contrast, the new Rolls-Royce Silver Wraith chassis would be available as a chassis only, which meant that there would be strong competition to secure orders for coachwork for it.

As for Daimler, the new DE27 and DE36 models announced in 1946 would also offer opportunities, but these were large cars intended for formal coachwork, and the market for them was never going to be very large. In addition, the coachbuilder Hooper belonged to the same BSA group as Daimler itself, which meant that the lion's share of coachwork was likely to be built in-house.

Nevertheless, a far smaller number of coachbuilders around the country would be competing for such work as did become available. There had already been a thinning of the ranks of British coachbuilders by 1938, as the smaller firms took stock of their future. Now, just five of the established major companies remained

in business: Abbott, Hooper, HJ Mulliner, Park Ward and James Young. The decision to make Freestone & Webb a sixth must have been a very hard one, but it seemed to be worth a gamble. So from some time in 1946, Freestone & Webb announced that they were back in the bespoke coachbuilding business. The likelihood is that they began by offering repair and refurbishment work on coachbuilt cars which had been in storage during the war years and were now being recommissioned for further use.

They had started work during late 1945, their first proper coachwork commission apparently being to fit a Hooper saloon-limousine body to a pre-war Rolls-Royce Wraith chassis. The chassis itself remains unidentified, as does the source of the body, but the job was numbered 1352 in the Freestone & Webb order book. This carried on from the aborted pre-war sequence, and the fact that it was allocated a body number at all rather suggests that a number of modifications were made when the body was fitted to the chassis. For Freestone & Webb it was a start, but nothing could have prepared them for the next commission that came their way – a deliberately flamboyant rebody of a pre-war Rolls-Royce Phantom III that was intended to win concours d'élégance events for its equally flamboyant owner in France.

The glamorous world for which this car was intended was very far removed from the difficult conditions that obtained back in Britain, and at Brentfield Road in particular. The order book reveals very few commissions for new coachwork during 1946, and no doubt one reason was that chassis supplies were very difficult. Customers simply could not obtain the chassis they wanted because car makers were obliged to follow the government policy of giving an absolute priority to exports. This situation would prevail for several more years, easing only in the early 1950s, and the order book has blank entries against several body numbers during this period. The probable explanation is that these were body numbers allocated in anticipation of a firm enquiry becoming a firm order, but that for one reason or another no chassis became available and so the anticipated body was not built.

No doubt Freestone & Webb had to put a great deal of effort into touting for business in the mid-1940s. As a trickle of chassis began to arrive from Rolls-Royce – a few Silver Wraith chassis and a small number of Bentley Mk VI types delivered in chassis-only form – the brightest light on the horizon was a low-volume contract for saloon-limousine bodies for the new post-war Daimler chassis.

As explained above, Daimler belonged to the BSA Group, which also owned the coachbuilder Hooper (which in turn had absorbed Barker in 1938). So there was plenty of in-house coachbuilding capacity to suit the new Daimler chassis. Nevertheless, Daimler did decide to farm out some of the coachwork for its new models to Freestone & Webb. The company was probably both surprised and thankful that it had been cultivating a relationship with Daimler at the time war had broken out in 1939, for the earlier link had now proved a life-saver at a critical time.

But Freestone & Webb needed more than this to become securely re-established; probably no more than four bodies for the Daimler contract were completed in 1946, and three or four in each of the subsequent years up to and including 1950. Nevertheless, the link with Daimler does appear to have led on to one more bespoke commission for Freestone & Webb, when Ivan Hendriks, a Jamaican businessman, ordered a four-door saloon on the DE36 chassis. The date of this commission is not clear, but the car appears to have been delivered in early 1949. Its design made clear that Freestone & Webb could still produce eye-catching and elegant coachwork, and the company must have been particularly proud of this one. Body number 1461 was built to design 3031 and made a masterful job of turning the vast Daimler DE36 chassis into a long, low, and attractively proportioned saloon. The car attracted a degree of attention in the British motoring press, and this must have done some good for Freestone & Webb's business.

Meanwhile, the company had been drawing up its offerings for the Rolls-Royce Silver Wraith and Bentley Mk VI chassis that became available in small numbers after mid-1946. For the Silver Wraith (at this stage in its original short-wheelbase form), there was design 3004 for a six-light saloon; over the years there would be multiple sub-variants of this, which could be had with or without a division. For the Bentley Mk VI, Freestone & Webb initially seem to have pinned their hopes on a two-door foursome drophead coupé with concealed head, and this certainly drew in the orders. Unfortunately, not one was ever built, and all five

The semi-razor-edge lines, wheel spats, and Hooper-inspired rear quarter-light shape were all fairly typical of Freestone & Webb bodies in his period. This advertisement for the company's stand at Earls Court in 1949 shows body number 1475 to design 3004/A2/F on Rolls-Royce Silver Wraith chassis WCB11. In fact, that car had been on the company's 1948 show stand, but in black-and-white it looked sufficiently similar to the car that was actually on the 1949 stand (number 1513, to design 3050/A/B) for few people to notice! The most obvious difference is actually in the shape of the over-riders.

orders were cancelled; no indication of the reason has so far come to light. More fruitful was design 3010, which was a typically clean-cut four-light saloon of which there were also multiple sub-variants. It was supplemented in 1947 by design 3038, with a more streamlined tail, which went on to become popular as business gradually improved.

Bespoke bodies could of course still be had to order, but they were few in number and there were just two on the Silver Wraith chassis before 1950. On the Bentley Mk VI chassis, there were three separate fixed-head coupé designs, and some went on to spawn sub-variants, but all were built either singly or in small numbers. Saloon coupé and a pair of bespoke four-door saloon designs for the Bentley chassis also all remained singletons.

As already noted, delivery dates in the period from 1946 to 1948 seem to be rather haphazard, and it is therefore difficult to be certain exactly how many bodies were delivered in a given year. However, as the table later in this chapter shows, 64 bodies were delivered in those three years, which gives an average of just over 21 bodies each year. In practice, there was a smaller number in 1946 and the annual totals gradually increased. Nevertheless, it must have been barely enough to keep the company viable, and whatever repair work came in must have been welcomed with open arms.

Hesitation, 1949

Austerity still ruled British life during 1949, but it looks as if things were beginning to return to normal at Brentfield Road. The orders seem to have been coming in, but within the wide spread of around 80 body

This remarkable photograph shows the specially commissioned Daimler saloon, body number 1461, in build. The panels have all been completed but the body has no glass or lighting. The sheer size of the car, on the huge DE36 straight-eight chassis intended for limousine bodies, is immediately apparent.

numbers probably associated with 1949 (it is hard to pinpoint exact start and finish points), no fewer than 31 bodies are listed as cancelled. One order is listed as a Bentley Mk VI standard steel saloon, presumably a car to which Freestone & Webb added a few individual touches of their own before delivering it.

These cancellations and exceptions reduce the likely total for 1949 to 36 bodies – which was nevertheless a very healthy figure when compared to the Freestone & Webb body output in the immediate post-war years. On top of it would have been two or three bodies for the Daimler contract.

The spectacular saloon body on Daimler DE36 chassis built in 1948 for Mr Hendriks had disappeared with him to Jamaica, but Freestone & Webb must have been very well aware of its appeal as a demonstration of their abilities. Daimler were using a picture of it on their sales catalogue for the DE27 and DE36 models, and *The Autocar* of 4 February 1949 reviewed it very favourably, noting that the car "would have won unstinted admiration if it had appeared at the London Show last autumn." So the company obtained a second DE36 chassis from Daimler and built what amounted to a modified replica of the Hendriks car to display at the Earls Court Show in September.

All the bodies not on Daimler chassis were for either the Bentley Mk VI or the Rolls-Royce Silver Wraith. Six-light saloon designs with razor-edge or toned-down "semi-razor-edge" features and various designs of rear wheel spat were the popular choice for both types, and despite their undeniable elegance there was a numbing similarity among the different variants. On the one hand, this could be seen as creating a distinctive Freestone & Webb style, but from a different perspective it could be seen as reflecting either a lack of new ideas or a deliberate reduction of variety to simplify production and keep costs in check at Brentfield Road.

FREESTONE & WEBB ANNUAL PRODUCTION TOTALS, 1946-1949

There remain some problems with completion dates, which may affect the figures here to a small extent. Nine bodies not included in the figures below were built between 1946 and 1949 but cannot yet be allocated a precise date.

Nevertheless, these calculated annual totals give a good idea of the output from Brentfield Road in the late 1940s. They relate to calendar years, and there is more detail about them in Chapter 6.

1945	2
1946	4
1947	23
1948	37
1949	36

Adding in the nine undated bodies, the total bodies for the five years from 1945 to 1949 is 111.

Chapter Six

THE COACHWORK 1945-1949

New chassis were in very short supply in the first few years after the war, and the first two bodies in the Freestone & Webb order book in 1945 were both on pre-war chassis. Many other coachbuilders did similar things, and there grew up a trade in so-called "replica" bodies, which re-created the elegant shapes of expensive pre-war coachwork on chassis that had survived the war but whose bodies had deteriorated beyond sensible repair. There is no indication that Brentfield Road indulged in this, although the company probably attracted a good deal of repair and recommissioning work in 1945-1946 just to keep itself ticking over until chassis supplies resumed and with them the demand for new bodies.

Those first two bodies were nevertheless interesting: one was a no doubt discreet Hooper Saloon Limousine that was transferred to an unidentified pre-war Rolls-Royce Wraith, and the other could hardly have been more spectacular, being a four-door, four-light sedanca de ville on the chassis of another pre-war Rolls-Royce – specifically a 1937 Phantom III.

The John Gaul Phantom

On that spectacular rebody, number 1353 in the Freestone & Webb order book, hangs a substantial and intriguing story all of its own. When new in 1937, its Phantom III chassis had been given a seven-passenger limousine body by the small Birmingham coachbuilder WC Atcherley. Like so many other cars of its type, the Phantom was stored during the war years, but in 1945 its existence came to the notice of Alfred John Gaul, usually known as John Gaul. Gaul had once been a car dealer, then a property tycoon, and had become a very wealthy man. He was a colourful if somewhat shady character who enjoyed spectacular

cars and had owned several bodied by the Parisian firm of Saoutchik. Though domiciled in England, he spent much of his time in the south of France, where he liked to be known as Sir John Gaul. Here, he clearly enjoyed the glamorous lifestyle and, with it, the local concours d'élégance events.

Gaul bought the chassis and commissioned Freestone & Webb to replace its limousine body with one that would be a guaranteed winner at such events when they resumed after the war. The order book records a date of November 1945, which may be when Gaul placed his order, but the car was not actually delivered until August 1946. In view of its complexity, it may well have taken much of the intervening period for the body to be completed.

Freestone & Webb drew up design number 2100 specially for the Gaul Phantom. The last known pre-war design number had been 2049, so this followed comfortably on from it. However, the number would stand alone, as a new sequence beginning probably at

This was Freestone & Webb's first post-war commission for a new body. The car was deliberately intended to be a spectacular concours d'élégance winner, and was built on a 1937 Rolls-Royce Phantom III chassis. Apparently commissioned in November 1945, it was delivered in August 1946. The unique sedanca de ville body, number 1353, shows that Freestone & Webb were still thinking along the lines established pre-war by their razor-edge bodies. (Rex Gray/ WikiMedia Commons)

Numerically, this was the first "proper" Freestone & Webb post-war body, 1354. It is on a Rolls-Royce Silver Wraith chassis, WTA37, and is a semi-razor-edge Saloon. The body design is 3004/1, and only this single example of the variant was built. Design 3004 and its variants became central to Freestone & Webb offerings for the Silver Wraith in the 1940s. (Real Car Company)

Design 3010 for the Bentley Mk VI was clearly related to design 3004 for the larger Silver Wraith chassis, and here is a 3010/D, number 1355, on the first Bentley MkVI chassis to be bodied by Freestone & Webb.

The Daimler limousine bodies were built to a standard design, and the identity of this one is not certain, but it was pictured when new in May 1949. Traces of the trademark razor-edge style are visible on the roof and around the rear quarters on this Daimler DE27, the shorter of the two chassis types that were given Freestone & Webb bodies.

3000 was initiated the following year. Design 2100 had traces of the company's trademark pre-war razor-edge detailing, plus burnished solid copper with a satin finish to face the long sweeping wings and running-boards. This feature later earned the car the nickname of "Gaul's Copper Kettle". The radiator grille, mouldings, lamps, bumpers and other metal work were copper-plated to match, and the copper colour made a striking contrast with the deep chianti red of the main body panels. Clearly, this was a no-expense-spared job, especially at a time of such great austerity.

The rear compartment contained two deep armchair seats upholstered in wine-coloured cloth and piped in a lighter colour. The rear of the division contained folding tables, a heater and a radio, all set in light burr walnut cabinet work. The car was reviewed in *The Autocar* of 27 September 1946, which added: "The division glass, the rear blind and the off-side front door window are electrically operated either from the instrument board or from switches on top of the rear cabinet. All operational switches are labelled with Old English lettering."

Gaul used the car extensively for concours d'élégance events in Cannes, Deauville and Monte Carlo before selling it in 1954. Since then it has had several more owners and, at the time of writing, was in the USA. As for John Gaul, he went on to run the Coronet Club in London's Soho district, and was fined in October 1962 for involvement with a prostitution racket. Gaul later disappeared abroad when he faced arrest after his wife was murdered in 1976, but the case against him was dropped in 1984 when a key prosecution witness changed his evidence.

Core designs

As the British motor industry sorted itself out in late 1945 and 1946, it became quite obvious that there would not be a wide variety of chassis available for domestic coachbuilders to body. Government restrictions meant there would be no imported types for the foreseeable future; some British makes were late in resuming manufacture, while a few never did; others were clearly going to follow the trend towards monocoque construction. So that left Rolls-Royce and Bentley as the major hope for an admittedly reduced number of coachbuilders.

It was not until 1946 that Crewe announced its plans for post-war production. There would be a Bentley chassis that would predominantly come with a standardised all-steel saloon body (although chassis would be available in limited numbers for bespoke coachwork), and there would be a related but larger Rolls-Royce type specifically intended for coachbuilt bodies. So Freestone & Webb's strategy had to be based around this, and during 1946 Brentfield Road prepared one basic design for each chassis, doubtless intending that each one should be flexible enough to allow for individual customer requests. These would be the core offerings and, the company must have hoped, order numbers would be swelled by bespoke individual commissions.

Unsurprisingly, both of these core designs carried on the razor-edge styling that had proved so popular in the later 1930s, adding changes to give at least an impression of newness. This was not the time for anything radically new because it was impossible to predict either the size of the market or the way customer tastes would go. So there were clear similarities between design 3004, a four-light saloon for the Rolls-Royce Silver Wraith, and design 3010 for the Bentley Mk VI (which had a four-light saloon body as standard). There were variants indicated by suffix letters (the earliest 3010 built, for example, was actually a 3010/D). The first examples of both bodies were built in early 1947, as examples of the new chassis became available.

During 1948, the 3004 family of designs remained central to Freestone & Webb's offerings for the Silver Wraith, and expanded to include a six-light variant as well. The four-light 3010 meanwhile remained the core design for the Bentley Mk VI, supplemented from the start of the year by a four-light alternative design numbered 3038. These three designs – 3004, 3010 and 3038 – remained available for 1949, and early in that year yet another new Bentley design (numbered 3046) was introduced, replacing the original 3010 of which the last example was built that summer.

These razor-edge designs generally had shallow windscreens, with a distinctive razor-edge outline to the front of the roof directly above them. Many had rear wheel spats, sometimes full spats and sometimes spats that were cut away to a greater or lesser extent.

This was the longer of the two Daimler limousine bodies, on the straight-eight DE36 chassis. This two-toned example is almost certainly body 1366, which was displayed on the Freestone & Webb stand at Earls Court in 1948. The number-plate, as would be typical of a show car, reads "FW 1949".

Razor-edges again, and there are some unmistakable Freestone & Webb design cues on this unique coupé body to design 3014. The chassis is a Rolls-Royce Silver Wraith, number WVA74, and the car was delivered in November 1947 with body number 1384.

There were several individual commissions in this period, and this all-weather body for a Rolls-Royce Silver Wraith had design number 3005. The chassis is number WTA44, and the car dates from April 1947. This is body number 1383.

There was only one of these bodies, to design 3027 on a Bentley Mk VI chassis (B239AJ). It is a most attractive coupé, in this case without the semi-razor-edge lines. The rear bulkhead contains a wind-up gramophone and a cocktail cabinet as well. The car was new in September 1947 and has body number 1386. (Klaus-Josef Rossfeldt)

This was yet another unique body, a foursome drophead coupé to design 3008. The lines are rounded and there is not a razor edge in sight; the absence of running-boards combines with pontoon wings and rear spats to give a very modern aspect for 1947. This is body 1388 on a Bentley MkVI chassis, B76AK. The customer was Percy Fritz Swain of Swain Holdings Ltd, the company that would later own Freestone & Webb. (Tom Clarke)

Body number 1391 is another variant of design 3004 for the Rolls-Royce Silver Wraith. This time it is 3004/A2, now a six-light saloon limousine with those extra side windows clearly influenced by the Hooper Teviot. The full spats with a flash to highlight them were probably unique to this car, although two other examples of the body were built. This one is on chassis WVA21 and dates from September 1947.

Designs were adapted, and the multiple variants of 3004, which included both four-light and six-light types, show just how much this was being done.

Most obvious from the Freestone & Webb order book, however, is that delivery dates were somewhat chaotic. No doubt both delays in the supply of chassis and periodic shortages of raw materials contributed to this. So it is not possible to divide the body numbers up in the same way as for earlier years, and this chapter has separate tables to show which bodies were completed in each year.

The Daimler contract

In 1945-1946, coachbuilders in general were only too pleased to attract work, and so it is no surprise that the contract which Freestone & Webb signed with Daimler in 1946 was not an exclusive one. Daimler introduced its two big post-war chassis in 1946, the

Numerically the first of a dozen bodies to design 3038, this is number 1403, on Bentley Mk VI chassis B370BH. The flat outer faces of the wings serve to emphasise the razor-edge lines elsewhere on the body. (Bill Wolf)

A different colour scheme gives a very different look to this body to design 3038, numbered immediately after the one pictured above. Body 1404 was mounted on Bentley Mk VI chassis B358BH. (Klaus-Josef Rossfeldt)

4.1-litre six-cylinder DE27 on a 138.4-inch wheelbase and the 5.4-litre eight-cylinder DE36 on a 147-inch wheelbase. Both were intended primarily for formal coachwork, and Daimler made arrangements with both Freestone & Webb and with Windovers to supply that coachwork. For Freestone & Webb, the deal was probably to build on demand as and when Daimler received an order.

It was not a large contract. Freestone & Webb allocated a batch of 25 body numbers, but only 18 bodies were actually built between 1946 and 1950, and the last seven numbers in the order book remained blank. Freestone & Webb drew up two versions of a four-door, six-light saloon-limousine design to suit the two sizes of Daimler chassis and the first example is annotated in the order book as "F&W standard Saloon and Limousine."

These were grand and deliberately formal bodies, which incorporated elements of the razor-edge designs that had been popular at the end of the 1930s. The most obvious difference between them was that the bodies for the DE36 chassis had a spare wheel alongside each side of the bonnet while those for the DE27 did not. They were ideal perhaps as mayoral transport or for wedding and funeral use, and as an example we know that one of them became the official car for the Bishop of Leeds.

The Hendriks Daimler

The massive Daimler DE36 chassis had been designed to take limousine bodies, but it also had great potential as the basis of a large and eye-catching motor show special. Daimler and Hooper capitalised on that for the

Design 3030 was produced for the actor Stewart Granger. This coupé on a Bentley Mk VI chassis again has rounded lines with pontoon wings and no running-boards. The bright stoneguard on the rear wing is an individual touch. Delivered in November 1947, this was body number 1408 and is on chassis number B288BH. (Klaus-Josef Rossfeldt)

Body number 1437 is yet another variant of design 3010, this time a 3010/E with six lights instead of four. Where the four-light 3010/A variant had no running-boards, 3010/E had both running-boards and outswept lower door panels. This one was new in 1948 on Bentley Mk VI chassis B424CF. (Klaus-Josef Rossfeldt)

Body number 1439 shows yet another variation on the two-door saloon theme. This is a pillarless four-light saloon coupé, delivered in 1947 to design 3029 on Bentley Mk VI chassis B392BH. (Tom Clarke)

The lines of the saloon bodies were softening by the time of this one to design 3050. It was number 1510 and was built on Rolls-Royce Silver Wraith chassis WFC32 in 1949. The body was equipped with a division, and in this picture, the quarter-window behind the rear door has been opened for ventilation. (Klaus-Josef Rossfeldt)

first post-war motor show at Earls Court in autumn 1948, displaying a quite remarkable drophead coupé that later became known as the Green Goddess on account of its colour. Their thinking seems not to have been in a vacuum, though: by this stage, it seems that Freestone & Webb were already working on a similar concept, in this case a four-door sports saloon on the DE36 chassis.

The result was delivered in early 1949, late enough not to avoid accusations of copying although according to *The Autocar* of 4 February 1949 it had been some two years in the making – and therefore pre-dated the Hooper show car. Body 1461 was built for Ivan R Hendriks, a Jamaican businessman who had apparently spent some time working with Daimler during the war years.

This body was quite remarkable from several points of view. Perhaps top of the list was that its sleek and curvaceous design concealed its real size, but it is worth emphasising that the design itself was a real triumph and a very clear demonstration of the talent then available within Freestone & Webb. It was also very different from other designs coming from the company at the time.

The DE36 chassis was standard except for an increased steering column rake that positioned the wheel some four inches lower than standard to allow the low build of the body. All the underbonnet metalwork was polished, and even the tools were specially plated and were stowed in a tray built into the boot lid. Although this was not the first Freestone & Webb body to have no running-boards, it was the first to eliminate them in favour of voluminous front wings that swept across the doors quite high up to terminate

Design 3010 for the Bentley Mk VI chassis was built in several variants until 1949. This is a 3010/A, still with traces of razor-edge lines, with body number 1413. It was on Bentley Mk VI chassis B103AJ and was delivered in 1947.

Quite unmissable on the Freestone & Webb stand at the first post-war Earls Court motor show in 1948 was this two-tone blue saloon. The four-wheel spats were probably inspired by a Franay body on a MkVI Bentley for the 1947 Paris show. Design 3046 went on to attract several orders – but without those spats – and lasted until 1952. This was body number 1476 on a Bentley Mk VI, B445CD.

The spectacular saloon body on Daimler DE36 chassis that was built in 1948 did not appear on that year's Earls Court stand, no doubt much to Freestone & Webb's chagrin. So they built another one to a slightly modified design (number 3051) and displayed it at the 1949 Show. The body was in Beige and the wings in Deep Maroon. This one had body number 1514.

against the leading edge of the rear wings. These front wings contained lockers that were accessible from inside the car. Although there were stylised swirls on the rear wheel spats, there was very little other ornamentation, and the whole car was painted a soft pastel grey colour called Silver Birch, with a fine gold coachline.

The interior was also very special, with seating for six on two full-width benches that were upholstered in leather of a slightly darker grey than the exterior paint. There was a cabinet in the rear centre, and from either side of this a table folded down. All the wood trim in the car was made from a finely figured, close-grain Jamaican type called Yellow Sanders, and the dashboard switches and steering wheel were made of Ivory.

Daimler showed a picture of this car next to their Green Goddess in some of their contemporary sales literature, but it must have been far too expensive to attract any orders – even though the Green Goddess attracted a few. *The Autocar* commented that it "may, perhaps, be the most expensive car built in this country since the war." Freestone & Webb did build a second car (with body number 1514) for display at the 1949 Earls Court Show, and this had some minor differences from the original design. It was painted Beige with contrasting wings in Deep Maroon, which helped it to look smaller than it really was, but still there were no more takers. Brentfield Road and Daimler had to remain content with the positive publicity that this car and the Hendriks original generated for them.

BODY DELIVERIES, YEAR BY YEAR

This table provides a quick reference guide to which bodies were delivered in each calendar year between 1945 and 1949, and also reveals how many bodies were built in each of those years. The overall total is 111 bodies, assuming that all those listed below were actually built.

1945 (Two bodies)
1352, 1353
Number 1352 was actually a Hooper body that had probably been built before the war. For these purposes, it is counted among Freestone & Webb's own creations.

1946 (Four bodies)
1358, 1359, 1361, 1369 – All these bodies were for the Daimler contract.

1947 (23 bodies)
1354, 1355, 1356, 1357, 1360, 1362, 1383, 1384, 1385, 1386, 1387, 1388, 1389, 1391, 1393, 1394, 1398, 1400, 1405, 1408, 1413, 1439, 1500

1948 (37 bodies)
1365, 1367, 1368, 1390, 1392, 1395, 1402, 1403, 1404, 1409, 1414, 1416, 1417, 1418, 1420, 1422, 1424, 1426, 1427, 1429, 1430, 1431, 1432, 1437, 1440, 1442, 1446, 1452, 1455, 1457, 1459, 1460, 1470, 1473, 1475, 1476, 1484

1949 (36 bodies)
1371, 1372, 1373, 1435, 1438, 1447, 1454, 1456, 1461, 1463, 1464, 1467, 1468, 1479, 1482, 1486, 1487, 1489, 1494, 1496, 1497, 1498, 1499, 1501, 1502, 1506, 1507, 1508, 1509, 1510, 1512, 1513, 1514, 1515, 1516, 1517

Unknown year (9 bodies)
1363, 1364, 1366, 1374, 1375 – all Daimlers (5)
1399, 1406 – Bentley Mk VI; no chassis numbers known, and it is possible that these two bodies were never built.
1401, 1441 – Rolls-Royce Silver Wraith; no chassis numbers known, and it is possible that these two bodies were never built.

The spectacular Hendriks Daimler is seen here being collected by its proud owner. The lines of the body are quite different from those of the standard Freestone & Webb saloons of the time, and incorporate some ideas – such as the wing line sweeping across the doors – that would not reach the company's mainstream designs until later.

THE 1945-1949 BODY LIST

This list has been compiled on the basis of surviving evidence and is the most complete available, but it should not be regarded as definitive. A small number of bodies within this list (such as no 1511) were delivered later than the end of 1949.

Body no	Design no and type	Date	Chassis type	Chassis no
1352	(Design number not recorded)			
	Four-light saloon limousine	Presumed 1945	Rolls-Royce Wraith	Not known
1353	2100 Sedanca de ville	1945, Nov	Rolls-Royce Phantom III	3CP38
1354	3004/1 Four-light saloon	1947, Apr	Rolls-Royce Silver Wraith	WTA37
1355	3010/D Saloon	1947, Jun	Bentley Mk VI	B242AK
1356	3010/D Saloon	1947, Jun	Bentley Mk VI	B97AJ
1357	3004/A/3 Four-light saloon	1947, Oct	Rolls-Royce Silver Wraith	WVA72
1358	3009/A Six-light saloon limousine	1946	Daimler DE36	51167
1359	3009 Six-light saloon limousine	1946	Daimler DE27	51064
1360	3009 Six-light saloon limousine	1947	Daimler DE27	51073
1361	3009/A Six-light limousine	1946	Daimler DE36	51198
1362	3009/A Six-light saloon limousine	1947	Daimler DE36	51210
1363	3009 Six-light saloon limousine	Not known	Daimler DE27	51113
1364	3009 Six-light saloon limousine	Not known	Daimler DE27	51104
1365	3009 Six-light saloon limousine	1948	Daimler DE27	51128
1366	3009/A Six-light saloon limousine	1948 See note	Daimler DE36	51234
1367	3009 Six-light saloon	1948	Daimler DE27	51273
1368	3009 Six-light saloon	1948	Daimler DE27	51282
1369	3009 Six-light saloon	1946	Daimler DE27	51290
1370	3009/A Six-light saloon limousine	1950	Daimler DE36	51739
1371	3009 Six-light saloon	1949	Daimler DE27	51302
1372	3009 Six-light saloon	1949	Daimler DE27	51310
1373	3009 Six-light saloon	1949	Daimler DE27	51308
1374	3009 Six-light saloon	Not known	Daimler DE27	51320
1375	3009/A Six-light saloon limousine	Not known	Daimler DE27	51328
1376-1382	NO ENTRY			
1383	3005 All-weather tourer	1947, Apr	Rolls-Royce Silver Wraith	WTA44
1384	3014 Fixed-head coupé	1947, Nov	Rolls-Royce Silver Wraith	WVA74
1385	3004 Four-light saloon	1947, Oct	Rolls-Royce Silver Wraith	WVA53
1386	3027 Fixed-head coupé	1947, Sep	Bentley Mk VI	B239AJ
1387	3013 Four-light Saloon	1947, July	Bentley Mk VI	B63AJ
1388	3008 Foursome drophead coupé	1947, May	Bentley Mk VI	B76AK
1389	3010/C Saloon	1947, July	Bentley Mk VI	B238AK
1390	3010/B Saloon	1948, Feb	Bentley Mk VI	B360BH
1391	3004/A2 Six-light saloon	1947, Sep	Rolls-Royce Silver Wraith	WVA21
1392	3004/C Four-light saloon with division	1948, Jun	Rolls-Royce Silver Wraith	WYA16
1393	3004/A Four-light saloon	1947, Dec	Rolls-Royce Silver Wraith	WYA4
1394	3004/A Four-light saloon	1947, Oct	Rolls-Royce Silver Wraith	WVA81
1395	3010/E Six-light saloon	1948, Jan	Bentley Mk VI	B374BH
1396	CANCELLED. Was to be Design 3008 (Foursome drophead coupé with concealed head) on Bentley Mk VI.			
1397	NO ENTRY			

THE 1945-1949 BODY LIST

1398	3004/A Four-light saloon	1947, Oct	Rolls-Royce Silver Wraith	WVA19
1399	3010/A Four-light saloon		Bentley Mk VI	Not recorded
1400	3010/A Four-light saloon	1947, Nov	Bentley Mk VI	B80BH
1401	Not recorded	Not known	Rolls-Royce Silver Wraith	Not known
1402	3010/A Four-light saloon	1948, Jan	Bentley Mk VI	B60BH
1403	3038 Saloon	1948, Feb	Bentley Mk VI	B370BH
1404	3038 Saloon	1948, Mar	Bentley Mk VI	B358BH
1405	3010/A Four-light saloon	1947, Dec	Bentley Mk VI	B84BH
1406	3010/A Four-light saloon		Bentley Mk VI	Not recorded
1407	CANCELLED. Was to be Design 3008 (Foursome drophead coupé with concealed head) on Bentley Mk VI B392BH; see 1439.			
1408	3030 Fixed-head coupé	1947, Nov	Bentley Mk VI	B288BH
1409	3038 Saloon	1948, Jan	Bentley Mk VI	B145BG
1410-1411	NO ENTRY			
1412	CANCELLED. Was to be Design 3008 (Foursome drophead coupé with concealed head) on Bentley Mk VI.			
1413	3010/A Saloon	1947, Aug	Bentley Mk VI	B103AJ
1414	3010/A Saloon	1948, May	Bentley Mk VI	B389BG
1415	CANCELLED			
1416	3004 Saloon	1948, Oct	Rolls-Royce Silver Wraith	WZB55
1417	3010/A Saloon	1948, Feb	Bentley Mk VI	B151BG
1418	3004 Saloon	1948, Oct	Rolls-Royce Silver Wraith	WZB25
1419	Incorrectly shown in the order book as a four-light saloon on Bentley Mk VI B381DG (see 1420).			
1420	3036/B Fixed-head Coupé	1948, Jun	Bentley Mk VI	B381BG
1421	NO ENTRY			
1422	3004/B Saloon	1948, July	Rolls-Royce Silver Wraith	WAB12
1423	NO ENTRY			
1424	3004/A Saloon	1948, May	Rolls-Royce Silver Wraith	WYA84
1425	CANCELLED. Was to be Design 3008 (Foursome drophead coupé with concealed head) on Bentley Mk VI.			
1426	3004 Saloon	1948, Apr	Rolls-Royce Silver Wraith	WYA62
1427	3030/A Fixed-head coupé	1948, Sep	Bentley Mk VI	B281BG
1428	CANCELLED. Was to be Design 3008 (Foursome drophead coupé with concealed head) on Bentley Mk VI.			
1429	3004 Saloon	1948, Jun	Rolls-Royce Silver Wraith	WZB42
1430	3004 Saloon	1948, Apr	Rolls-Royce Silver Wraith	WYA68
1431	3010/E Six-light saloon	1948, July	Bentley Mk VI	B395BG
1432	3004/A Saloon	1948, Aug	Rolls-Royce Silver Wraith	WYA74
1433	NO ENTRY			
1434	CANCELLED. Was to be Bentley Mk VI.			
1435	3004/B Saloon	1949, Jan	Rolls-Royce Silver Wraith	WAB46
1436	CANCELLED. Was to be 3010/A on Bentley Mk VI.			
1437	3010/E Six-light saloon	1948, Aug	Bentley Mk VI	B424CF
1438	3047/B Six-light saloon	1949, Oct	Rolls-Royce Silver Wraith	WFC89
1439	3029 Four-light saloon coupé	1947, Jun	Bentley Mk VI	B392BH
1440	3004/B Saloon	1948, Oct	Rolls-Royce Silver Wraith	WZB19
1441	Not recorded	Not known	Rolls-Royce Silver Wraith	Not recorded
1442	3010/E Saloon	1948, Aug	Bentley Mk VI	B202CF
1443	CANCELLED. Was to be 3010/E on Bentley Mk VI.			
1444	CANCELLED. Was to be 3004/2 on Rolls-Royce Silver Wraith.			
1445	CANCELLED. Was to be 3038 on Bentley Mk VI.			
1446	3038 Saloon	1948, Mar	Bentley Mk VI	B446CF
1447	3038 Saloon	1949, Feb	Bentley Mk VI	B474DA
1448	CANCELLED. Was to be 3004/2 on Rolls-Royce Silver Wraith.			
1449	CANCELLED. Was to be 3010/E on Bentley Mk VI.			
1450	3046/C Six-light saloon	1950, Jan	Bentley Mk VI	B89EW
1451	NO ENTRY, but Owner Name shown as CS Shrubshall.			
1452	3010/E Six-light saloon	1948, July	Bentley Mk VI	B198CF
1453	CANCELLED. Was to be 3004/2 on Rolls-Royce Silver Wraith.			
1454	3004/2 Six-light saloon	1949, Apr	Rolls-Royce Silver Wraith	WDC72
1455	3010/E Six-light saloon	1948, July	Bentley Mk VI	B391BG
1456	3038 Saloon	1949, Jan	Bentley Mk VI	B185CD
1457	3038 Saloon	1948, Dec	Bentley Mk VI	B181CD
1458	CANCELLED.			
1459	3004/B Saloon	1948, Sep	Rolls-Royce Silver Wraith	WZB37
1460	3037/D Fixed-head coupé	1948, Dec	Bentley Mk VI	B333CD
1461	3031 Sports saloon	1949, See note	Daimler DE36	51238
1462	Complete standard P/S car from Bentley Motors			
1463	3046/C Six-light saloon	1949, Jan	Bentley Mk VI	B260DA
1464	3004/A/2 Saloon with division	1949, Apr	RR Silver Wraith	WDC34
1465	CANCELLED. Was to be 3004/2 on Rolls-Royce Silver Wraith.			

THE 1945-1949 BODY LIST

1466	CANCELLED. Was to be 3010/E on Bentley Mk VI.			
1467	3004/2 Six-light saloon	1949, Jan	Rolls-Royce Silver Wraith	WCB7
1468	3004/A/2 Saloon with division	1949, Oct	Rolls-Royce Silver Wraith	WFC46
1469	CANCELLED. Was to be 3010/E on Bentley Mk VI.			
1470	3038 Saloon	1948, Dec	Bentley Mk VI	B252DA
1471	CANCELLED. Was to be Bentley Mk VI.			
1472	CANCELLED. Was to be 3010/E on Bentley Mk VI.			
1473	3004/B Saloon	1948, Nov	Rolls-Royce Silver Wraith	WAB65
1474	CANCELLED.			
1475	3004/A/2/F Six-light saloon with division	1948, Aug	Rolls-Royce Silver Wraith	WCB11
1476	3046 Six-light saloon	1948, Nov	Bentley Mk VI	B445CD
1477	CANCELLED. Was to be 3010/E on Bentley Mk VI.			
1478	CANCELLED. Was to be 3010/E on Bentley Mk VI.			
1479	3038 Saloon	1949, Jan	Bentley Mk VI	B262DA
1480	CANCELLED. Was to be 3038 on Bentley Mk VI.			
1481	CANCELLED. Was to be 3038 on Bentley Mk VI.			
1482	3004/C Saloon with division	1949, Jun	Rolls-Royce Silver Wraith	WDC39
1483	CANCELLED. Was to be 3004/A2 on Rolls-Royce Silver Wraith.			
1484	3038 Saloon	1948, Dec	Bentley Mk VI	B254DA
1485	CANCELLED. Was to be Bentley Mk VI.			
1486	3010/E Six-light saloon	1949, July	Bentley Mk VI	B443DZ
1487	3047/2A Six-light saloon limousine	1949, Jun	Rolls-Royce Silver Wraith	WFC7
1488	CANCELLED. Was to be Bentley Mk VI, for entertainer George Formby via Marylebone Garages.			
1489	3029/A Four-light saloon coupé	1949, Feb	Bentley Mk VI	B380DA
1490	CANCELLED. Was to be 3004/A2/F on Rolls-Royce Silver Wraith.			
1491	CANCELLED. Was to be Bentley Mk VI.			
1492	CANCELLED. Was to be Bentley Mk VI.			
1493	CANCELLED. Was to be 3038 on Bentley Mk VI.			
1494	3047/1 Saloon with division	1949, July	Rolls-Royce Silver Wraith	WDC88
1495	3046 Six-light saloon	1950, Feb	Bentley Mk VI	B203EW
1496	3046 Six-light saloon	1949, Apr	Bentley Mk VI	B383DZ
1497	3029/A Four-light saloon coupé	1949, Apr	Bentley Mk VI	B327DZ
1498	3038 Saloon	1949, Aug	Bentley Mk VI	B180EY
1499	3046 Six-light saloon	1949, Jun	Bentley Mk VI	B337DZ
1500	3047 Saloon with division	1947, Oct	Rolls-Royce Silver Wraith	WVA75
1501	3038 Saloon	1949, Nov	Bentley Mk VI	B376EY
1502	3050 Six-light saloon with division	1949, Aug	Rolls-Royce Silver Wraith	WFC68
1503	CANCELLED. Was to be Rolls-Royce Silver Wraith.			
1504	CANCELLED. Was to be Bentley Mk VI.			
1505	CANCELLED. Was to be Bentley Mk VI.			
1506	3047/2 Saloon with division	1949, May	Rolls-Royce Silver Wraith	WDC94
1507	3046/1 Six-light saloon	1949, Mar	Bentley Mk VI	B93DZ
1508	3047/B/2 Six-light saloon	1949, May	Rolls-Royce Silver Wraith	WZB54
1509	3046/C Six-light saloon	1949, July	Bentley Mk VI	B405DZ
1510	3050 Six-light saloon with division	1949, Aug	Rolls-Royce Silver Wraith	WFC32
1511	3056 Drophead coupé	1950, Aug	Rolls-Royce Silver Wraith	WFC69
1512	3046/C Six-light saloon	1949, Oct	Bentley Mk VI	B45EW
1513	3050/A/B Six-light saloon with division	1949, Oct	Rolls-Royce Silver Wraith	WGC19
1514	3051 Sports saloon	1949	Daimler DE36	52801
1515	3029/C Four-light saloon coupé	1949, Oct	Bentley Mk VI	B488EY
1516	3046/C Six-light saloon	1949, Nov	Bentley Mk VI	B133EW
1517	3046/C Six-light saloon	1949, Dec	Bentley Mk VI	B301EW

Notes

1364 The body type is not recorded in the Freestone & Webb order book but was presumably a Six-light saloon limousine to design 3009.

1366 This car is believed to have been on the Freestone & Webb stand at Earls Court in 1948. The date of its completion is based on this.

1375 The order book records this body as a 3009/A design, which would be for the DE36 chassis. Daimler historian Brian Smith has established that the chassis was a DE27, so the design was correctly a 3009.

1376-1382 These numbers were probably reserved against further orders from Daimler, but were not used.

1419 & 1420 The chassis card for B381BG shows that the intention was to mount a "Sports Saloon (4 door) by Freestone & Webb Ltd". This would be consistent with the entry for body 1419. The probability is that the customer changed his mind about the style he wanted and that a new body number was therefore allocated.

1461 This was the spectacular car for Mr Hendriks. It was completed in early 1949. The modified copy was built as body number 1514.

1475 This car was displayed on the Freestone & Webb stand at Earls Court in 1948.

1476 This car was displayed on the Freestone & Webb stand at Earls Court in 1948. It had spats on all four wheels, but otherwise retained the standard 3046 body design.

1512 This car was displayed on the Freestone & Webb stand at Earls Court in 1949.

1513 This car was displayed on the Freestone & Webb stand at Earls Court in 1949.

1514 This car was displayed on the Freestone & Webb stand at Earls Court in 1949. Its date of completion has been estimated from that.

1515 This car was displayed on the Freestone & Webb stand at Earls Court in 1949.

Chapter Seven

PROUD DECLINE 1950-1958

By 1950, it was quite clear that traditional coachbuilding was dying. In Britain, Freestone & Webb were one of just five major coachbuilders discreetly vying with one another for the business that remained, and in the company of HJ Mulliner, Park Ward, Hooper and James Young, Freestone & Webb was the smallest and the most vulnerable.

In West Germany, the post-war economic devastation had left no demand for luxury products like coachbuilt bodies, and in France most of the major coachbuilders had already gone to the wall or were in difficulties. Only in Italy, where a rather different business model kept several small artisan-type companies afloat, was there any sign that the craft might have a longer-term future. And so it proved, as Italian car styling became predominant in the 1950s and 1960s.

Whatever the reasons, Freestone & Webb seem to have been marking time over the next few years. This was perhaps not the right moment to invest time and effort in new designs because the chassis supply situation was still not stable; although the order book shows only one cancellation during 1950, there are several blank entries for the following year, no doubt reflecting occasions when anticipated orders failed to materialise.

Brentfield Road was of course not alone in facing these difficulties. All the leading British coachbuilders were playing for time with cautious designs, and many series-built saloon bodies had similarities. The Hooper Teviot, a Park Ward saloon and the six-light Freestone & Webb bodies all clearly came from the same school of thought; it was less a case of copying than of huddling together for comfort. There was certainly no real excitement about the Freestone & Webb stand at Earls Court in 1950, and even the introduction of a new boot shape and raised wing lines that ran back across the doors and eliminated the traditional running-boards had minimal impact, because these new features were harnessed to otherwise familiar shapes.

A more fundamental change also had its effect on the coachbuilder, however. The final bodies for the Daimler limousines were built in 1950, and these would be the last bodies that Freestone & Webb built on any chassis other than Rolls-Royce and Bentley. All the Daimler coachbuilding work was taken back in-house (where it was entrusted to Hooper),

FREESTONE & WEBB ANNUAL PRODUCTION TOTALS, 1950-1958

All figures here relate to calendar years and are based on delivery dates. There remain some problems with completion dates, which may affect the individual year totals here. Nevertheless, these figures do give a good idea of the output from Brentfield Road in its final years. For more detail, please see Chapter 8.

1950	30
1951	29
1952	33
1953	22
1954	26
1955	26
1956	25
1957	11
1958	9

The total for the decade was 211 bodies.

and there simply were no other separate chassis available to take coachbuilt bodies. It was the same right across Europe; as monocoque construction became the norm, the role of the coachbuilder had to change, and many companies closed for good in the early 1950s.

Freestone & Webb nevertheless clung on, as one of that small group of top-class British coachbuilders capable of providing coachwork for Rolls-Royce and Bentley chassis. Like their colleagues in the business, they continued to build coachwork that was very different indeed from the shapes and styles that were generally available from the volume car manufacturers, and these designs had a certain olde-worlde charm about them. But they were what the customers wanted, and would continue to be so for the next few years.

So there were no exciting new designs from Brentfield Road for the next few years, and even when the new Bentley R Type arrived in 1951 and the long-wheelbase Rolls-Royce Silver Wraith appeared in 1952, the first Freestone & Webb designs for them were simply adaptations of those that had gone before. Six-light saloons and limousines, with sweeping lines that still retained traces of the razor-edge style and mostly had partly spatted rear wheels, were still the order of the day. There had meanwhile been one subtle change: front doors were now usually hinged on the bulkhead rather than the central pillar, as had been the Freestone & Webb standard since 1945.

It would be wrong to blame Freestone & Webb for a lack of imagination, of course. They were only building what the customers wanted, and many of those customers undoubtedly had a conservative turn of mind. There were still problems with materials supplies, and rationing did not end in Britain until 1953; all this made any attempt to predict future fashions a hazardous business. Chassis supplies also seem to have been problematical. The situation fluctuated wildly, too: in 1950 there had been just one blank entry in the order book, but in later years there were as many as 58 blanks (the figure for 1953). This may well have been an effect of the uncertainty over Purchase Tax during 1952, as buyers waited for the "temporary" high rate of 66⅔% that had been imposed during in 1951 to be eased, which did not happen until April 1953.

Nevertheless, some fresh new designs began to appear in 1953. Most notable among them was one that took its inspiration from the so-called Empress Line developed by Hooper. This "new look" – which was what its designer Osmond Rivers called it when

Freestone & Webb's interpretation of the Hooper "Empress" style became a strong seller in the 1950s. This advertisement for the company's stand at Earls Court in 1952 shows one. If the picture really is the show car, then it is body 1698 on a Bentley MkVI chassis.

it appeared – was first seen on a Rolls-Royce Silver Wraith at Earls Court in 1949, although it took its familiar name from the Daimler chassis on which it appeared in 1952. Its most striking characteristic was the elimination of the rear wings as separate volumes. Instead, the front wings swept right back to the base of the tail, and a particularly smooth line was achieved by using full spats over the rear wheels. Without the need for separate rear wings, a further advantage was that the full width of the body could be devoted to the passenger cabin.

So, did Freestone & Webb simply copy the Hooper design? The fact is that the new Hooper-esque lines blended well with the semi-razor-edge

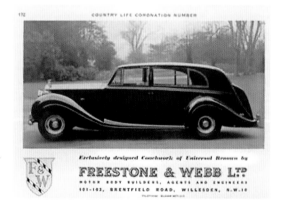

This advertisement from the Coronation issue of Country Life *magazine shows a limousine body to design 3110 on a Rolls-Royce Silver Wraith chassis. Echoes of the older styles remained in formal and conservative bodies like this one.*

lines of existing Freestone & Webb designs – so well that they seemed like a logical evolution from them. An interesting transitional design appeared as a coupé on the company's 1952 show stand (body number 1695) and shows the way design was already heading at Brentfield Road. Also worth noting is that the early Freestone & Webb bodies suffered from some rather fussy door shut lines ahead of the rear wheelarch, which were not tidied up until autumn 1955, when the Hooper solution was adopted. Nevertheless, their chrome-framed windscreens were always far more elegant than the rather functional-looking rubber-glazed type associated with the Hooper bodies.

A distinguishing feature of many early bodies to the "Empress" style was large flat bumpers, but these were not universal; the full spats were nevertheless invariable. Over the next few years, elements of this new style came to affect several of the body designs from Brentfield Road as Freestone & Webb adapted it in their own way. The results were unarguably successful (with a few notable exceptions) and delivered what were probably the most attractive of the company's 1950s bodies. Whether they were

Dated December 1953, this picture shows the beautifully appointed interior of a Freestone & Webb limousine. The body has not been positively identified but is very likely to have been number 1646 on a Rolls-Royce Silver Wraith, which was delivered in January 1954. Note the buttons on the door for the electric windows, then considered the height of luxury.

more or less aesthetically pleasing than their Hooper contemporaries is something that will probably excite argument for many more years, but what is undeniable is their success: the last examples were built in 1957.

Something borrowed, something new

By 1954, it must have been clear that the volume of bodies constructed at Brentfield Road was unlikely ever to attain its former levels, although there would certainly have been a degree of optimism about the impending arrival of new chassis from Crewe. These

Customers would be shown beautifully-produced coloured drawings of coachwork proposals, and this one shows one of the "Empress" styles, design 3206/A for the Rolls-Royce Silver Cloud chassis.

FEATURES OF THE MID-1950S BODIES

Freestone & Webb never abandoned traditional composite wood-and-metal construction for their bodies, and were the only one of the five major British coachbuilders in the 1950s who did not to go over to all-metal construction.

By the mid-1950s, they were proud of the curved windscreens with slim pillars they were incorporating into their coachwork, claiming that these gave better vision for the driver. It may be that Show catalogues stressed these features as one of the more obvious ways in which the Freestone & Webb "Empress" style coachwork differed from the Hooper original.

Coachwork was typically delivered with two-colour paint. Upholstery was generally in leather, piped to match or to contract with the main colour, but limousines might have cloth for the rear seats. Cabinetwork generally had a high-gloss Burr Butt walnut veneer, and gloveboxes typically had a semi-circular shape. Very much typical of the period were picnic sets housed in recesses in the front doors, and many bodies had picnic tables in the backs of the front seats, with glass tops and chrome-plated edging.

Air conditioning was often fitted, along with a demister-type back light, and there might be a perspex panel in the roof, with a sliding inner shutter. The 1955 show cars had remote electric locking for the bonnet and fuel filler door.

Limousines might have a hand-wound reclining mechanism for the rear seat, and the centre rear armrest might contain items such as a swivel mirror, cigar box and cigarette box. Limousine rear compartments might have one or more occasional seats that doubled as footrests when not in use.

The division in limousines might have electrically operated drop-glass, and this glass might also be curved rather than flat. The division in some cars was fitted with an electric revolving cocktail cabinet, and electric rear door windows were also available.

The traditional coachbuilder's plate is seen here on body 1695, on a Silver Wraith chassis for the 1952 Earls Court Show. The body number is just visible in the rectangle on the right. Below is an interesting additional plate, recording the fact that the body was restored by Hooper & Co (Coachbuilders) Ltd, who had once been one of the leading builders of coachwork for Rolls-Royce chassis. (Bill Wolf)

materialised in the autumn as the Rolls-Royce Silver Cloud and the Bentley S Type, and Freestone & Webb undoubtedly put in a bid to obtain some examples as soon as they possibly could.

No doubt recognising that deliveries would not be immediate, the company nevertheless started planning its new designs for the two new chassis early, and had its ideas in place by the end of 1954. Resources were obviously not infinite, and Brentfield Road chose to develop a design that would suit both the Bentley and the Rolls-Royce models (they were, after all, essentially the same car). However, a stroke of genius in the circumstances was to develop a version of the design that would suit the outgoing Rolls-Royce Silver Dawn and Bentley R-type chassis, so that the sleek new lines would attract custom as soon as possible.

As design 3165 (Silver Dawn) and 3191 (R Type), this appeared over the summer of 1954 in what might be called prototype form. It then became 3191/A for the Bentley S Type chassis that began to arrive in the summer, and seems to have been known as the Special Sports Saloon. Design 3191 brought some fresh ideas into play. Although its front end was conventionally rounded and not unlike the standard front of an R Type Continental, this was a six-light saloon body. The most striking new features were at the rear, where the wing line was broken by a kick-up that hinted at the embryonic tail fins seen on some late 1940s American cars. But the real uniqueness lay in the way each wing became a separate structure aft of the rear window, leaving a gap between the sides of the boot and the wing itself.

On this occasion, Freestone & Webb could certainly not be accused of copying another company's design, and it is possible with a little imagination to trace the inspiration for that unusual rear wing treatment back to Brentfield Road's own early-1930s "shouldered" designs for the Bentley 8-litre and 3½-litre chassis.

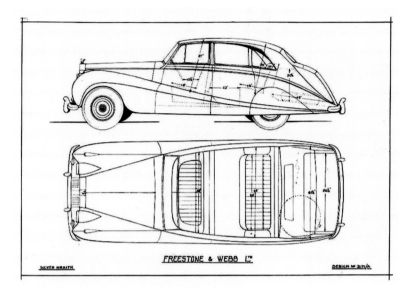

The Special Sports Saloon was certainly distinctive and would not be copied elsewhere, and its features appeared on a number of other bodies from Freestone & Webb, notably for the Rolls-Royce Silver Cloud, of which the first examples passed through Brentfield Road in 1956.

Orders for coachwork on the Rolls-Royce Silver Wraith chassis now began to drop off. It was, after all, an elderly design by the middle of the 1950s and the arrival of the Silver Cloud and Bentley S Type twins would have signalled to many potential customers that a new Rolls-Royce limousine chassis must be on the way. On the Silver Cloud and S Type, the popular choices were the latest versions of the Empress style designs, adapted to suit the newer chassis.

The beginning of the end

Meanwhile, AJ Webb had begun to think about retiring; by 1954 he was well over 70 years old. So,

This is the coachbuilder's dimensional drawing for another of the Empress styles, this time design 3171/A for the Silver Wraith chassis.

THE EMPRESS LINE DESIGNS

Disambiguation is a wonderful thing, and is also the purpose of this table, which lists the different Freestone & Webb designs that were inspired by Osmond Rivers' original "Empress line". Each of them had variants and sub-variants, which are listed in Appendix C. Note that Freestone & Webb themselves never described these bodies as Empress-line types.

ID no	Type	Date	Chassis type
3093	Six-light saloon	between 1952 and 1954.	Bentley Mk VI and R Type
3163	Six-light saloon	1954 and 1955	Rolls-Royce Silver Dawn
3171	Six-light touring limousine	1954 to 1958	Rolls-Royce Silver Wraith
	There was a four-light variant as well.		
3199	Six-light saloon	built between 1955 and 1958	Bentley S Type
3206	Six-light saloon	built between 1956 and 1958	Rolls-Royce Silver Cloud

Swan song: this was
Freestone & Webb's
advertisement in the
catalogue of the 1957
Earls Court Show, the last
one at which the company
would have a stand. They
had been awarded a gold
medal for coachwork for
eight successive years, and
1957 would make it nine
in a row.

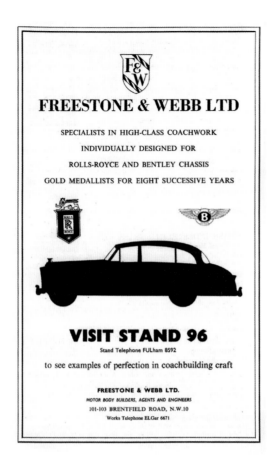

F&W

FREESTONE & WEBB LTD

SPECIALISTS IN HIGH-CLASS COACHWORK

INDIVIDUALLY DESIGNED FOR

ROLLS-ROYCE AND BENTLEY CHASSIS

GOLD MEDALLISTS FOR EIGHT SUCCESSIVE YEARS

VISIT STAND 96

Stand Telephone FULham 8592

to see examples of perfection in coachbuilding craft

FREESTONE & WEBB LTD.

MOTOR BODY BUILDERS, AGENTS AND ENGINEERS

101-103 BRENTFIELD ROAD, N.W.10

Works Telephone ELGar 6671

with assistance from his friend Reggie Beaumont-Thomas (who had spent some time as Freestone & Webb's Managing Director in the early 1930s), he put the company up for sale. The asking price, according to research by John de Campi, was £70,000 all-in.

It seems that there was no rush of bidders, and no buyer had been found by the end of 1954. The Webb and Beaumont-Thomas families regularly spent Christmas together, and it was on Christmas morning 1954 that Webb was found dead at the Albion Hotel in Brighton, where they were staying. John de Campi adds some scurrilous detail: "Webb didn't wear pajamas and, since he was a small man, he was buried in Reggie's wife's pajamas!"

Inevitably, some management changes must have followed at Freestone & Webb. By summer 1956, the position of Managing Director was held by Major TK Williams, who had once been chief tester with the original Bentley company. Len Hedges had become chief designer, having earlier been with HJ Mulliner. However, it is not clear when these two gentlemen joined the company; they might have been there before AJ Webb's death. One way or the other, it must by this time have been obvious to those working at

Brentfield Road that this was the beginning of the end for the company. Sales were already at a low ebb, and the future for the bespoke coachbuilding business looked bleak.

In fact, 1956 had brought a very interesting development in the shape of a striking new front end design, in which each headlamp was cowled and mounted in a wing front shaped into a more or less triangular panel. It is not quite clear when this first appeared, but it was in place before Motor Show time in October and was first seen by the public at large at that show. The new front end was grafted onto existing designs, including the popular Bentley (3191/A) and Rolls-Royce Silver Cloud (3206) saloon types, and also appeared on some new designs.

It is hard not to imagine that this new design was something of a desperate appeal for attention, at a time when Freestone & Webb needed all the orders they could get and their future was looking bleak. Yet the new front end seemed to have the right appeal, and it very much looks as if a few older cars were returned to Brentfield Road to have the new features grafted on to them.

One more notable body from 1956 bore witness to Freestone & Webb's willingness to take on commissions for attention-grabbing coachwork. This was an extraordinary limousine on the Silver Wraith chassis, built for Mitchell Engineering and featuring what is probably best described as a flamboyantly futuristic body design with a great deal of curved glass. Eye-catching it certainly was; whether it was also attractive is a matter of personal opinion. It is certainly open to question whether AJ Webb would ever have agreed to build such a body if he had still been running the company, but perhaps he would have taken the view that his successors clearly did: any business is good business in a time of crisis. Nevertheless, there were no repeat orders for this design.

By the beginning of 1957, negotiations about the future of Freestone & Webb must have been well under way, and in May that year they reached a conclusion. The company would become part of the Swain Group, which at the time also owned the HR Owen chain of dealerships that retailed Rolls-Royce and Bentley cars, among others. The exact details of the arrangement are not clear, but John de Campi quotes a purchase price of "about £10,000". It was a fraction of the original asking price, but there was nothing Freestone & Webb could do in these circumstances. The deal probably allowed for existing orders to be fulfilled but anticipated that no more orders would be taken. There was, sadly, no longer a rôle for an old-style bespoke coachbuilder in the world of the late 1950s.

Much the same attitude prevailed elsewhere, too. So, for example, in 1959 the once great coachbuilder HJ Mulliner was bought out by Rolls-Royce and merged with the company's existing Park Ward division to become its bespoke coachbuilding arm under the name of Mulliner Park Ward. Hooper, meanwhile, closed down in late 1959 after learning of Crewe's plans to use monocoque construction for the next Rolls-Royce and Bentley models.

So those last few orders were fulfilled, and although there were enough of them to keep the company busy beyond the end of the year and into 1958, this was a period of winding down. Just a dozen bodies came from Freestone & Webb during 1957, and three of those were really delayed deliveries from earlier. Established designs prevailed, although there was one bespoke body on the Silver Wraith chassis, which by this time was known to be going out of production and to be giving way to a long-wheelbase version of the Silver Cloud.

If all this sounds rather mundane and gloomy, there was nevertheless clear evidence of a proud spirit remaining at Freestone & Webb in 1957, and somebody within the company took the decision that it should go out in a blaze of glory. So that year's expected Earls Court show exhibits – a Silver Wraith limousine and a Silver Cloud saloon – were accompanied by a real show-stopper. Quite clearly built to impress the crowds at the Motor Show in October, it was a two-door, two-seat drophead coupé with prominent American-style tail fins and American-style two-tone paintwork on a Silver Cloud chassis. There was even a special sales brochure for it; Freestone & Webb did not intend to give up that easily.

One of the factors that made this car such a sensation was its flagrant waste of space: the Silver Cloud chassis was far too big to suit a two-door body and so there was a long rear deck that was given over to luggage accommodation. The popular press got hold of the story that the buyer had bought it to use on his honeymoon and dubbed it the "Honeymoon Express", a name that caught the public imagination and has persisted to the present day, although it was not in any sense official. The convertible roof was power-operated and when retracted was completely concealed under a metal tonneau cover. And, of course, the front end incorporated Freestone & Webb's distinctive triangular panels around the headlights. The Honeymoon Express has retained its appeal right through to the present day and, if it was not the most attractive design that Freestone & Webb ever produced, it was certainly one of the most memorable. It was also the last. There would be no more new designs after number 3243/C – although a variant of it on Bentley chassis would be built to meet a customer order during 1958.

The last half-dozen bodies to bear the Freestone & Webb name were built at Brentfield Road in the first half of 1958. They included a final Silver Wraith and a long-wheelbase Silver Cloud, its design adapted from an earlier one for the standard-wheelbase chassis.

THE HONEYMOON EXPRESS CARS

There were three bodies built to the Honeymoon Express design, and over the years their identities have become blurred as mistakes in identification have been made. The three cars were as follows:

Body number 1827 on Rolls-Royce Silver Cloud SED179
This was the original 1957 Earls Court show car, built to design number 3243/C. It was originally painted Dark Green with Shell Grey side panels, and had a Grey convertible top. The seats were in Light Grey hide piped with dark green.
The car was initially sold to James Ives, and had registration number ULM 69. Later in life it appears to have been repainted in blue with fawn side panels, and reupholstered in tan leather. In that condition, it was displayed for a time at the Petersen Museum in the USA.

Body number 1831 on Bentley S-type B377EK
The second car was on a Bentley chassis, and is said to have been Black with Garnet side panels (although the picture on p130 suggests otherwise) and red seats. The body had minor differences from the first example and was built to design number 3243/B. The first registration number of this car was BOB 1, but the car has also been registered as MC 98, PSU 269, 509 NOJ, and possibly EMH 12. This car also seems to have been displayed at the Petersen Museum in the USA.

Body number 1833 on Rolls-Royce Silver Cloud SGE270
The last of the three cars has become the best known, probably because it was not only the last built to that design but also the last car that Freestone & Webb completed. It was ordered through the dealer HR Owen and was delivered to Arnold Moreton, who put the registration number AM 2375 on it. His car was originally blue with grey side panels and a blue convertible top. Like the first Honeymoon Express, it had design number 3243/C.

How the mighty are fallen…. by 6 October 1958, when this picture was taken, the Unity Works buildings were being used as a distribution centre for vans and trucks.

But there were also two bodies with the Honeymoon Express design that had stolen the limelight at Earls Court the previous year. Probably not part of the original close-down plan, their construction was nevertheless authorised. One was on a Bentley S Type chassis, and the other was on a Silver Cloud chassis. This car, with Freestone & Webb body number 1833, was completed in June and was the very last car to be completed at Brentfield Road. As they must have wished from the time it became clear that the end was inevitable, Freestone & Webb went out with dignity and in style.

… and afterwards

From mid-1958, Freestone & Webb became a showroom name associated with the HR Owen dealership chain, although the Unity Works site remained in the ownership of the Webb family. The company continued in business at a fairly low level,

undertaking repairs and refurbishments for coachbuilt cars, but it was no longer a coachbuilder in the traditional sense.

The business closed in the mid-1960s and the buildings that had once been the Freestone & Webb workshops were demolished, the site of 101-103 Brentfield Road becoming a branch office of a car rental company. The adjacent site (105-119 Brentfield Road) was subsequently chosen for the spectacular BAPS Shri Swaminarayan Mandir, more familiarly known as the Neasden Temple and the largest Hindu temple outside India. This opened in 1995. By 2018, the former Freestone & Webb site was again scheduled for redevelopment, this time with housing under the Brent Local Plan.

The ownership of the Freestone & Webb name had meanwhile gone through some complicated changes. In 1959, the Owen dealerships were sold to Swain Group (Motors), which in 1961 was acquired by the Provincial Traction Company to protect the name (according to The Times of 3 July 1961). By 1961, the coachbuilder Harold Radford had also become part of the Swain Group, and in 1963 the rights to the Freestone & Webb name were sold on to Radford. Radford, too, changed hands in the mid-1960s. In the late 1970s or early 1980s, the Freestone & Webb name and emblem were used on a leaflet advertising the Avon-Stevens convertible based on a Jaguar XJC coupé. The company was then described as providing Rolls-Royce Spares, Restorations and Service.

The rights to the company name subsequently lapsed. In 1990, a new company called Freestone & Webb Limited was incorporated and registered at Companies House by a Bentley enthusiast, who put it up for sale together with his 1935 Bentley 3½-litre Brougham saloon at an auction in 2010. "It is now offered, together with the car, as asset and debt free, offering a once-in-a-lifetime opportunity to own not only a fine motor car, but also an iconic piece of British automotive coachbuilding history," said a spokesman for Historics at Brooklands, which auctioned the Bentley on Wednesday 2 June that year at its Brooklands, Weybridge centre, along with 65 other classic and collectors' cars. By 2017, the company was still listed but was classified as dormant.

During the 1970s, HR Owen produced this leaflet with the Freestone & Webb name, promoting restoration work and spare parts for Rolls-Royce cars. The car illustrated is an Avon Stephens convertible conversion of the Jaguar XJC coupé, which was available through the company, but there is no evidence that it was ever branded as a Freestone & Webb product.

Chapter Eight

THE COACHWORK 1950-1958

1950

The new decade did not bring any radically new design ideas in its wake, and in fact 1950 started it off with a lower body total from Brentfield Road than the year before. One of those bodies was the last of the Daimler limousine contract, but the others were all on Bentley Mk VI or Rolls-Royce Silver Wraith chassis

The first of the bodies delivered in 1950 (that Daimler excepted) was numbered 1511, and the last one was numbered 1567. As the lists below show, there were several blank entries in the order book between those two numbers, although perhaps surprisingly only one actual cancellation.

There was probably still some repair and

Saloon design 3046 was still very much alive and well during 1950, and a dozen bodies were built, some to variant 3046/C (bodies 1527-1534) and others to 3046/C/F (1535-1538). This is a 3046/C dating from September 1950, and is almost certainly body number 1534 on Bentley MkVI B497EW.

The high wing line that swept across the doors had earlier been seen on the Hendriks Daimler, and began to appear on other bodies during 1950, eliminating the running-boards at the same time. However, the Freestone & Webb order book describes this body, to design 3070/B, as having the lines of the "Park Ward 1949 Show job." A similar saloon with division, to design 3070/A, would appear on the Freestone & Webb stand at Earls Court in 1950. The chassis of the car pictured is a Rolls-Royce Silver Wraith, WHD44. This is body number 1539.

Freestone & Webb remained happy to take on individual commissions, and this one was certainly unusual. The body design was number 3068 and was a utility estate for a left-hand-drive Rolls-Royce Silver Wraith chassis, LWHD73. Despite the utility nature, its lines are rather elegant. This one was new in September 1950 and had body number 1541.

Those newly raised wing lines are in evidence again on this saloon coupé with design number 3073. The chassis is a Bentley Mk VI, B351GT, and the car promoted Freestone & Webb's skills at the Earls Court Show in 1950. Body number 1542 was painted Red and Grey.

recommissioning work being done on older bodies, but only one of the new bodies in 1950 was for an older chassis. Number 1533, one of the popular six-light saloons for the Bentley Mk VI, replaced an estate car body by David Joel that was less than a year old. In 1953, Freestone & Webb fitted a David Joel estate car body onto a new Bentley R Type chassis, and it would be a remarkable coincidence if the two bodies were not one and the same!

The core designs for 1950 were numbered 3046 (a six-light saloon for the Bentley Mk VI) and 3050 (a six-light design for the Silver Wraith). They were joined at

Earls Court in the autumn by design 3070, another saloon for the Silver Wraith. Among these, the major success was the 3046/C variant for the Bentley Mk VI, which accounted for 11 of the bodies completed that year; variant 3046/C/F brought in another five orders.

On the Silver Wraith chassis, the 3050/A/B variant brought in a handful of sales and was considered good enough to be shown at Earls Court in the autumn to attract sales for the following year. Its most notable new feature, if a subtle one, was that its front doors were hinged at the front rather than from the centre pillar like other Freestone & Webb four-door designs; the same feature appeared on design 3070, a saloon for the Silver Wraith chassis, and it would become common on new designs from now on. Also at Earls Court was a saloon coupé (design 3073) for the Bentley Mk VI, but although it continued into the era of the Bentley R Type, it was not a major success. Other designs were sold in only penny numbers.

One other body worthy of comment is the single

The older style of wing line that ran below the doors was still in evidence on this Earls Court Show exhibit, though. Body number 1544 is a six-light saloon with division, to design 3050/A/B, on Rolls-Royce Silver Wraith WHD76. Freestone & Webb had displayed a body of exactly the same design on their stand in 1949, a fact that highlights their slow progression towards new ideas at this time.

Saloon design 3046/C/F is seen here on Bentley MkVI B195HP. The two-tone colour scheme emphasises the elegant lines of the coachwork and the division between the colours differs from that on the 3046/C body pictured earlier. The wheel spats are another obvious difference between the two variants of the design. This car had body number 1548 and was new in March 1951 to AJ Webb himself, although he kept it only until November that year before selling it on. (Real Car Company)

"utility" (estate car) to design 3068 that Freestone & Webb built on a left-hand-drive Rolls-Royce Silver Wraith. With wing lines similar to those on their contemporary closed bodies for the Silver Wraith, Freestone & Webb made quite a stylish job of this wooden-bodied estate. It is tempting to wonder how much inspiration they took from the David Joel body they had removed earlier in the year, and which was sitting in the workshop awaiting a new owner…

1951

The core designs from Brentfield Road for the first three quarters of 1951 were again numbers 3046 (six-light saloon, Bentley Mk VI), 3050 (limousine, Rolls-Royce Silver Wraith) and 3070 (Silver Wraith saloon). The biggest success was once again design 3046, with 11 copies delivered of the 3046/C/F variant (although there is a question mark over one) and a single example of the older 3046/C. Perhaps most noticeable from the list of 1951 bodies was that there was now very little call for genuinely bespoke designs.

Bodies on the Bentley chassis accounted for 21 of the 31 delivered during the year, and the other ten were of course all for the Rolls-Royce Silver Wraith. They were saloons, saloons with division, and limousines, although only saloon design 3070, introduced at Earls Court in 1950, attracted as many as three customers – and those were for two different variants.

There were new designs at Earls Court in the autumn, of course. For the Bentley chassis, a new six-light design numbered 3082/C featured a higher

wing line on an otherwise largely familiar shape, and attracted five more orders. Both existing core designs for the Silver Wraith were replaced, too, and the new saloon with division 3091/A and six-light saloon 3092 would go on to have reasonable careers. Although the designs were recognisably related to the earlier razor-edge and semi-razor-edge shapes, the nearest thing to a knife-edge crease on most of these new bodies was now the edge of the Rolls-Royce bonnet. Front doors were hinged at their leading edges, and on design 3092, so were the rear doors.

This rear view of body number 1558, a 3046/C/F saloon, shows that razor-edges were still in evidence during 1951. This example dates from June that year, and was on Bentley MkVI B10LJ. (Andrew Bone/ Wikimedia Commons)

This very upright and formal limousine body had design number 3074/A/B, and was new during 1951, although only two were built. The rear wheel spat with its offset cutaway is a slightly uncomfortable feature, but was considered stylish at the time. The body is number 1575 and is on Rolls-Royce Silver Wraith WME15, new in April 1951.

Body number 1577 was the only example built to design 3081, a six-light saloon with division. It was new in April 1951, on Rolls-Royce Silver Wraith chassis WLE27. This original "works" photograph shows its unusual faux wicker-work side panels. The body was later removed and transferred to another Silver Wraith, WVH110, and WLE27 received all-weather body number 1745. That was originally mounted on a long-wheelbase Silver Wraith chassis, so some adjustment was necessary! The all-weather body now survives with faux wicker-work side panels like those on the original saloon.

Design 3082/C added a new, raised wing line to more familiar shapes for the Bentley Mk VI chassis. As was now the case with new designs, the front doors were hinged at their leading edges. This example on chassis number B6MD was another exhibit at the 1951 Earls Court Show, and was body number 1611.

Another new design in 1951 was number 3091, but just one body (1610) was built to the original six-light saloon design, even though there were a few more to a variant design. Not much was new here; the offset cutaway in the wheel spat and the lines on the wing valances were really grafted on to established shapes, although the front doors were now hinged at their leading edges. This car, on Rolls-Royce Silver Wraith chassis WOF3, was a Freestone & Webb exhibit at the 1951 Earls Court Show.

This was the third exhibit at Earls Court in 1951, and this time is a variant of an older design, actually a 3046/C/F. The straighter waistline and the differently shaped wings are noticeable by comparison with the car pictured earlier, while the offset cutaway of the wheel spats introduces a contemporary note. This is body number 1612 on a Bentley Mk VI, B8MD. (Frank Dale & Stepsons)

The curvaceous lines of this lovely coupé to design 3087 show early 1950s Freestone & Webb style at its finest. The chassis is Rolls-Royce Silver Wraith WOF54 and the car was new in February 1952, with body number 1571.

This rear view of the same car shows that spats with an offset cutaway were still in favour, and the way that bright waist moulding divides above the rear wing is a reminder of 1930s designs. Just one other body to this design was built.

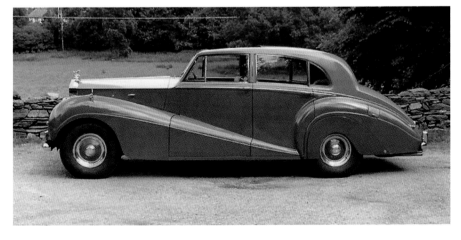

This six-light saloon design, number 3092, was introduced at Earls Court in 1951 and proved quite popular; there would eventually be seven bodies to the basic design and two others of a variant with division. This one is body number 1617. The cutaway in the rear wheel spat is in fact central to the wheel, but the wing shape makes it look offset. (Real Car Co)

1952

If the front-end proportions and wire wheels look odd, that is because the chassis is actually a 1937 Rolls- Royce Phantom III, 3CP118. Otherwise, this new two-door body provided in 1952 was in line with contemporary Freestone & Webb styles. It had design number 3089 and body number 1634.

As always, there are problems with establishing which bodies really were completed at Brentfield Road this year, but the total seems to have been 33. This year's core design for the Bentley chassis was number 3082, the six-light saloon which had been introduced at Earls Court in 1951 and became 1952's strongest seller with ten examples. Four of these were on the new R Type chassis; the others were on the Mk VI; nine had variant 3082/C and one was a 3082/D.

Other bodies on the Bentley Mk VI chassis were less numerous. Two were drophead coupés, both variants of design 3077 (and one was on a left-hand drive chassis). The only other two were six-light saloons to design 3093/A, the first of the "Empress" designs and a new one in the Freestone & Webb catalogue. This design was adapted for the R Type as well, and one of

the first two R Types supplied to Freestone & Webb carried it at the 1952 Earls Court Show.

The company was still struggling to find a strong-selling design for the Silver Wraith, and may again have been biding its time until examples of the new long-wheelbase chassis became available. Its 1952 bodies were the usual collection of saloons, saloons with division, and limousines, the strongest sellers being the two new designs introduced at Earls Court the previous autumn. Even so, variants of saloon design 3091 and of six-light saloon 3092 sold just three examples each.

Much more exciting were the coupés on the Silver Wraith chassis, which allowed the Freestone & Webb talent to shine. There was just one to design 3087, a real beauty with running-boards and cutaway spats

Body number 1641 was the prototype of Freestone & Webb's interpretation of the Hooper "Empress" style, and was completed in spring 1952. This six-light design, number 3093/A, was rather sleeker than the Osmond Rivers original, and the full-width windscreen with its slim pillars was much neater than the rubber-glazed Hooper type. Unlike the Hooper design, all doors were hinged on their forward edges, and on early bodies of this type there was a rather awkward shut line for the door just ahead of the rear wheel spat. The flat bumpers were used on all early examples. The chassis is a Bentley MkVI, B390MD.

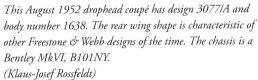

This August 1952 drophead coupé has design 3077/A and body number 1638. The rear wing shape is characteristic of other Freestone & Webb designs of the time. The chassis is a Bentley MkVI, B101NY. (Klaus-Josef Rossfeldt)

This rear view of the same car with convertible top erected shows the hinged cover panel that concealed the retracted canvas to give the car clean lines when open. This panel was seen on other Freestone & Webb drophead bodies of the period. The two-tone paintwork works well but appears not to be original to the car. (Klaus-Josef Rossfeldt)

Formal limousines were represented by design 3110/A for the long-wheelbase Rolls-Royce Silver Wraith. Two examples were built, plus a third with a variant of the design. The coachwork drawing for the design was dated October 1952, and this body, number 1646, was completed in January 1953. It was on chassis number ALW39. The smooth lines of this modern-looking body contrast with the elderly family saloon that has crept into the background.

(body 1571), and there were two to design 3107, a magnificently proportioned body with high wing lines, full spats and a sweeping tail. One of these represented the company at Earls Court that year, along with a saloon limousine to design 3090/B – the only one that would ever be made.

As the coupé bodies for the Silver Wraith showed, Freestone & Webb could still come up with some interesting and attractive designs when given a chance – and the company was given one more chance to shine during 1952. The vogue for rebodying pre-war chassis was more or less dead by this time, but one customer appeared with a 1937 Rolls-Royce Phantom III and asked for a new coupé body to be put on it. Thoroughly modern in design, and yet retaining a classic elegance from the proportions of the Phantom chassis, design 3089 was a huge success, and it is regrettable that only the one example was ever built.

Body 1698 introduced the Empress-inspired saloon design to the public at Earls Court in 1952. This formidably expensive car did not find a buyer until June 1953, when it went to the West German Embassy in London. The amber turn signals were added later, and the car still survives as an example of the coachbuilder's best work. It is on Bentley MkVI chassis B12RT. (Klaus-Josef Rossfeldt)

This coupé follows the Freestone & Webb trend towards higher wing lines, and the full rear wheel spats work well. Design 3107 represents a half-way house between the older semi-razor-edge designs from Brentfield Road and the Hooper-inspired saloons that would soon become staple fare. Body number 1695 is on Rolls-Royce Silver Wraith chassis WVH6 and was on the Freestone & Webb stand at Earls Court in 1952. (Bill Wolf)

1953

Only 29 bodies left Brentfield Road during 1953, and the order book for the period again has large quantities of body numbers against which there is no entry. As suggested in Chapter 7, this may well have been one of the results of uncertainty about rates of Purchase Tax in the early part of the year. Yet all was not doom and gloom. Initial customer response to the Freestone & Webb designs for the latest chassis from Crewe – the long-wheelbase Rolls-Royce Silver Wraith and the Bentley R-type – was encouraging.

Of those 29 bodies, 14 were on Silver Wraith chassis. There were ten of the older types and four of the new long-wheelbase models. On the short-wheelbase chassis there were five six-light saloons to design 3092 (one a variant), two to design 3091 (one a variant), one saloon to 3070, and a single example of the lovely coupé 3087. For the new long-wheelbase Silver Wraith, there were two new designs, the appropriately formal looking limousine 3110/A and the touring limousine 3131/A with a higher wing line. Neither brought any radically new ideas to the Freestone & Webb repertoire, but of course their target customers probably did not

want any such frivolities. Both appeared in the first half of the year, but both were also displayed at Earls Court in the autumn as new designs.

The close similarity between the Bentley Mk VI chassis and its R Type replacement allowed older designs to be carried over. Just one Mk VI chassis left Brentfield Road during 1953, with the much-liked six-light saloon body 3082/C; the same design also began to appear on the new R Types. A second existing design applied to the R Type was saloon coupé 3073, of which one was built. The Empress style six-light saloon 3093/A, showcased on an R Type chassis at Earls Court in the autumn of 1952, attracted no fewer than six orders. It was a design that would endure until Freestone & Webb's final days.

The remaining body on Bentley R Type chassis during 1953 was a four-light saloon to design 3132, clearly inspired by Park Ward designs and in the event destined to remain unique. Freestone & Webb also fitted one second-hand utility body to a Bentley Mk VI chassis; this body has not been counted among the total of bodies constructed by the company itself.

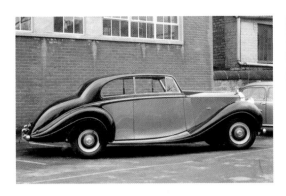

Progress in design: body 1663 is the second of the two coupé bodies built to design 3087. The earlier one (number 1571) was built in 1952, and this one was completed exactly a year later, in February 1953. Two-tone paintwork apart, the two bodies are superficially the same – but on this later car the doors are hinged at the front rather than at the rear. The chassis is a Rolls-Royce Silver Wraith, WVH42. (Tom Clarke)

Design 3110/A/L was the later variant of the limousine design 3110/A, pictured above. The two-tone paintwork would have been suitably eye-catching for the Freestone & Webb stand at Earls Court in 1953 on which this car was displayed. However, the only other visible difference from the earlier body is that this one appears not to have semaphore indicators in the B/C pillars. It was on Rolls-Royce Silver Wraith chassis BLW58.

1954

There was a slight drop in the Freestone & Webb output for 1954, to 26 bodies. This year, there were two core body designs for the Bentley chassis, the old six-light saloon 3082 and the new Empress-line saloon 3093. For the Silver Wraith, design 3131 was a touring limousine and design 3171 was a new touring saloon with the distinctive Empress lines. But there would be a new look from the autumn, as a wholly new design

appeared with variants to suit the Rolls-Royce Silver Dawn and Bentley R Type chassis.

The Rolls-Royce Silver Wraith accounted for the majority of chassis to pass through Brentfield Road, the total of 13 consisting of one final short-wheelbase type and 12 long-wheelbase types. The coachwork for the short-wheelbase chassis was a six-light saloon with division to existing design 3091/A. On the long-

The Empress style was easy enough to adapt for the Rolls-Royce Silver Dawn chassis, and design 3163 was really a mildly altered 3093, as used on the Bentley MkVI. This fine example has body number 1740 and was new in April 1954 on chassis SNF107. (RL GNZLZ/ Wikimedia Commons)

wheelbase chassis, there were seven bodies to three variants of design 3131, six being four-light touring limousines and one a six-light saloon, and new Empress-line touring saloon 3171/A provided two bodies, one of which became an Earls Court exhibit in the autumn.

The high wing line disguises the length of the Rolls-Royce Silver Wraith chassis on this coupé to design number 3183. However, the lines are not completely happy, and body number 1753 remained a one-off on chassis number CLW39. The car was new in December 1954.

By October 1954, when body number 1754 was completed, the Freestone & Webb limousine design for the Rolls-Royce Silver Wraith chassis had evolved further, although the rear doors were still rear-hinged. This is design 3131/L on chassis CLW37, which at some stage in its life was fitted with the straight-eight engine designed for the Phantom IV chassis. (Klaus-Josef Rossfeldt)

As this view makes clear, softer lines were now the order of the day at Brentfield Road. Even so, there is a clear line of descent from the earlier razor-edged designs. (Klaus-Josef Rossfeldt)

The remaining three Silver Wraith bodies were all unique designs. It was most unusual to see a new all-weather tourer by this time, but one was built to design 3160. There were then a limousine with design 3170/A and a coupé with design 3183. The wing lines of the coupé were uncharacteristically uncomfortable, and the body was not an unqualified success.

This year also saw the first examples of the Rolls-Royce Silver Dawn pass through the Brentfield Road workshops. In truth, the chassis was that of the Bentley R Type but retuned for refinement rather than speed, and it was not difficult for Freestone & Webb to adapt existing coachwork designs to suit it. Of the four Silver Dawn chassis that were bodied during 1954, three had an Empress-line six-light saloon designated 3163, and a fourth had the first example of a new design, numbered 3165.

Design 3165 would have long-term importance. It would later be described in Earls Court Show catalogues as a Special Sports Saloon, and was a genuinely new design that had probably been drawn up in anticipation of the forthcoming Rolls-Royce Silver Cloud and Bentley S Type chassis, as it presaged their longer and sleeker lines. The single body on a Silver Dawn chassis was completed in May 1954; it was followed in October by a version of the design (numbered 3191) on a Bentley R Type, and in that guise appeared on the coachbuilder's stand at Earls Court. These two bodies can be considered the prototypes of a design that continued right through into Freestone & Webb's final days.

As for the R Type Bentley, the customers seemed to like the bodies already on offer. Five examples were bodied with versions of design 3093, a six-light Empress-line saloon first seen on the Mk VI chassis in 1952, and two more with the ever-popular 3082/C six-light saloon that dated back as far as 1951. There was also a single drophead coupé that was a version of design 3077 seen on Bentley Mk VI chassis in 1952. It would be the only example built on the R Type chassis.

New at Earls Court in 1954, this touring limousine to design 3171/A showed that Freestone & Webb were now completely comfortable with these elegant, sweeping lines. The long wheelbase of the Rolls-Royce Silver Wraith chassis (number DLW44) is a help, and the result is a major success, with a much neater shut line for the rear door than on earlier bodies. The characteristic flat bumpers remain in use with body number 1760, which was the show model.

Far less formal, and no doubt deliberately so, is this saloon with division on Rolls-Royce Silver Wraith DLW45. New in March 1955, body number 1759 was the only one built to design 3192/A.

This rear view of the same car reveals how large the elegantly shaped boot must have been.

1955

There were more changes in the Freestone & Webb designs for 1955 as the chassis available changed once again. This year saw the last Bentley R Type and Rolls-Royce Silver Dawn types pass through the workshops, and the first of the new Bentley S Types. There would be none of the new Rolls-Royce Silver Cloud models this year, but there were plenty of the long-standing Silver Wraith models.

In fact, the Silver Wraith accounted for the lion's share of the 1955 bodies, with 12 of the 25 built. The majority were to familiar designs: seven of the Empress-line 3171 touring limousine (including variants), and three of the older 3131 touring limousine first seen in 1953. A single saloon with division to design 3192/A and a single limousine to design 3190 completed the list, and each remained the only one of its type.

The Silver Dawns were few and far between, and just two were bodied, both with the Empress-line 3163 Saloon design. On the Bentley R Type chassis, the core design was Empress-line 3093, as introduced for the Mk VI chassis in 1952, and there were five examples of it. Then there was one with the new Special Sports Saloon body 3191.

As Freestone & Webb had doubtless planned from the start, the Special Sports Saloon was adapted to suit

the new Bentley S Type chassis, where it became design 3191/A. The first of these bodies was displayed at Earls Court that year, but the second may well have become the first of this design to have the modified front end with cowled headlights. It is difficult to be sure, because it looks as if some owners returned their cars to Freestone & Webb to have this new design fitted once it became available.

There was also, of course, an Empress-line body (3199) for the S Type chassis. Three examples of this one were built, and all of them probably had standard S Type bumpers and over-riders instead of the flat bumpers associated with earlier bodies to the same design on the R Type chassis.

Design 3131/A/L was described as a Touring Limousine, and the two-colour paintwork certainly takes some of the formality away from the shape. Eight bodies were built to this design, plus more of variants; this is body number 1746. It is a January 1955 car on Rolls-Royce Silver Wraith chassis CLW31, late enough to have the small built-in headlamps instead of the large free-standing type seen on the earlier 3131/A variant. (Klaus-Josef Rossfeldt)

A radically new design was previewed on some late R Type Bentley chassis, and was then revised to suit the Silver Cloud and S Type. Early examples had the headlamps perched a little uncomfortably on the nose of each wing, but they were now mounted within cowled panels. All of them had the striking new rear wing design, with a gap between wing and boot. This is body 1786, described in the 1955 Earls Court Show catalogue as a Special Sports Saloon, and finished in Shell Grey over Dark Violet. It may have been the first with the cowled headlamp panels. The body design was number 3191/A, of which seven would be built; the chassis is a Bentley, B486AN.

Existing designs were adapted to suit the new Rolls-Royce Silver Cloud and Bentley S Type models in 1955. Design 3199 was the Bentley version, and picked up on the improvements introduced for the long-wheelbase Silver Wraith design, number 3171/A. There were 13 bodies to this design; this is number 1777, on chassis B464AN. It was new in December 1955. (Klaus-Josef Rossfeldt)

1956

There were 26 new bodies from Brentfield Road during 1956 – 12 on the Bentley S Type, nine on the Rolls-Royce Silver Cloud, and five on the Rolls-Royce Silver Wraith. In addition, the order book shows a "Standard Steel Saloon" (otherwise unidentified) that passed through the workshops. Destined for the impresario Lew Grade, this was probably a Rolls-Royce Silver Cloud and presumably came in for some special fittings to be added.

Despite the interest generated by Freestone & Webb's Special Sports Saloon design with its unorthodox rear wing lines and cowled headlamps, it was the Empress-line bodies that continued to dominate proceedings during 1956. They were in the majority on all three types of chassis.

On the Bentley chassis, there were six of the Empress-line bodies to design 3199. Four of the Special Sports Saloons to design 3191/A were built, plus one to design 3191, and there was a single example of a derivative design with altered rear wing lines. This was numbered 3224/1, and was displayed at Earls Court that year in the hope of generating more orders.

The picture was much the same for the Silver Clouds, where five bodies had Empress-line design 3206 (or a variant), and two bodies were built to design 3194, which was a Special Sports Saloon with a slightly modified rear wing line. There were then two individual designs, each with its own interest. One was a coupé to design 3210/A. Despite oversized blind rear quarters, this was an attractive design that deserved to be repeated but never was. The other was a special two-door saloon to design 3193, built to order for the Armenian-British

businessman and socialite Nubar Gulbenkian. A most impressive design, this took the elements of the Empress line and grafted them very successfully onto the long-wheelbase Silver Wraith chassis.

As for the Silver Wraith, customer interest had declined dramatically, perhaps in anticipation of the arrival of a long-wheelbase Silver Cloud as the basis for limousine bodies. There were two Empress-line touring limousines to design 3171/A, of which one was displayed at Earls Court. A single example was bodied as a 3131/A touring limousine, and then on display at Earls Court in the autumn was a new limousine design, number 3225, that incorporated the wing line and front end of the Special Sports Saloons.

The Rolls-Royce equivalent of design 3199 for the Bentley S Type chassis was numbered 3206. This is it on Silver Cloud chassis SWA56, dating from March 1956 and the first Silver Cloud to pass through the Freestone & Webb workshops. The body number is 1782.

There was only ever one of these elegant coupés to design 3210/A. Clear here are the cowled rear lights that matched the cowled headlamps. Body 1804 was new in June 1956 on Silver Cloud chassis SWA108.

Rolls-Royce Silver Cloud chassis ALC1 carried the first of only two long-wheelbase examples of body 3191. It was built for the 1957 Earls Court Show, with body number 1826 in Tyrolean Green over Cactus Green.

Would AJ Webb have approved? This special commission was a Limousine design, number 3222 and (perhaps fortunately) only one was ever built. Body number 1813 on Rolls-Royce Silver Wraith FLW26 was delivered in December 1956 and has always been controversial. (Klaus-Josef Rossfeldt)

The cowled headlamps and separate rear wings of designs 3191/A and 3194 were here tried out on a four-light saloon with division for a Rolls-Royce Silver Wraith chassis, FLW68. There was only one example of design 3230, which was delivered in July 1957. This is body number 1822.

1957

Just 13 bodies were completed at Brentfield Road during 1957, the small number being a sure sign that the end of coachwork construction was near for Freestone & Webb. Four were on Bentley chassis; four were on the Rolls-Royce Silver Cloud, including one on the new long-wheelbase chassis; and five were on the Silver Wraith. There were some bizarre happenings with the design numbers, too, or at least with their recording in the order book. A Rolls-Royce version of saloon design 3224/1 was numbered as 3224/SC (for Silver Cloud, presumably), while a long-wheelbase version for Rolls-Royce chassis of design 3191 – seen on both R Type and S Type Bentleys in different variants – retained the number 3191 without any identifying suffix. Nevertheless, a design drawing of it that survives shows the number as 3191/LWB.

Beginning, then, with the Silver Wraiths, four of them were touring limousines with Empress-line design 3171 in two different variants. The fifth was a one-off saloon with division to design 3230, which was

Among the special features of body number 1813 was a drinks cabinet that could be raised from behind the rear seat.

It was probably a try-out for a design that could have been used on the long-wheelbase Silver Cloud when that arrived, but it was not a great success and was not repeated.

Then, of course, there was the unique glass-roof limousine for Mitchell Engineering, design number 3222. This has already been described in Chapter 7, and it remains controversial to this day.

Enthusiasts have to wonder how such a rare and elegant car can descend into such a heartbreaking state. This was ALC1 with body 1826 as it survived in 2014. The likely cost of restoration must have been a major hindrance to a successful sale. Nevertheless this picture does show the cowled headlamps characteristic of Freestone & Webb designs in this period. (Klaus-Josef Rossfeldt)

This is body 1826 on ALC1 yet again, this time demonstrating the way Freestone & Webb designs of the time separated the rear wings from the boot compartment.

The original Honeymoon Express was finished in Dark Green and Shell Grey, and was displayed at Earls Court in 1957 on Freestone & Webb's last motor show stand. This was body number 1827 to design 3243/C

another attempt to make a limousine-like design from the Special Sports Saloon lines.

Three of the Bentleys had Empress-line bodies with design 3199, and the fourth was another of the new 3191/A Special Sports Saloons. Just one Empress-line 3206 was built on a Silver Cloud chassis. The other three Silver Clouds had three different designs. One was a Rolls-Royce version of last year's 3224/1 limousine for the Bentley (this was 3224/SC); one was a long-wheelbase derivative of the Special Sports Saloon (called 3191); and the third was the infamous Honeymoon Express, described more fully in Chapter 7.

Even though body production was now at a low ebb, no fewer than four of those bodies appeared on the Freestone & Webb stand at Earls Court in 1957. There was one Bentley S Type, the long-wheelbase Silver Cloud, a Silver Wraith Limousine, and the Honeymoon Express. If nothing else, it was a remarkably eclectic collection that showcased the coachbuilder's abilities to the full.

The tail fins were very much in fashion in 1957, thanks to American influence, but many people considered them rather vulgar and not at all in keeping with a Rolls-Royce. This is the original car again.

A power-operated convertible top was a quite advanced feature for 1957, and was pictured here midway through its cycle.

1958

Freestone & Webb staff completed the company's last seven bodies in 1958, probably finishing work in October or November on the last one – which was not the last one numerically.

To the last, the Empress-line designs predominated, with one 3199 saloon on Bentley S Type chassis and two 3206 saloons on Silver Cloud chassis. Then there was a second limousine body to design 3191 on a long-wheelbase Silver Cloud, and a copy of the 1956 Show limousine 3225 was completed for another Silver Cloud chassis.

But pride of place went to the two copies of the Honeymoon Express from the 1957 Show. One – the only one – was built on a Bentley S Type chassis, and the other was built on a Silver Cloud chassis, like the original. That car had the honour of taking the highest number, and the last, in the Freestone & Webb order book.

The second long-wheelbase 3191 body was on Silver Cloud chassis ALC10 and had number 1829. It was new in February 1958, and these pictures make clear that the search for new styling features had certainly not harmed Freestone & Webb's ability to produce an elegant piece of coachwork.
(Klaus-Josef Rossfeldt)

Design number 3243/B was the Bentley variant of the Honeymoon Express, and the sole example was built on S Type chassis B377EK. It was delivered in November 1958 but was probably completed some time earlier. With body number 1831, it was the second of the three Honeymoon Express cars. The small convertible top – the same on all three cars – did look rather lost on such a long body.

BODY DELIVERIES, YEAR BY YEAR

This table provides a quick reference guide to which bodies were delivered in each calendar year between 1950 and 1958, and also reveals how many bodies were built in each of those years. The overall total is 223 bodies, assuming that all those listed below were actually built.

1950 (33 bodies)
1370, 1450, 1495, 1511, 1518, 1520, 1521, 1522, 1523, 1524, 1525, 1526, 1527, 1528, 1529, 1530, 1531, 1532, 1533, 1534, 1536, 1537, 1538, 1539, 1540, 1541, 1542, 1543, 1544, 1546, 1547, 1552, 1567

1951 (31 bodies)
1535, 1548, 1549, 1550, 1551, 1553, 1558, 1562, 1564, 1565, 1570, 1572, 1575, 1577, 1581, 1582, 1583, 1585, 1587, 1588, 1603, 1609, 1610, 1611, 1612, 1615, 1616, 1619, 1623, 1626, 1631

1952 (33 bodies)
1554, 1556, 1571, 1573, 1574, 1578, 1580, 1589, 1590, 1592, 1593, 1595, 1600, 1601, 1605, 1617, 1620, 1625, 1627, 1628, 1629, 1634, 1638, 1640, 1641, 1642, 1644, 1647, 1654, 1691, 1695, 1696, 1698

1953 (29 bodies)
1632, 1636, 1637, 1646, 1650, 1656, 1663, 1671, 1697, 1708, 1709, 1713, 1714, 1716, 1717, 1718, 1719, 1720, 1721, 1722, 1723, 1725, 1726, 1727, 1728, 1730, 1731, 1732, 1734

1954 (26 bodies)
1693, 1724, 1729, 1733, 1736, 1738, 1739, 1740, 1742, 1743, 1744, 1745, 1747, 1748, 1749, 1750, 1753, 1754, 1755, 1756, 1757, 1758, 1760, 1761, 1762, 1763

1955 (25 bodies)
1735, 1746, 1751, 1752, 1759, 1764, 1765, 1766, 1767, 1768, 1769, 1770, 1771, 1772, 1774, 1775, 1776, 1777, 1778, 1781, 1784, 1786, 1787, 1788, 1794

1956 (26 bodies)
1773, 1779, 1780, 1782, 1785, 1790, 1791, 1792, 1793, 1795, 1796, 1797, 1799, 1801, 1803, 1804, 1807, 1808, 1809, 1811, 1812, 1813, 1815, 1816, 1817, 1818

1957 (13 bodies)
1783, 1789, 1805, 1814, 1819, 1820, 1821, 1822, 1823, 1824, 1825, 1826, 1827

1958 (7 bodies)
1800, 1828, 1829, 1830, 1831, 1832, 1833

BODY NUMBERS 1518 TO 1599

This range of body numbers follows on from the list for 1949. The list has been compiled on the basis of surviving evidence, is the most complete available, and may be regarded as reasonably definitive. The tables divide the body numbers into blocks of one hundred (approximately) for ease of reference.

Body no	Design no and type	Date	Chassis type	Chassis no
1518	3029/C Four-light saloon coupé	1950, Feb	Bentley Mk VI	B189EW
1519	CANCELLED. Was to be 3050/A/B on Rolls-Royce Silver Wraith.			
1520	3046/C Six-light saloon	1950, Feb	Bentley Mk VI	B46FV
1521	3046/C Six-light saloon	1950, Mar	Bentley Mk VI	B67FU
1522	3046/C Six-light saloon	1950, Feb	Bentley Mk VI	B408FV
1523	3050/A/B Six-light saloon with division	1950, Mar	Rolls-Royce Silver Wraith	WGC50
1524	3050/B Six-light saloon	1950, May	Rolls-Royce Silver Wraith	WGC99
1525	3050/A/B Six-light saloon with division	1950, July	Rolls-Royce Silver Wraith	WHD15
1526	3050/B Six-light saloon	1950, July	Rolls-Royce Silver Wraith	WHD27
1527	3046/C Six-light saloon	1950, Apr	Bentley Mk VI	B291FU
1528	3046/C Six-light saloon	1950, Apr	Bentley Mk VI	B143FU
1529	3046/C Six-light saloon	1950, July	Bentley Mk VI	B533FU
1530	3046/C Six-light saloon	1950, May	Bentley Mk VI	B403FU
1531	3046/C Six-light saloon	1950, May	Bentley Mk VI	B297FU
1532	3046/C Six-light saloon	1950, May	Bentley Mk VI	B411FU
1533	3046/C Six-light saloon	1950 See note	Bentley Mk VI	B340EY
1534	3046/C Six-light saloon	1950, Sep	Bentley Mk VI	B497EW
1535	3046/C/F Six-light saloon	1951, Jan	Bentley Mk VI	B139HP
1536	3046/C/F Six-light saloon	1950, Jun	Bentley Mk VI	B287FU
1537	3046/C/F Six-light saloon	1950, Jun	Bentley Mk VI	B293FU
1538	3046/C/F Six-light saloon	1950, July	Bentley Mk VI	B3GT
1539	3070/B Saloon with division	1950, Aug	Rolls-Royce Silver Wraith	WHD44
1540	3046/C/F Six-light saloon	1950, Nov	Bentley Mk VI	B373GT
1541	3068 Utility (estate)	1950, Sep	Rolls-Royce Silver Wraith	LWHD73
1542	3073 Saloon coupé	1950, Nov	Bentley Mk VI	B351GT
1543	3070/A Saloon	1950, Nov	Rolls-Royce Silver Wraith	WHD86
1544	3050/A/B Six-light saloon with division	1950, Nov	Rolls-Royce Silver Wraith	WHD76
1545	"Pressed Steel Saloon"			
1546	3029/C Four-light saloon coupé	1950, Nov	Bentley Mk VI	B1GT
1547	3047/B Six-light saloon	1950, Dec	Rolls-Royce Silver Wraith	WHD72
1548	3046/C/F Six-light saloon	1951, Mar	Bentley Mk VI	B195HP
1549	3070 Saloon	1951, Feb	Rolls-Royce Silver Wraith	WLE29

BODY NUMBERS 1518 TO 1599

1550	3073 Four-light saloon coupé	1951 See note	Bentley Mk VI	Not known
1551	3073 Four-light saloon coupé	1951, July	Bentley Mk VI	B196KM
1552	3046/C/F Six-light saloon	1950, Dec	Bentley Mk VI	B145HP
1553	3046/C/F Six-light saloon	1951 See note	Bentley Mk VI	Not known
1554	3046/C/F Six-light saloon	1952, Jan	Bentley Mk VI	B202MD
1555	NO ENTRY			
1556	3082/C Six-light saloon	1952, Aug	Bentley Mk VI	B97NY
1557	NO ENTRY			
1558	3046/C/F Six-light saloon	1951, Jun	Bentley Mk VI	B10LJ
1559	NO ENTRY			
1560	NO ENTRY			
1561	NO ENTRY			
1562	3046/C/F Six-light saloon	1951, Jan	Bentley Mk VI	B237HP
1563	Bentley Mk VI Standard Steel			
1564	3046/C/F Six-light saloon	1951, Apr	Bentley Mk VI	B163JN
1565	3029/C Four-light saloon coupé	1951, Jan	Bentley Mk VI	B91GT
1566	NO ENTRY			
1567	3070/A Saloon	1950, Dec	Rolls-Royce Silver Wraith	WLE20
1568	NO ENTRY			
1569	NO ENTRY			
1570	3046/C/F Six-light saloon	1951, Sep	Bentley Mk VI	B209LH
1571	3087 Coupé	1952, Feb	Rolls-Royce Silver Wraith	WOF54
1572	3046/C Six-light saloon	1951, Sep	Bentley Mk VI	B178LJ
1573	3091/A Six-light saloon with division	1952, Jun	Rolls-Royce Silver Wraith	WOF51
1574	3092 Six-light saloon	1952, Jun	Rolls-Royce Silver Wraith	WOF65
1575	3074/A/B Limousine	1951, Apr	Rolls-Royce Silver Wraith	WME15
1576	NO ENTRY			
1577	3081 Six-light saloon with division	1951, Apr	Rolls-Royce Silver Wraith	WLE27
1578	3070 Saloon	1952, Jan	Rolls-Royce Silver Wraith	WOF21
1579	NO ENTRY			
1580	3082/C Six-light saloon	1952, Apr	Bentley Mk VI	B133MB
1581	3046/C/F Six-light saloon	1951, May	Bentley Mk VI	B110KM
1582	3046/C/F Six-light saloon	1951, Apr	Bentley Mk VI	B106KM
1583	3074/A/B Limousine	1951, Aug	Rolls-Royce Silver Wraith	WME40
1584	NO ENTRY			
1585	3082/C Six-light saloon	1951, Sep	Bentley Mk VI	B79LH
1586	NO ENTRY			
1587	3050/A/CE Limousine	1951, July	Rolls-Royce Silver Wraith	WME88
1588	3082/C Six-light saloon	1951, July	Bentley Mk VI	B169KL
1589	3070/E Saloon	1952, Jan	Rolls-Royce Silver Wraith	WOF41
1590	3047/C Six-light saloon	1952, Apr	Bentley Mk VI	B70NZ
1591	NO ENTRY			
1592	3046/C/F Six-light saloon	1952	Bentley Mk VI	B178EY
1593	3091/A Six-light saloon with division	1952, Oct	Rolls-Royce Silver Wraith	WSG62
1594	NO ENTRY			
1595	3050/A/C Limousine	1952, Feb	Rolls-Royce Silver Wraith	WOF53
1596	NO ENTRY			
1597	NO ENTRY			
1598	NO ENTRY			
1599	NO ENTRY			

Notes
1533 The date of completion is an assumption.
1539 The order book notes, "as lines of 1949 Park Ward show job."
1540 This car was displayed on the Freestone & Webb stand at Earls Court in 1950.
1542 This car was displayed on the Freestone & Webb stand at Earls Court in 1950.
1543 This car was displayed on the Freestone & Webb stand at Earls Court in 1950.
1544 This car was displayed on the Freestone & Webb stand at Earls Court in 1950.
1545 This was presumably a Standard Steel Bentley Mk VI that passed through the Freestone & Webb workshops for some minor coachwork modifications. The description is taken from the order book.
1550 The date of completion is an assumption.
1553 The date of completion is an assumption.
1563 Presumably like number 1545, this one passed through the Freestone & Webb workshops for some minor coachwork modifications.
1577 This body was later transferred to WVH110, an August 1954 Rolls-Royce Silver Wraith.
1592 This was a rebody of an October 1949 chassis. The original body was fitted by coachwork dealer Cooper of Putney.

BODY NUMBERS 1600 TO 1699

This list has been compiled on the basis of surviving evidence, is the most complete available, and may be regarded as reasonably definitive. The tables divide the body numbers into blocks of one hundred (approximately) for ease of reference.

Body no	Design no and type	Date	Chassis type	Chassis no
1600	3046/C/F Six-light saloon	1952, Aug	Bentley Mk VI	B103NY
1601	3091 Six-light saloon	1952, Feb	Rolls-Royce Silver Wraith	WOF37
1602	NO ENTRY			
1603	3046/C/F Six-light saloon	1951, Nov	Bentley Mk VI	B139LH
1604	NO ENTRY			
1605	3046/C/F Six-light saloon	1952, Jan	Bentley Mk VI	B44MD
1606	NO ENTRY			
1607	NO ENTRY			
1608	NO ENTRY			
1609	3092 Saloon	1951, Oct	Rolls-Royce Silver Wraith	WOF2
1610	3091/A Saloon limousine	1951, Oct	Rolls-Royce Silver Wraith	WOF3
1611	3082/C Six-light saloon	1951, Nov	Bentley Mk VI	B6MD
1612	3046/C/F Six-light saloon	1951, Nov	Bentley Mk VI	B8MD
1613	NO ENTRY			
1614	NO ENTRY			
1615	3070/A Saloon	1951 See note	Rolls-Royce Silver Wraith	WVA70
1616	3070/A Saloon	1951, Jun	Rolls-Royce Silver Wraith	WME52
1617	3092 Six-light saloon	1952, May	Rolls-Royce Silver Wraith	WOF58
1618	NO ENTRY			
1619	3082/C Six-light saloon	1951, Nov	Bentley Mk VI	B9LH
1620	3082/C Six-light saloon	1952, July	Bentley Mk VI	B317MB
1621	NO ENTRY			
1622	NO ENTRY			
1623	3082/C Six-light saloon	1951, Aug	Bentley Mk VI	B3LH
1624	NO ENTRY			
1625	3082/C Six-light saloon	1952, Apr	Bentley Mk VI	B84NZ
1626	3050/A/D Limousine	1951, Nov	Rolls-Royce Silver Wraith	WME86
1627	3082/C Six-light saloon	1952, Mar	Bentley Mk VI	B392MD
1628	3082/C Six-light saloon	1952, Feb	Bentley Mk VI	B256MD
1629	3082/C Six-light saloon	1952, Jun	Bentley Mk VI	B107NY
1630	NO ENTRY			
1631	3046/C/F Six-light saloon	1951 See note	Bentley Mk VI	B297FU
1632	3070/A Saloon	1953, Jan	Rolls-Royce Silver Wraith	WVH17
1633	NO ENTRY			
1634	3089 Four-light coupé	1952, Jun	Rolls-Royce Phantom III	3CP118
1635	NO ENTRY			
1636	3092 Six-light saloon	1953, Mar	Rolls-Royce Silver Wraith	WVH64
1637	3082/C Six-light saloon	1953, Dec	Bentley Mk VI	B473NY
1638	3077/A Drophead coupé	1952, July	Bentley Mk VI	B101NY
1639	NO ENTRY			
1640	3082/C Six-light saloon	1952, Aug	Bentley Mk VI	B291NY
1641	3093/A Six-light saloon	1952, Apr	Bentley Mk VI	B390MD
1642	3077 Drophead coupé	1952, Mar	Bentley Mk VI	B200LMD
1643	NO ENTRY			
1644	3093/A Six-light saloon	1952, Jun	Bentley Mk VI	B86NZ
1645	NO ENTRY			
1646	3110/A Limousine	1953, Jan	Rolls-Royce Silver Wraith	ALW39
1647	3082/C Six-light saloon	1952, Jun	Bentley Mk VI	B146NZ
1648	NO ENTRY			
1649	NO ENTRY			
1650	3082/C Six-light saloon	1953, Jan	Bentley R Type	B81RS
1651	NO ENTRY			
1652	NO ENTRY			
1653	NO ENTRY			
1654	3092/A Six-light saloon with division	1952, Jun	Rolls-Royce Silver Wraith	WSG2
1655	NO ENTRY			

BODY NUMBERS 1600 TO 1699

1656	3082/C Six-light saloon	1953, Apr	Bentley R Type	B94SR
1657	NO ENTRY			
1658	NO ENTRY			
1659	NO ENTRY			
1660	NO ENTRY			
1661	NO ENTRY			
1662	NO ENTRY			
1663	3087 Coupé	1953, Feb	Rolls-Royce Silver Wraith	WVH42
1664	NO ENTRY			
1665	NO ENTRY			
1666	NO ENTRY			
1667	NO ENTRY			
1668	NO ENTRY			
1669	NO ENTRY			
1670	NO ENTRY			
1671	3092 Six-light saloon	1953, May	Rolls-Royce Silver Wraith	WVH49
1672	NO ENTRY			
1673	NO ENTRY			
1674	NO ENTRY			
1675	NO ENTRY			
1676	NO ENTRY			
1677	NO ENTRY			
1678	NO ENTRY			
1679	NO ENTRY			
1680	NO ENTRY			
1681	NO ENTRY			
1682	NO ENTRY			
1683	NO ENTRY			
1684	NO ENTRY			
1685	NO ENTRY			
1686	NO ENTRY			
1687	NO ENTRY			
1688	NO ENTRY			
1689	NO ENTRY			
1690	NO ENTRY			
1691	3107 Coupé	1952, Dec	Rolls-Royce Silver Wraith	WVH22
1692	NO ENTRY			
1693	3082/C Six-light saloon	1954, Feb	Bentley R Type	B206UM
1694	NO ENTRY			
1695	3107 Coupé	1952, Oct	Rolls-Royce Silver Wraith	WVH6
1696	3082/D Six-light saloon	1952, Nov	Bentley R Type	B4RT
1697	3090/B Saloon limousine	1953, Aug	Rolls-Royce Silver Wraith	WVH5
1698	3093/A Six-light saloon	1952, Oct	Bentley R Type	B12RT
1699	NO ENTRY			

Notes
1609 This car was on the Freestone & Webb stand at Earls Court in 1951.
1610 This car was on the Freestone & Webb stand at Earls Court in 1951.
1611 This car was on the Freestone & Webb stand at Earls Court in 1951.
1612 This car was on the Freestone & Webb stand at Earls Court in 1951.
1615 This was a rebody; the date is an assumption. WVA70 was new in November 1947 with a Park Ward saloon body.
1619 & 1620, 1623 & 1625 These four bodies to the same design can probably be considered as a batch, although their completion dates varied considerably.
1631 This may have been less a new body than a comprehensive rebuild of the old one. It replaced body number 1531, which dated from 1950, but was in fact to the latest variant of the same design (3046/C/F instead of 3046/C). A likely explanation is that the original body was damaged in an accident and that the customer liked it enough to want the same again. Freestone & Webb then obliged, adding the latest updates. In such circumstances, it seems quite likely that some elements of the original body would have been retained as well. The car was also re-registered in 1951.
1634 This was a re-body of a 1937 Rolls-Royce Phantom III chassis.
1695 This car was on the Freestone & Webb stand at Earls Court in 1952.
1696 This car was on the Freestone & Webb stand at Earls Court in 1952.
1697 This car was on the Freestone & Webb stand at Earls Court in 1952.
1698 This car was on the Freestone & Webb stand at Earls Court in 1952, and had taken over four months to complete as a showcase for the company's skills. It was one of the most expensive cars at the Show, with a price of £6500. As its current owner notes: "the average working wage in 1952 was about £5 a week, or £250 a year. At the Earls Court Show you could have bought an Aston Martin DB2 at £2500, together with a Jaguar XK120 at £1200, and a Morris Minor at £600. Then you could have gone out and bought a large detached house with the other £2300, all for the price of this car." Its first owner was the West German Embassy in London, which took delivery in June 1953 and retained the car until 1979.

BODY NUMBERS 1700 TO 1799

This list has been compiled on the basis of surviving evidence, is the most complete available, and may be regarded as reasonably definitive. The tables divide the body numbers into blocks of one hundred (approximately) for ease of reference.

Body no	Design no and type	Date	Chassis type	Chassis no
1700	NO ENTRY			
1701	NO ENTRY			
1702	NO ENTRY			
1703	NO ENTRY			
1704	NO ENTRY			
1705	NO ENTRY			
1706	NO ENTRY			
1707	NO ENTRY			
1708	3092 Six-light saloon	1953, Jan	Rolls-Royce Silver Wraith	WSG70
1709	3110/A Limousine	1953, Apr	Rolls-Royce Silver Wraith	ALW33
1710	NO ENTRY			
1711	NO ENTRY			
1712	NO ENTRY			
1713	3093/A Six-light saloon	1953, Apr	Bentley R Type	B56RT
1714	3092 Six-light saloon	1953, May	Rolls-Royce Silver Wraith	WVH44
1715	NO ENTRY			
1716	3093/A Six-light saloon	1953, May	Bentley R Type	B123SP
1717	3091 Six-light saloon	1953, Apr	Rolls-Royce Silver Wraith	WVH58
1718	3093/A Six-light saloon	1953, May	Bentley R Type	B121SP
1719	3131/A Four-light touring limousine	1953, Jun	Rolls-Royce Silver Wraith	ALW42
1720	3132 Saloon	1953, Oct	Bentley R Type	B382SR
1721	3091/A Six-light saloon with division	1953, July	Rolls-Royce Silver Wraith	WVH98
1722	3073 Four-light saloon coupé	1953, July	Bentley R Type	B333SP
1723	3082/C Six-light saloon	1953, July	Bentley R Type	B5TO
1724	3131/A/L Touring limousine	1954, Feb	Rolls-Royce Silver Wraith	BLW59
1725	3110/A/L Limousine	1953, Sep	Rolls-Royce Silver Wraith	BLW58
1726	3093/A Six-light saloon	1953, Nov	Bentley R Type	B142TN
1727	3082/C Six-light saloon	1953, Oct	Bentley R Type	B140TN
1728	3092/A Six-light saloon with division	1953, Sep	Rolls-Royce Silver Wraith	WVH100
1729	3091/A Six-light saloon with division	1954, Mar	Rolls-Royce Silver Wraith	WVH105
1730	3082/C Six-light saloon	1953, Sep	Bentley R Type	B399TO
1731	3093/A Six-light saloon	1953, Oct	Bentley R Type	B387TO
1732	See note Two-door, six-light utility	1953, Aug	Bentley R Type	B110TN
1733	3093/A Six-light saloon	1954, Apr	Bentley R Type	B214UM
1734	3093/A Six-light saloon	1953, Dec	Bentley R Type	B101UL
1735	3171/A Touring limousine	1955, May	Rolls-Royce Silver Wraith	DLW134
1736	3082/C Six-light saloon	1954, Apr	Bentley R Type	B106UM
1737	NO ENTRY			
1738	3093/A Six-light saloon	1954, Jan	Bentley R Type	B104UM
1739	3131/A/L Four-light touring limousine	1954, Apr	Rolls-Royce Silver Wraith	BLW96
1740	3163 Six-light saloon	1954, Apr	Rolls-Royce Silver Dawn	SNF107
1741	NO ENTRY			
1742	3093/A Six-light saloon	1954, May	Bentley R Type	B6WH
1743	3170/A Limousine	1954, Nov	Rolls-Royce Silver Wraith	DLW8
1744	3165 Special Sports Saloon	1954, May	Rolls-Royce Silver Dawn	SOG46
1745	3160 All-weather tourer	1954, Sep	Rolls-Royce Silver Wraith	LCLW9
1746	3131/A/L Touring limousine	1955, Jan	Rolls-Royce Silver Wraith	CLW31
1747	3171/A Touring limousine	1954, Nov	Rolls-Royce Silver Wraith	CLW32
1748	3077/A/P Drophead coupé	1954, Oct	Bentley R Type	B204WH
1749	3131/A/L Touring limousine	1954, Jun	Rolls-Royce Silver Wraith	BLW93
1750	3131/A/L Touring limousine	1954, Jun	Rolls-Royce Silver Wraith	CLW12
1751	3093/A/L Six-light saloon	1955, July	Bentley R Type	B4WH
1752	3131/A/L Touring limousine	1955, May	Rolls-Royce Silver Wraith	DLW69
1753	3183 Coupé	1954, Dec	Rolls-Royce Silver Wraith	CLW39
1754	3131/L Six-light saloon	1954, Oct	Rolls-Royce Silver Wraith	CLW37
1755	3163 Six-light saloon	1954, Aug	Rolls-Royce Silver Dawn	SOG50

BODY NUMBERS 1700 TO 1799

1756	3093/A/L Six-light saloon	1954, July	Bentley R Type	B2WH
1757	3163 Six-light saloon	1954, July	Rolls-Royce Silver Dawn	SOG48
1758	3131/A/L Touring limousine	1954, July	Rolls-Royce Silver Wraith	LCLW34
1759	3192/A Saloon with division	1955, Mar	Rolls-Royce Silver Wraith	DLW45
1760	3171/A Touring limousine	1954, Oct	Rolls-Royce Silver Wraith	DLW44
1761	3131/A Touring limousine	1954, Oct	Rolls-Royce Silver Wraith	DLW43
1762	3191 Special Sports Saloon	1954, Oct	Bentley R Type	B30YD
1763	3093/A/L Six-light saloon	1954, Oct	Bentley R Type	B32YD
1764	3190 Limousine	1955, Mar	Rolls-Royce Silver Wraith	DLW83
1765	3163 Six-light saloon	1955, July	Rolls-Royce Silver Dawn	STH53
1766	3163 Six-light saloon	1955, Oct	Rolls-Royce Silver Dawn	STH55
1767	3191 Special Sports Saloon	1955, Jan	Bentley R Type	B248YD
1768	3093/A/L Six-light saloon	1955, Apr	Bentley R Type	B318YD
1769	3171 Touring limousine	1955, Sep	Rolls-Royce Silver Wraith	DLW72
1770	3093/A/L Six-light saloon	1955, Feb	Bentley R Type	B326YD
1771	3093/A/L Six-light saloon	1955, Apr	Bentley R Type	B324YD
1772	3171/A Touring limousine	1955, May	Rolls-Royce Silver Wraith	DLW94
1773	3199 Six-light saloon	1956, Apr	Bentley S Type	B3AP
1774	3171 Touring limousine	1955, July	Rolls-Royce Silver Wraith	DLW154
1775	3093/A/L Six-light saloon	1955, Apr	Bentley R Type	B320YD
1776	3171/A Touring limousine	1955, Jun	Rolls-Royce Silver Wraith	DLW138
1777	3199 Six-light saloon	1955, Dec	Bentley S Type	B464AN
1778	3171/A Touring limousine	1955, Jun	Rolls-Royce Silver Wraith	DLW137
1779	3191/A Special Sports Saloon	1956, Jan	Bentley S Type	B23AP
1780	3199 Six-light saloon	1956, Jan	Bentley S Type	B458AN
1781	3131/A/L Touring limousine	1955, July	Rolls-Royce Silver Wraith	DLW160
1782	3206 Six-light saloon	1956, Mar	Rolls-Royce Silver Cloud	SWA56
1783	3191/A Special Sports Saloon	1957, Sep	Bentley S Type	B202LAN
1784	3191/A Special Sports Saloon	1955, Nov	Bentley S Type	B204AN
1785	3131/A/L/3 Touring limousine	1956, Jan	Rolls-Royce Silver Wraith	ELW8
1786	3191/A Six-light saloon	1955, Nov	Bentley S Type	B486AN
1787	3171/A Touring limousine	1955, Nov	Rolls-Royce Silver Wraith	ELW3
1788	3199 Six-light saloon	1955, Nov	Bentley S Type	B474AN
1789	3171/A Touring limousine	1957, Jun	Rolls-Royce Silver Wraith	ELW33
1790	3171/A Touring limousine	1956, May	Rolls-Royce Silver Wraith	ELW57
1791	3194 Six-light saloon	1956, July	Rolls-Royce Silver Cloud	SXA49
1792	3191/A Special Sports Saloon	1956, Apr	Bentley S Type	B121AP
1793	3191/A Special Sports Saloon	1956, Mar	Bentley S Type	B83AP
1794	3199 Six-light saloon	1955, Dec	Bentley S Type	B212AN
1795	3199 Six-light saloon	1956, Mar	Bentley S Type	B7AP
1796	3193 Two-door saloon	1956, Feb	Rolls-Royce Silver Cloud	SWA42
1797	3194 Six-light saloon	1956, Mar	Rolls-Royce Silver Cloud	SWA48
1798	Standard Steel Body			
1799	3199 Six-light saloon	1956, Jun	Bentley S Type	B289AP

Notes
1724 This car was on the Freestone & Webb stand at Earls Court in 1953.
1725 This car was on the Freestone & Webb stand at Earls Court in 1953.
1726 This car was on the Freestone & Webb stand at Earls Court in 1953.
1727 This car was on the Freestone & Webb stand at Earls Court in 1953.
1732 This was a rebody, using a second-hand body made by David Joel Ltd. The body is likely to have been the one removed from Bentley Mk VI B340EY in 1950 (see 1533).
1751 The Freestone & Webb order book records this as a "demo" car, so presumably it became what the chassis manufacturers always liked to describe as a "trials car" – in plain language, a demonstrator.
1760 This car was on the Freestone & Webb stand at the 1954 Earls Court Show.
1761 This car was on the Freestone & Webb stand at the 1954 Earls Court Show.
1762 This car was on the Freestone & Webb stand at the 1954 Earls Court Show.
1763 This car was on the Freestone & Webb stand at the 1954 Earls Court Show.
1773 This was the first Bentley S Type to be bodied by Freestone & Webb.
1782 This was the first Rolls-Royce Silver Cloud to be bodied by Freestone & Webb. Note, however, the 1956 date.
1783 This car was built for Jack Warner of the Warner Bros film studios in the USA.
1785 This car was displayed on the Freestone & Webb stand at Earls Court in 1955.
1786 This may have been the first 3191/A body with the cowled headlamp design, but see reservations expressed in the main text.
1787 This car was displayed on the Freestone & Webb stand at Earls Court in 1955.
1798 This was probably a Rolls-Royce Silver Cloud, SYB168, that was delivered to impresario Lew Grade in May 1956.

BODY NUMBERS 1800 TO 1833

This list has been compiled on the basis of surviving evidence, is the most complete available, and may be regarded as reasonably definitive. The tables divide the body numbers into blocks of one hundred (approximately) for ease of reference.

Body no	Design no and type	Date	Chassis type	Chassis no
1800	3206 Six-light saloon	1958, Jun	Rolls-Royce Silver Cloud	SWA74
1801	3191/A Special Sports Saloon	1956 presumed	Bentley S Type	B297AP
1802	CANCELLED			
1803	3199 Six-light saloon	1956, May	Bentley S Type	B281AP
1804	3210/A Coupé	1956, Jun	Rolls-Royce Silver Cloud	SWA108
1805	3206 Six-light saloon	1957, Jan	Rolls-Royce Silver Cloud	SZB149
1806	CANCELLED			
1807	3206 Six-light saloon	1956, July	Rolls-Royce Silver Cloud	SXA117
1808	3191 Special Sports Saloon	1956, Aug	Bentley S Type	B144BA
1809	3206 Six-light saloon	1956, Sep	Rolls-Royce Silver Cloud	SXA123
1810	CANCELLED			
1811	3206 Six-light saloon	1956, Jun	Rolls-Royce Silver Cloud	SYB20
1812	3199 Six-light saloon	1956, Aug	Bentley S Type	B138BA
1813	3222 Special limousine	1956, Dec	Rolls-Royce Silver Wraith	FLW26
1814	3224/SC Six-light saloon	1957, Mar	Rolls-Royce Silver Cloud	SYB24
1815	3206/A Six-light saloon	1956, Nov	Rolls-Royce Silver Cloud	SZB95
1816	3171/A Touring limousine	1956, Dec	Rolls-Royce Silver Wraith	FLW8
1817	3224/1 Six-light saloon	1956, Dec	Bentley S Type	B354CK
1818	3225 Limousine	1956, Nov	Rolls-Royce Silver Wraith	FLW25
1819	3199 Six-light saloon	1957, Jan	Bentley S Type	B53CM
1820	3171/M Touring limousine	1957, May	Rolls-Royce Silver Wraith	FLW76
1821	3171/A Touring limousine	1957, Apr	Rolls-Royce Silver Wraith	FLW77
1822	3230 Saloon with division	1957, July	Rolls-Royce Silver Wraith	FLW68
1823	3199 Six-light saloon	1957, Apr	Bentley S Type	B286LEG
1824	3171/A Touring limousine	1957, Oct	Rolls-Royce Silver Wraith	FLW94
1825	3199 Six-light saloon	1957, Oct	Bentley S Type	B532EG
1826	3191 Limousine	1957, Oct	Rolls-Royce Silver Cloud LWB	ALC1
1827	3243/C Two-seat sports drophead coupé	1957, Oct	Rolls-Royce Silver Cloud	SED179
1828	3206 Six-light saloon	1958, Feb	Rolls-Royce Silver Cloud	SED337
1829	3191 Special Sports Saloon	1958, Feb	Rolls-Royce Silver Cloud	ALC10
1830	3225 Limousine	1958, Oct	Rolls-Royce Silver Wraith	HLW11
1831	3243/B Two-seat sports drophead coupé	1958, Nov	Bentley S Type	B377EK
1832	3199 Six-light saloon	1958, May	Bentley S Type	B402FA
1833	3243/C Two-seat sports drophead coupé	1958, Jun	Rolls-Royce Silver Cloud	SGE270

Notes

1815 This car was displayed on the Freestone & Webb stand at Earls Court in 1956.
1816 This car was displayed on the Freestone & Webb stand at Earls Court in 1956.
1817 This car was displayed on the Freestone & Webb stand at Earls Court in 1956.
1818 This car was displayed on the Freestone & Webb stand at Earls Court in 1956.
1824 This car was displayed on the Freestone & Webb stand at Earls Court in 1957 but was not delivered until a year later.
1825 This car was displayed on the Freestone & Webb stand at Earls Court in 1957 but was not delivered until January 1958.
1826 This car was displayed on the Freestone & Webb stand at Earls Court in 1957.
1827 This car was displayed on the Freestone & Webb stand at Earls Court in 1957 and was delivered in January 1958.
1829 This was the second and last long-wheelbase Silver Cloud to receive Freestone & Webb coachwork.
1831 On the face of it, this would appear to be the last body actually delivered by Freestone & Webb.

Appendix A

FREESTONE & WEBB LONDON SHOW CARS

Freestone & Webb did not take a stand at the annual Olympia Show before 1926. The show relocated to Earls Court in 1937.

1926
OCTOBER 21-30
Freestone & Webb had Stand 81, where they showed two cars.

1. Hispano-Suiza 37.2hp, with Weymann saloon body
This was a four-door body, listed here as number (26/38).

2. Voisin 16-60hpwith four-door, touring body
This body had four doors and a folding roof of the "transformable" type. It had seating for four or five passengers. It is listed here as number (26/39).

1927
OCTOBER 13-22
Freestone & Webb had Stand 80, where they showed two cars.

1. Bentley 6½-litre, with coupé de ville body
The body was panelled in fabric and the head was covered in enamelled leather. There were tool boxes on the step-boards. The body had five seats, including two folding occasional seats. Upholstery was in plain fawn West of England cloth except for the driver's seat, which was in plain English leather. Cabinet work was in burr walnut. Hay believes this was probably on chassis PR2307, the body for which is listed here as number (28/24). An alternative possibility is that it was on chassis BX2403, listed here as number (27/18).

2. Crossley 20.9hp, with Weymann saloon body
The body was panelled in black fabric. It had five seats and the upholstery was in brown hide, with cabinet work in black ebony inlaid with a white ivory line. This body is listed as number (27/35).

1928
OCTOBER 11-20
Freestone & Webb had Stand 79, where they showed two cars.

1. Bentley 4½-litre, with Weymann saloon body
The body was a four-door, four-light type with a vee-screen, and was painted in two shades of brown. This body has not been identified beyond doubt but was probably (28/36), on chassis XR3327.

2. Mercedes 36-220 (ie S), with coachbuilt saloon body
The body was a four-door, four-light saloon in Battleship Grey over Mojave Brown and with metal grilles in place of steps. There were sunken floors front and rear and the front seats were on Leveroll fittings. Upholstery was in mottled grain grey leather over pneumatic cushions, with harewood cabinet work inlaid with an ivory and violet line. This body is listed as number (28/34).

1929
OCTOBER 17-26
Freestone & Webb had Stand 70, where they showed two cars.

1. Bentley 4½-litre supercharged, with Grafton Coupé body
The body had triangular rear quarter-windows and was painted dark grey over light grey. The glass was by Triplex and the cabinet work was in burr walnut. This body is listed as number (29/43).

2. Bentley 6½-litre, with limousine body
The body was painted in dark brown over beige-brown tôle souple. The glass was by Triplex and the cabinet work was in burr walnut. There was a sliding, detachable drop-light partition. This body was number (29/44).

Note: Bentley Motors exhibited for the first time at the Paris Salon in 1929, and among their exhibits was a Speed Six with Freestone & Webb Weymann saloon body. Hay identifies the car as KR2695, which had the body numbered (30/23).

1930
OCTOBER 16-25
Freestone & Webb had Stand 67, where they showed two cars.

1. Bentley 8-litre, with Weymann metal-panelled body
The body was a four-door, four-light design with a fabric roof and built-in trunk, and was painted in dark grey over birch grey. Upholstery was in brown leather and cabinet work in figured walnut, with a companion in the rear quarter. Hay identifies the car as YF5009. The body is listed here as number (30/36) and also had Freestone & Webb body number 965.

2. Mercedes-Benz type SS, with Weymann two-door body
The body had fabric panels, cycle wings, a chrome waistline and a small streamlined step. It was painted black. The upholstery was in brown leather and the cabinet work in burr walnut. This body is listed as number (30/7).

Note: The Bentley 8-litre, YF5009, was also at the Scottish Show in 1930, on the stand of J Buchanan & Co.

1931
OCTOBER 15-24

Freestone & Webb had Stand 120, where they showed two cars.

1. Mercedes-Benz 15-75 (ie 370S), with drophead coupé body

The body had two doors, light metal screen pillars and offset and shaped scuttle and waist mouldings. The windows were frameless, and there was a trunk to which access was from inside the body. The body was painted in black and yellow, and the interior was in brown leather, with a single sideways-facing rear seat. This body is listed as number (31/20). The total price for this car was £1225, and the body cost £475.

2. Sunbeam 20hp, with saloon body

This was a four-door panelled body with tee iron centre pillars, frameless windows and a built-in luggage trunk. It was painted in Fawn with darker Fawn mouldings, and was upholstered in Brown Vaumol leather. It is listed as number (31/21).

The total price for this car was £1045, and the body cost £495.

Note: On Stand 11, importers LC Rawlence & Co Ltd showed an Ansaldo 3½-litre eight-cylinder with a metal panelled Weymann saloon body by Freestone & Webb. This is listed as number (31/22). The total price for this car was £1175, and the body cost £480.

1932
OCTOBER 13-22

Freestone & Webb had Stand 190, where they showed two cars.

1. Delage 29.4hp, with coupé body

This was a two-door, four-seat panelled body, in two-tone green with bright red fine lines. The doors had Silent Travel patented vertical locks and the upholstery was in green leather. This body is listed as number (32/19).

2. Talbot 95, with saloon body

This was a four-door, four-light "coachbuilt panelled" saloon with a Pytchley sliding roof. It was painted black with a white fine line. There were Leveroll mountings for the front bucket seats, Silentbloc door locks, and brown leather upholstery. This body is listed as number (32/20).

1933
OCTOBER 12-21

Freestone & Webb had Stand 29, where they showed three cars.

1. Alvis Speed 20 SB, with pillarless saloon body

This was body number 1064, painted in two-tone grey with brown hide upholstery.

2. Delage 4-litre (ie D8), with two-door saloon body

Motor Sport describes this as a close-coupled four-light saloon body. It was painted maroon and had a chrome waist moulding. The body was number 1061.

3. Lagonda 3-litre, with coupé de ville body

This was painted in Deep Royal Blue and black. It was presumably body number 1059.

Note: The Motor Sport report implies that there were five cars on the stand. These were the Alvis (described as a Crested Eagle), the Delage, a Rolls-Royce with closed bodywork, a Rolls-Royce with open bodywork, and an Alfa Romeo "2.3-litre long chassis, with two-seater body". The Alfa Romeo may well have been at the show, and was pictured in the magazine's report. It was actually a 1750SS model and carried body number 1053.

1934
OCTOBER 11-20

Freestone & Webb had Stand 17, where they showed two cars.

1. Bentley 3½-litre, with saloon body

This was body number 1113 to design number 1507, and was painted in two-tone blue and grey with a chrome plated waist moulding, recessed spare wheel, and sliding sunshine roof. (The Motor reported it as two-tone grey.) The upholstery was in blue/grey leather, and the wood fillets in light and dark walnut. There were two fitted suitcases.

2. Daimler 25hp Straight Eight, with saloon-limousine body

This was body number 1114 to design number 1518. It was a four-door, four-light type with removable division and was painted maroon with black wings and a black waist moulding.

Note: There was also a Hispano-Suiza 30hp with Freestone & Webb coachwork on the stand of J Smith & Co (Motor Agents) Ltd, the sole Hispano concessionaires in the UK. This was body number 1116, to design 1521, a close-coupled two-door saloon body that was painted maroon.

1935
OCTOBER 17-26

Freestone & Webb had Stand 31, where they showed four cars.

1. Alvis 3½-litre, with pillarless saloon body

This was body number 1173 to design number 1609 and was one of a batch of four cars bodied for Alvis. The body was a four-door, four-light Saloon and was painted in Olympia Blue. The upholstery was in light blue leather.

2. Bentley 3½-litre, with Brougham saloon body

This was body number 1169 to design number 1617, which was the first version of the razor-edge Brougham Saloon to be presented to the public. (There had been one example of an earlier design, number 1598.) The Bentley had chassis number B125EJ, and the car was finished in Birch Grey with chrome mouldings and a sliding sunshine roof. The interior was upholstered in grey leather, with wood fillets in ebony with a pewter inlay. There were three fitted suitcases.

3. Talbot 3½-litre, with fixed-head coupé body

This was body number 1176 to design 1601/A. It had a sliding roof and two fitted suitcases. The exterior was Nutmeg Brown and Dark Fawn, and the upholstery was in Hazel Brown; woodwork was solid walnut with a gloss finish.

4. Hispano-Suiza K6, with two-door sports saloon body

This was body number 1182 to design number 1629 and was a four-light type. It was finished in Chianti Red and probably had red upholstery; the woodwork was in Plum mottled mahogany with an ivory inlay.

1936

OCTOBER 15-24

Freestone & Webb had Stand 31, where they showed four cars.

1. Bentley 4¼-litre, with Brougham Saloon body

This was body number 1214 to design number 1755, the third iteration of the razor-edge Brougham Saloon. The body was finished in Duck Egg Green with a Black roof and pillars, and the upholstery was in green-grey leather, with headlining and carpets to tone in. Features were a chrome waist moulding, wheel discs and a cover for the rear-mounted spare wheel. There were dual windscreen wipers with an interior wiping blade. The interior also had fillets of Harewood inlaid with green stringing, and there were three fitted suitcases.

2. Daimler 3½-litre with four-light saloon body

This was body number 1216.

3. Lagonda LG45, with Brougham saloon body

This was body number 1215.

4. Alvis 4.3-litre SA, with streamlined-tail saloon body

This was body number 1217.

1937

OCTOBER 14-23

Freestone & Webb had Stand 18, where they showed four cars.

1. Daimler 4½-litre with touring limousine body

This was body number 1264 and was fitted with an electric division.

2. Mercedes-Benz 540K with touring saloon body

This was body number 1265.

3. Bentley 4¼-litre with Brougham saloon body

This was body number 1266 to Design 1880, painted in Duck Egg Green and Black, with green-grey leather upholstery and fillets of Harewood with black bevelled surround. (The overall scheme was very similar to that of the 1936 Show car.) Lady's and gentleman's companions in rear quarters with mirror backs; front seats adjustable for rake; stainless steel tread mouldings with rubber inserts; fitted tool tray within bootlid.

4. Daimler 3½-litre with touring saloon body

This was body number 1267.

1938

OCTOBER 13-22

Freestone & Webb had Stand 84, where they showed five cars.

1. Bentley 4¼-litre with Brougham saloon body

This was body number 1278, painted in maroon and black, with a special chamfered chrome waist moulding and a cover for the spare wheel. Upholstered in beige leather; fillets etc in burr walnut with bevelled surrounds, lady's and gentleman's companions in rear quarters with mirror backs; driver's seat adjustable for rake. Fitted tool tray within bootlid.

2. Lagonda V12 with Brougham saloon body

This was body number 1289.

3. Daimler 4½-litre with touring limousine body

This was body number 1314.

4. Mercedes-Benz 540K with touring saloon body

This was body number 1315.

5. Daimler 4-litre with touring saloon body

This was body number 1316.

1939

The Earls Court Show was cancelled because of the outbreak of war. Freestone & Webb records show that the coachbuilder had intended to exhibit three cars on its stand. These were:

1. Daimler 4½-litre touring limousine with body number 1342.

2. Daimler 4½-litre touring saloon with body number 1343.

3. Lagonda V12 with razor-edge saloon body number 1345.

1948

OCTOBER 27-NOVEMBER 6

Freestone & Webb had Stand 117, where they showed three cars.

1. Bentley Mk VI with six-light saloon body

This was body number 1476 to design 3046. It had a sunshine roof and was painted in Forget-me-Not Blue with Novo Blue wings and running-boards. The upholstery was in Powder Blue leather with a Silver-Grey cloth headlining. All four wheels were concealed by spats. The rear blind and driver's door window were electrically operated and the rear quarter-lights had sliding inner sections of opaque Purdah glass.

2. Daimler DE36 with saloon limousine body

This body was to design 3009/A and was probably number 1366. A sunshine roof was fitted over the front compartment, and the division glass and rear blind were electrically operated. The body was painted in Champagne with Black wings and bonnet panels, and the interior was upholstered in Beige leather with contrasting piping.

3. Rolls-Royce Silver Wraith with six-light saloon body with division

The body was to design 3004/A/2/F and had number 1475. The division glass, driver's door window and rear blind were all electrically operated, and the adjustable rear quarter-lights were fitted with sliding inner opaque Purdah glass. The body was painted in Duck Egg Green with wings and lower panels in Maroon, and the rear compartment had Maroon cloth upholstery while the front was in Maroon leather with Duck Egg Green piping.

1949

SEPTEMBER 28-OCTOBER 8

Freestone & Webb had Stand 118, where they showed four cars.

This year, the company was awarded the first of its nine consecutive Gold Medals for coachwork at the show.

1. Bentley Mk VI with sports saloon body

This was body number 1512. It was painted metallic blue and silver grey and had a sunshine roof. The upholstery was in powder blue leather and there were tables to the rears of front seats. The cost of £5811-10-0 was made up of £3735-0-0 basic plus £2076-10-0 Purchase Tax.

2. Bentley Mk VI with saloon coupé body

This was body number 1515 and was painted two-tone beige. There were electric door windows. The upholstery was brown and there were folding tables to the rears of the front seats. The cost of £5811-10-0 was made up of £3735-

0-0 basic plus £2076-10-0 Purchase Tax, and was the same as for the Bentley listed above.

3. Rolls-Royce Silver Wraith with six-light saloon body with division

This was body number 1513 and was painted in Silver and Black. There was a transparent panel in the roof above the rear seats.

4. Daimler DE36 with sports saloon body

This was body number 1514 to design 3051. It was painted Beige with Deep Maroon wings.

1950
OCTOBER 18-28

Freestone & Webb had Stand 117, where they showed four cars.

This year, the company was awarded the second of its nine consecutive Gold Medals for coachwork at the show.

1. Bentley Mk VI with six-light sports saloon body

This was body number 1540 to design 3046/C/F. It was painted in Oxford Blue over Dragonfly Blue, and had a sunshine roof and sliding purdah glasses inside the rear quarter-lights. The upholstery was in Powder Blue leather with contrasting piping and there were tables on the backs of the front seats. The body incorporated Freestone & Webb air conditioning.

2. Bentley Mk VI with saloon coupé body

This was body number 1542, painted in Gris Irisé over Rouge Irisé (irisé is French for "iridescent", or what is now called metallic paint). It had a sunshine roof. The upholstery was in Grey leather with contrasting piping and there were picnic tables on the backs of the front seats. The body incorporated Freestone & Webb air conditioning.

3. Rolls-Royce Silver Wraith with six-light saloon body with division

This was body number 1544, to design 3050/A/B, with a sun roof over the rear compartment that incorporated a Perspex panel and a sliding inner shutter. The rear quarter-lights had sliding inner purdah glasses. The paintwork was in Maroon and Light Grey, and the upholstery in Grey with Maroon piping, with leather in the front compartment and cloth in the rear. The electrically-operated division incorporated folding picnic tables and a cocktail cabinet, and the rear door windows and blind were electrically operated.

4. Rolls-Royce Silver Wraith with four-light saloon body with division

This was body number 1543, to design 3070/A, and had a sun roof over the front compartment and an electrically-operated rear blind. It was painted in Vineyard Green and lighter Vert Casanova. The seats were upholstered in Green leather with Dark Green piping, and the woodwork used walnut and burr veneers with a high-gloss finish. The electrically-operated division incorporated folding picnic tables and a press-button radio.

1951
OCTOBER 17-27

Freestone & Webb had Stand 99, where they showed four cars.

This year, the company was awarded the third of its nine consecutive Gold Medals for coachwork at the show.

1. Bentley Mk VI with saloon body

This was body number 1611, to design 3082/C. It was painted in two shades of grey and had a sunshine roof and purdah glass to the rear quarter-lights. The upholstery was in grey leather, and there were adjustable bucket-type front seats with folding tables on their rears. The cost of £6410-7-10 was made up of £4120-0-0 basic plus Purchase Tax of £2290-7-10.

2. Bentley Mk VI with sports saloon body

This was body number 1612, to design 3046/C/F. It was painted Black and Cream and had a sunshine roof and sliding purdah glasses in the rear quarter-lights. The upholstery was in beige with black piping and there were folding tables on the backs of the front seats. The cost of £6254-16-8 was made up of £4020-0-0 basic plus Purchase Tax of £2234-16-8.

3. Rolls-Royce Silver Wraith with saloon body

This was body number 1609, to design 3092.

4. Rolls-Royce Silver Wraith with saloon limousine body

This was body number 1610, to design 3091/A.

1952
OCTOBER 22-NOVEMBER 1

Freestone & Webb had Stand 104, where they showed four cars.

This year, the company was awarded the fourth of its nine consecutive Gold Medals for coachwork at the show.

1. Rolls-Royce Silver Wraith with coupé body

This was body number 1695 to design 3107. It was painted in Imperial Beige and darker Beryl Brun and incorporated Freestone & Webb air conditioning and a "thermally heated backlight". The bench front seat had a split backrest and there was accommodation for five or six passengers. The upholstery was in Light Chocolate Brown leather and there was a detachable headrest for the left-hand rear seat. The woodwork was in Olive Ash veneer with a semi-matt finish, and a sliding drawer under the left-hand rear seat contained a dictaphone.

2. Rolls-Royce Silver Wraith with saloon limousine body

This was body number 1697 to design 3090/B, and was painted Light Grey over Deep Maroon. The rear quarter-lights had sliding inner opaque purdah glasses, and there was a sun roof over the rear compartment with a Perspex panel and sliding shutter. The rear door windows and division were electrically operated, and the division incorporated picnic tables and a cocktail cabinet. There were two occasional seats. The upholstery was Maroon, with leather in the front compartment and cloth in the rear, both with Green-Grey piping. Woodwork was in walnut and special flare veneers with a high gloss finish.

3. Bentley R Type with saloon body

This was body number 1698 to design 3093/A. It had a sun roof over the front compartment and was finished in Green Jewelescence and Black. The upholstery was in Pastel Green with darker green piping, and the wood veneers were of Olive Ash Burr Butt with a high-gloss finish. There were picnic tables in the backs of the front seats, and the car incorporated Freestone & Webb air conditioning.

4. Bentley R Type with saloon body

This was body number 1696 to design 3082/D, finished in dark Vert Golconde and Jaune Pollen Irisé (silver-green). It had a sun roof over the front compartment and sliding purdah glasses inside the rear quarter-lights. The upholstery was in Pastel Green with Dark Green piping and the woodwork used Burr Butt veneers. There were picnic tables in the backs of the front seats, and the boot contained a lightweight fitted suitcase set.

1953
OCTOBER 21-31

Freestone & Webb had Stand 103, where they showed four cars.

This year, the company was awarded the fifth of its nine consecutive Gold Medals for coachwork at the show.

1. Rolls-Royce Silver Wraith with touring limousine body

This was body number 1724, to design 3131/A/L. It had a Perspex sunroof over the rear compartment, with an inner shutter, and was painted in Black and Blanc Saffrane. The upholstery was in Light Beige with black contrast piping, and the woodwork was in walnut and special flare veneers. The division contained a cocktail cabinet and an electrically operated drop-glass.

2. Rolls-Royce Silver Wraith with limousine body

This was body number 1725, to design 3110/A/L, finished in Black and Special Beige (ref 141). The rear compartment was trimmed in Fawn cloth and the front in Brown leather, each with matching piping, and the woodwork was in walnut and special burr butt walnut veneer. The division contained a cocktail cabinet and an electrically operated drop-glass, and the rear door windows were electrically operated. The rear quarter-lights had sliding inner purdah glasses and Freestone & Webb air conditioning was fitted. There was provision on the roof for a luggage rack to be fitted.

3. Bentley R Type with saloon body

This was body number 1726, to design 3093/A. The paintwork was in Brundore Irisé and Pink Beige, and the interior was in Beige leather with contrasting piping to match the Brundore Irisé paint. There were folding picnic tables in the backs of the front seats and all woodwork was in walnut burr butt veneers. Recesses in the front doors contained picnic requisites for four people and there was a sunshine roof over the rear compartment.

4. Bentley R Type with saloon body

This was body number 1727, to design 3082/C, and was painted in Violet Maroon (ref 290) and Beige Corona Irisé. The upholstery was in Silver Green leather with Maroon piping, and the woodwork was in mahogany with mahogany flare veneer. Freestone & Webb air conditioning was fitted, and there was a set of lightweight fitted suitcases in the boot.

1954
OCTOBER 20-30

Freestone & Webb had Stand 102, where they showed four cars.

This year, the company was awarded the sixth of its nine consecutive Gold Medals for coachwork at the show.

1. Rolls-Royce Silver Wraith with touring limousine body

This was body number 1760, to design 3171/A and was a six-seater with an electrically-operated division and electric rear door windows. The roof contained a Perspex panel with an inner sliding shutter, and the body was finished in Black and Pink Beige. The interior was upholstered in Beige leather and the front doors incorporated recesses to accommodate picnic requisites. Woodwork was in high-gloss walnut and special walnut flare veneer, and there were two picnic tables and a cocktail cabinet in the back of the division.

2. Rolls-Royce Silver Wraith with touring limousine body

This was body number 1761, to design 3131/A, finished in Black and Blue. It had an electrically operated division that incorporated two picnic tables and a cocktail cabinet, and two occasional seats. The upholstery was in Fawn, with leather at the front and cloth in the rear compartment, and the high-gloss woodwork was in walnut and special Burr Butt. There was also a set of suitcases in the boot.

3. Bentley R Type with six-light saloon body

This was body number 1762, to design 3191. It had a crocodile-type boot with a picnic table that hinged out of it, and a lightweight suitcase set was provided. The body was painted in Gris Londres over Black and the interior was upholstered in Grey leather, with high-gloss Burr Butt veneers and picnic tables in the backs of the front seats. Freestone & Webb air conditioning was incorporated.

4. Bentley R Type with six-light saloon body

This was body number 1763, to design 3093/A/L, finished in Dark Green and Pastel Green and fitted with a sun roof over the rear compartment. The seats were upholstered in Light Green leather with contrasting piping, and the woodwork was in Burr Butt walnut. There were picnic tables on the backs of the front seats, picnic requisites in recesses in the front doors, and the body incorporated Freestone & Webb air conditioning.

1955
OCTOBER 19-29

Freestone & Webb had Stand 104, where they showed four cars.

This year, the company was awarded the seventh of its nine consecutive Gold Medals for coachwork at the show.

The two Silver Wraith exhibits were on chassis ELW3 and ELW8, but it is not clear beyond doubt which of the descriptions below applies to which body. The probability is that no 1 below, finished in Black and Blanc Saffrane was ELW3 with body number 1787. The other one had body number 1785.

1. Rolls-Royce Silver Wraith with touring limousine body

Four-door, six-light Saloon Limousine with division, painted in Black and Blanc Saffrane. Six/seven seater with rear seat reclinement adjustable by winder mechanism. Centre rear arm rest with swivel mirror, cigar box and cigarette box. Single occasional seat on right-hand side of rear compartment, doubling as a footrest when not in use. Upholstery in cream beige hide. Air conditioning and demister type back light. Picnic requisites for four people housed in front door recesses; set of suitcases in boot. Interior woodwork in Burr Butt walnut veneer finished in high gloss; division with two folding picnic tables built into rear, with mirror backs; sliding picnic table in centre of instrument board. Revolving cocktail cabinet in rear of division. Electric division with curved glass; electric rear door windows; clock on dash and in rear of division. Press-button radio below dash centre with a speaker in rear parcel board; fixed perspex roof panel with inner sliding shutter.

2. Rolls-Royce Silver Wraith with touring limousine body

Four-door, six-light Saloon Limousine with division, painted in Violet Maroon and Pink Beige. Two occasional rear seats, doubling as footrests. Beige cloth rear trim with own piping and leather with own piping at the front. Air conditioning and demister type back light. Interior woodwork in Burr Butt walnut veneer finished in high gloss. Rear of division with two folding picnic tables incorporating self-positioning mirrors to backs; centre mirrored back cabinet with auto switch, housing ashtray and cocktail requisites. Quick-lift front door windows and winding rears; electric curved glass division. Press-button radio in top of centre cabinet with extension speaker and separate volume control on instrument board. Rear compartment with perpsex panel sunshine roof and inner shutter.

3. Bentley S Type with Special Sports Saloon body

This was body number 1786 to design 3191/A, painted in Shell Grey over Dark Violet. Grey leather upholstery with grey piping; Burr Butt wood veneers cross-banded and finished in high gloss; picnic tables in front seat backs and below instrument panel; mirror in passenger side glove box. Press-button radio with extension speaker in rear parcel shelf. Picnic requisites for four people housed in front door recesses; air conditioning. Electrically locking bonnet and fuel filler door.

4. Bentley S Type with Special Sports Saloon body

This was body number 1788 to design 3199, painted in Dark Green over Beige Corona Irisé. Curved windscreen and demister type back light. Light Green leather upholstery with matching piping. Picnic tables in front seat backs and under dash (latter with perspex top with rings to hold drinking vessels), and picnic requisites for four people housed in front doors. Press-button radio with extension speaker in rear parcel shelf. Front compartment with fixed perpsex panel and inner sliding shutter. Remote locking bonnet and electric fuel filler door.

1956
OCTOBER 17-27

Freestone & Webb had Stand 109, where they showed four cars.

This year, the company was awarded the eighth of its nine consecutive Gold Medals for coachwork at the show.

1. Rolls-Royce Silver Wraith with touring limousine body

This was body number 1816, to design 3171/A, painted in Black over Sahara Beige. It was a 6/7 seater with division; aircon, rear window demister; picnic requisites in front doors; division contains electric revolving cocktail cabinet; electric curved division glass; electric rear door windows; perspex roof panel with sliding shutter.

2. Rolls-Royce Silver Wraith with limousine body

This was body number 1818, to design 3225, and was painted Black. It was described as a Pullman Limousine with division; 9 seats; fawn cloth trim to rear and hide to front; rear demister; aircon; quick-lift driver's door window; electric curved glass in division; perspex roof panel over rear, with shutter.

3. Bentley S Type with six-light saloon body

This was body number 1817 to design 3224/1, and was painted in Gris Irisé over Rouge Irisé. The upholstery was red and there were picnic requisites in the front doors, and air conditioning.

4. Rolls-Royce Silver Cloud with six-light saloon body

This was body number 1815 to design 3206/A, painted in Dark Green over Pastel Green. The upholstery was in light green hide. There were picnic tables; picnic requisites in the doors, and a perspex panel with shutter over the front compartment; air conditioning.

1957
OCTOBER 16-26

Freestone & Webb had Stand 96, where they showed four cars.

This year, the company was awarded the last of its nine consecutive Gold Medals for coachwork at the show.

1. Rolls-Royce Silver Wraith with touring limousine body

This was body number 1824, to design 3171/A, and was painted in Maroon over Golden Beige. The upholstery was in beige hide. The 6/7-seater body had a division with electric curved glass and an electric revolving cocktail cabinet. It was fitted with air conditioning, a rear window demister, picnic requisites in the front doors, electric rear windows, and a perspex roof panel with sliding shutter. There was provision for safety belts.

2. Bentley S Type with six-light saloon body

This was body number 1825, to design 3199, and was painted in Dark Blue over Pastel Blue with Cream hide upholstery. It had a rear demister, aircon, picnic requisites in the doors, and provision for safety belts.

3. Rolls-Royce Silver Cloud LWB with limousine body

This was body number 1826, to design 3191, painted in Tyrolean Green over Cactus Green. The upholstery was in green hide; picnic requisites were fitted in doors and there was provision for safety belts.

4. Rolls-Royce Silver Cloud with two-seats sports drophead coupé body

This was body number 1827, to design 3243/C. It was painted in Dark Green with Shell Grey side panels and a Grey hood. The upholstery was in Light Grey hide piped with dark green. Power hood and concealed decking; electric aerial; picnic requisites in doors; aircon; safety belt provisions.

Appendix B

FREESTONE & WEBB COACHWORK BY CHASSIS MAKER

ALFA ROMEO
Freestone & Webb built only one known body on an Alfa Romeo chassis. This was a rakish two-seater sports on a 1750SS chassis in 1933.

ALVIS
Alvis was a maker of high-class sporting chassis, and a total of nine examples received Freestone & Webb coachwork between 1933 and 1936. All had four-light pillarless saloon bodies. Four were on the Speed 20 chassis in 1933-1934, four more on the 3½-litre chassis in 1934-1935, and the final body was on a 4.3-litre chassis in 1936.

ANSALDO
The Italian Ansaldo was not a very well-known make in Britain, although it had enjoyed some sporting successes in the 1920s. The concessionaires were based in Albemarle Street, in London's fashionable West End. Freestone & Webb were commissioned to build only one body, which was a four-light saloon on the 3½-litre straight-eight chassis in 1931.

BENTLEY
Freestone & Webb constructed bodies for Bentley chassis throughout their life as a coachbuilder, and on every variety of Bentley chassis except for the post-war Continentals and the long-wheelbase S Type. There were 483 bodies in all on Bentley chassis. This total makes Bentley by far the most numerous of all the chassis bodied by Freestone & Webb, and is around 150 greater than the total of the second most numerous chassis, which were by Rolls-Royce.

For the "WO" period models, there were 109 bodies on the 3-litre chassis, 65 on the 4½-litre, 45 on the 6½-litre, 13 on the 8-litre and 12 on the 4-litre. On the Derby models, there were 39 on the 3½-litre chassis and 34 on the 4¼-litre. On the post-war chassis, there were 111 for the Mk VI, 31 on the R Type, and 23 on the S Type.

BUGATTI
There were probably just three Freestone & Webb bodies on Bugatti chassis. The earliest was a fabric saloon in 1925; there was a Weymann saloon on a Type 46 chassis in 1930 (although this is not proven beyond doubt); and the last was a four-door sports saloon on a Type 46 chassis, built for Victor Rothschild in 1933.

BUICK
Just one Buick carried a Freestone & Webb body, which was a seven-seater limousine built in 1934. The precise identity of the chassis is in doubt; the order book records it as a Master 8, although that model was not current in 1934, and the chassis number recorded makes no sense.

CORD
Freestone & Webb built a single body on the front-wheel-drive Cord chassis from America. The chassis would have been the type usually called the L-29 (although not by its makers), and the body was an extraordinary two-door touring saloon that was largely designed by the customer. It was delivered in 1931.

CROSSLEY
There were probably five bodies on Crossley chassis during the 1920s. All were Weymann saloons except for one that was built with a folding-head saloon body in 1926. Probably four of the Crossley chassis were 20.9hp types; the fifth, in 1928, was a Super Six.

DAIMLER
Freestone & Webb built far more bodies on Daimler chassis than is generally realised, with a grand total of 43 between 1934 and 1949.

The first known body on a Daimler chassis was a pillarless saloon in 1934 on the 20hp LQ2 model. This was followed later in the year by a saloon limousine on the 25hp straight-eight chassis.

There were seven bodies on the 3½-litre straight-eight in 1936-1937, one a sports saloon, one a Brougham saloon, and five touring saloons. Only touring limousines were built for the 4½-litre straight-eight, of which there were four in 1938 and two more in 1939. On the 4-litre there was a single touring limousine in 1938, which was followed by five "semi-touring" saloons in 1939.

Daimler was also the only make other than Bentley and Rolls-Royce to receive Freestone & Webb bodies after the war. The coachbuilder constructed 18 limousine bodies (out of a planned 25) between 1946 and 1949; 13 were on the DE27 chassis and just five on the DE36. There were also two sports saloon bodies on the DE36, one in 1948 and the second in 1949.

DARRACQ
Only one Darracq chassis received a body by Freestone & Webb. This was a T23 chassis built in France and bodied as a touring saloon for the dealer Albemarle Motors in 1939.

DELAGE
A total of 30 or 31 Delage chassis are thought to have been bodied by Freestone & Webb between 1925 and 1938. The earliest was a two-door Weymann saloon in 1925 and there may have been another saloon in 1926; the chassis under body (26/44) has not been identified beyond doubt. A third saloon was built in 1927.

Next came a fabric-bodied tourer on the DMS chassis in 1928, and a fabric saloon in 1930. There were then two bodies on the eight-cylinder chassis, one a D8S in 1932 and the other a D8 in 1933. In 1938 Freestone & Webb appear to have taken over from Coachcraft a contract with the Delage importer University Motors to build batches of bodies on the D6-70 chassis. A dozen saloon bodies and a dozen drophead coupé bodies are recorded, and in all cases the bodies were built to the Coachcraft designs. Construction of these bodies may have continued into 1939.

FORD
Just one Freestone & Webb body is known on a Ford chassis. This was an open four-seater sports type that was built on an 8hp chassis for Betaway Motors in 1934.

FRAZER-NASH BMW
The British importers of BMWs from 1934 were AFN Ltd of Isleworth, who made some modifications to them and added their own badges, rebranding them as Frazer-Nash BMWs. AFN also commissioned coachwork for a number of these chassis.

Freestone & Webb built just two bodies for Frazer-Nash BMWs. One was a unique Brougham coupé in 1937 on what was probably a 326 chassis. The other was a razor-edge touring saloon in 1938 that was definitely on a 326.

HISPANO-SUIZA
The British importers for Hispano-Suiza cars were J Smith & Co in London, and they commissioned several bodies from Freestone & Webb between 1926 and 1937. Possibly all seven known bodies were built to their order.

The earliest of these were on the H6B chassis, which typically had a 6.6-litre engine and a 133-inch wheelbase. The first was a six-light Weymann saloon in 1926. Two sedanca de ville bodies followed in 1928, and a fabric-bodied sportsman's coupé in 1930.

The K6 model introduced in 1934 had a 5.2-litre engine and came with two different wheelbase sizes. In Britain, it was known as a 30hp model or a 30/120. Freestone & Webb's first body for one of these was a two-door Silentbloc saloon on the short-wheelbase chassis in 1934. A four-light fixed-head coupé followed in 1936. The final body was a four-light saloon limousine built in 1937, the last year of the K6's manufacture.

HUDSON

Only one body is known on a Hudson chassis. This was a special light four-door cabriolet on a Terraplane 8 chassis in 1936.

INVICTA

The only known Freestone & Webb body on an Invicta chassis was a sporting drophead coupé on a 1930 S Type.

ITALA

Itala was another make that was probably only ever bodied once by Freestone & Webb. That body was a six-light saloon built in summer 1926.

LAGONDA

As Lagonda began to move its range more up-market in the 1930s, so it turned to independent coachbuilders to produce appropriate bodywork. Freestone & Webb were commissioned to build a total of 22 bodies on Lagonda chassis between 1933 and 1939.

Of these, just one was on the 3-litre long-wheelbase chassis, and was a coupé de ville for the dealer Jack Barclay in 1933. There were then 16 on the 4½-litre chassis in 1934-1935; 13 were drophead coupés, two were fixed-head coupés, and one was a close-coupled two-door saloon.

A single razor-edge saloon was built on the LG45 chassis in 1936, and the last four bodies were on V12 chassis in 1938-1939. Two were touring saloons and two were Brougham saloons.

LANCHESTER

There were three bodies on Lanchester chassis. These were a Weymann saloon in July 1926, a limousine in July 1929, and a drophead coupé in late 1932.

LA SALLE

The only known Freestone & Webb body on a La Salle chassis was a saloon built in 1928.

MERCEDES

Only one body is known on a Mercedes chassis prior to the merger of Daimler and Benz to create Mercedes-Benz. This was a Weymann saloon built in 1925.

MERCEDES-BENZ

Freestone & Webb must have formed links with British Mercedes-Benz Ltd, the London importers, as soon as that company was established in 1926. Between then and 1938, 22 Mercedes-Benz chassis are known to have been bodied at Brentfield Road.

The earliest was a six-light saloon in 1926 on either the 400 or the 630 chassis. There were then no more until 1928, when no fewer than six bodies were built; three were saloons, one a drophead coupé, one a tourer and one a special roadster. Three of these were on the supercharged Type S chassis.

In 1929-1930, there were nine overtly sporting bodies of various types, probably all on the Type SS chassis. In complete contrast, there was also an odd and rather old-fashioned looking saloon on a 460 Nürburg chassis in 1929. Then in 1931, there was a single drophead coupé on the 370S Mannheim chassis.

The remaining four bodies were on the supercharged 540K chassis and were built in 1937-1938. One was a saloon and the other three were touring saloons, and one of those three was delivered to the German Embassy.

PACKARD

There were six known bodies on Packard chassis between 1925 and 1938. Two were built in 1925 – a sunroof saloon on the 333 Six chassis and a "fully-collapsible sedan" on the 433 Six. A single Weymann saloon followed in 1926 on the eight-cylinder 336 chassis.

There was one touring limousine on the Packard 8 chassis in 1934, and then two rather grand razor-edged limousines on the Super 8 chassis in 1938 were the last of this American make to have Freestone & Webb coachwork.

ROLLS-ROYCE

The earliest Rolls-Royce chassis bodied by Freestone & Webb was in 1924, and the last in 1958. In the intervening years, there were bodies for every variety of Rolls-Royce chassis except the Phantom IV. Totals should be qualified with the word "approximately" in some cases, because of a number of bodies built for a particular type of chassis but for which no chassis details have been found.

The overall total was 321 bodies, and the individual figures were as follows:

40/50	1
Twenty	8
20/25	87
25/30	28
Wraith	11 (including one post-war rebody)
Phantom I	6
Phantom II	20 (including Continental)
Phantom III	16 (including two post-war rebodies)
Silver Wraith	121
Silver Dawn	6
Silver Cloud	17 (including two long-wheelbase chassis)

SUNBEAM

There were three bodies on Sunbeam chassis. These were a saloon on a 1925 3-litre, another saloon on a 35hp chassis in 1927, and an unidentified body (probably a saloon) on a 20hp model in 1931.

TALBOT

Freestone & Webb built five known bodies on Talbot chassis between 1932 and 1936. The earliest was a panelled four-light saloon on a 1932 95 chassis, and there was a second four-light saloon on the 95 chassis in 1933.

On the BG 110 3½-litre chassis there was a single close-coupled two-door saloon in 1935, which was followed by two four-door versions of the same design in 1936.

VOISIN

There were probably just two bodies on Voisin chassis, a tourer in 1926 and a coupé de ville in 1927. Details of the chassis are unclear but the earlier is described in the Freestone & Webb order book as a 16-60, which appears to have been the British designation of the C11 model. The later car was probably on the same type of chassis.

CHASSIS MANUFACTURERS AT A GLANCE

(in descending order of quantity)

Bentley	483
Rolls-Royce	321
Daimler	43
Delage	30 (or 31)
Lagonda	22
Mercedes-Benz	22
Alvis	9
Hispano-Suiza	7
Packard	6
Talbot	5
Crossley	5
Bugatti	3
Lanchester	3
Sunbeam	3
Frazer-Nash BMW	2
Voisin	2
Alfa Romeo	1
Ansaldo	1
Buick	1
Cord	1
Darracq	1
Ford	1
Hudson	1
Invicta	1
Itala	1
La Salle	1
Mercedes	1

Appendix C

FREESTONE & WEBB DESIGN NUMBERS AND QUANTITIES BUILT

The earliest design numbers so far discovered date from 1933 and are shown in the Freestone & Webb order book. There were probably earlier ones as well. There are many gaps in the numbers, all of which relate to designs that were actually built. It is reasonable to suppose that the missing numbers were for designs that, for one reason or another, were not built. Variants of a design were normally shown with a suffix letter, as in 3004/A, although the meaning of some of the suffix letters is obscure. Towards the end of the company's life, there were also some inconsistencies in the use (or non-use) of suffix letters to indicate variants.

DESIGN NO.	TYPE	DATES	CHASSIS TYPES	REMARKS
1200/A	Two-light fixed-head coupé	1933	Rolls-Royce 20/25	Three bodies: 1027, 1028 &1033.
1225	All-weather	1933	Talbot 95	One body: 1034.
1247/A	Sports saloon	1933	Rolls-Royce Phantom II Continental	One body: 1060.
1272	Four-light swept-tail saloon	1933	Rolls-Royce 20/25	One body: 1026.
1275	Continental saloon	1933	Rolls-Royce 20/25	Two bodies: 1024 & 1025. (There may have been earlier examples as well, before the start of the surviving order book.)
1275/A	Continental saloon	1933	Rolls-Royce 20/25	Five bodies: 1029, 1030, 1038, 1039 & 1040.
1275/B	Continental saloon	1933-1934	Rolls-Royce 20/25	Nine bodies: 1046, 1047, 1049, 1050, 1051, 1056, 1057, 1077 & 1078.
1275/C	Continental saloon	1933-1935	Rolls-Royce 20/25	Seven bodies: 1052, 1066, 1067, 1107, 1108, 1112 & 1133.
1281	Four-light saloon coupé	1933	Rolls-Royce 20/25	Two bodies: 1037 & 1048.
1281/A	Four-light saloon coupé	1933-1934	Rolls-Royce 20/25	Two bodies: 1065 & 1084.
1281/B	Two-light fixed-head coupé	1934	Rolls-Royce 20/25	Three bodies: 1104, 1105 & 1106.
1283	Six-light saloon with division	1933	Rolls-Royce 20/25	Two bodies: 1031 & 1043. See also note on 1044.
1283/C	Six-light saloon	1936	Rolls-Royce 20/25	One body: 1193.
1286	Limousine	1933	Rolls-Royce 20/25	One body: 1032.
1296	Saloon	1933	Rolls-Royce 20/25	One body: 1036.
1299/A	Four-door sports saloon	1933	Bugatti Type 46	One body: 1035.
1306	Saloon; also with division	1933-1934	Rolls-Royce Phantom II / Rolls-Royce Phantom II Continental	Three bodies: 1041, 1068 & 1103.
1307	Saloon	1933	Rolls-Royce 20/25	One body: 1042.
1318	Two-seater sports	1933	Alfa Romeo 1750SS	One body: 1053.
1324	Two-door sedanca coupé	1933-1934	Rolls-Royce 20/25	Two bodies: 1054 & 1062.
1338	Coupé de ville	1933	Lagonda 3-litre (LWB)	One body: 1059.
1369	Fixed-head coupé	1933	Rolls-Royce Phantom II Continental	One body: 1063.
1372	Four-light pillarless saloon	1933-1934	Alvis Speed 20	Two bodies: 1064 & 1076.
1377/A	Four-light saloon coupé	1935	Rolls-Royce 20/25	One body: 1136.
1381	Saloon	1934	Rolls-Royce 20/25	One body: 1083.
1399	Four-light pillarless saloon	1934	Daimler 20hp LQ2	One body: 1070.
1403	Saloon	1934-1935	Rolls-Royce 20/25	Four bodies: 1069, 1092, 1120 & 1121.
1404	Four-light pillarless saloon	1934	Alvis Speed 20	Two bodies: 1071 & 1072.
1422	Three-position drophead coupé	1934	Bentley 3½-litre	One body: 1086.
1423	Foursome drophead coupé	1934	Lagonda 4½-litre	Eight bodies: 1073, 1074, 1075, 1080, 1085, 1095, 1096 & 1097.
1423/A	Foursome drophead coupé	1934	Lagonda 4½-litre	One body: 1099.
1424/A	Four-light fixed-head coupé	1934	Lagonda 4½-litre	One body: 1089.
1424/B	Four-light fixed-head coupé	1934	Lagonda 4½-litre	One body: 1091.
1424/C	Two-light fixed-head coupé	1934	Lagonda 4½-litre	One body: 1102.
1436	Sports saloon	1934	Bentley 3½-litre	One body: 1081.
1436/A	Sports saloon	1934	Bentley 3½-litre	One body: 1109.
1441	Sports saloon	1934-1935	Bentley 3½-litre	Two bodies: 1082 & 1163.
1441/A	Sports saloon	1934-1935	Bentley 3½-litre	Six bodies: 1100, 1101, 1117, 1119, 1129 & 1137.
1446	Open four-seater sports	1934	Ford 8hp	One body: 1079.
1460	Pillarless saloon coupé	1934	Bentley 3½-litre	One body: 1090.
1461	Limousine (7 seats)	1934	Buick Master 8	One body: 1088.
1462	Saloon with division	1934	Rolls-Royce 20/25	One body: 1098.

1463	Drophead coupé with dickey	1934	Rolls-Royce Phantom II Continental	One body: 1094.
1470	Two-light saloon coupé	1934	Bentley 3½-litre	One body: 1093.
1478	Saloon	1934	Rolls-Royce 20/25	One body: 1087.
1499	Drophead coupé	1934	Rolls-Royce Phantom II Continental	One body: 1110.
1501	Four-light touring limousine	1934	Packard 8	One body: 1111.
1507	Sports saloon	1934-1935	Bentley 3½-litre	11 bodies: 1113, 1130, 1131, 1132, 1134, 1135, 1136, 1138, 1139, 1158, 1166.
1507/C	Sports saloon	1935	Bentley 3½-litre	One body: 1159.
1512	Coupé de ville	1934	Rolls-Royce Phantom II	Two bodies: 1115 & 1127.
1518	Four-light saloon limousine	1934	Daimler 25hp	One body: 1114.
1520	Two-light, three-position drophead coupé	1934	Bentley 3½-litre	One body: 1118.
1521	Two-door, close-coupled saloon	1934	Hispano-Suiza 30hp (SWB)	One body: 1116.
1528	Limousine	1934	Rolls-Royce 20/25	One body: 1122.
1535	Saloon with division	1935	Rolls-Royce Phantom II Continental	One body: 1124.
1536	Saloon with division	1935	Rolls-Royce 20/25	One body: 1123.
1540	Three-position drophead coupé	1934	Bentley 3½-litre	One body: 1128.
1554	Four-light saloon coupé	1937	Bentley 4¼-litre	One body: 1233.
1555	Foursome drophead coupé	1935	Lagonda 4½-litre	Three bodies: 1142, 1143 & 1144.
1560	Four-light close-coupled saloon	1935	Lagonda 4½-litre	One body: 1157.
1562	Saloon	1936-1937	Rolls-Royce 20/25	Two bodies: 1210 & 1237.
1567	Saloon; also with division	1935	Rolls-Royce 20/25	Ten bodies: 1145, 1146, 1147, 1148, 1149, 1150, 1151, 1152, 1164 & 1167.
1568	Sedanca coupé	1935	Rolls-Royce 20/25	One body: 1160.
1569	Four-light fixed-head coupé	1935	Rolls-Royce 20/25	Four bodies: 1153, 1154, 1155 & 1156.
1577	Four-light fixed-head coupé	1935	Bentley 3½-litre	One body: 1161.
1579	Pillarless saloon	1935	Bentley 3½-litre	One body: 1162.
1586	Four-door all-weather tourer	1935	Bentley 3½-litre	One body: 1140.
1592	Four-light fixed-head coupé	1935	Rolls-Royce 20/25	One body: 1141.
1598	Brougham saloon	1935	Bentley 3½-litre	One body: 1165.
1601/A	Two-door, four-light close-coupled FHC	1935	Talbot 3½-litre	One body: 1176.
1609	Four-light pillarless saloon	1935	Alvis 3½-litre	Four bodies: 1172, 1173, 1174 & 1175.
1614	Two-light, three-position drophead coupé	1935	Bentley 3½-litre	One body: 1171.
1615	Limousine	1937	Rolls-Royce 25/30	One body: 1168.
1617	Brougham saloon	1935-1937	Bentley 3½-litre Bentley 4¼-litre	Nine bodies: 1169, 1177, 1178, 1179, 1180, 1185, 1188, 1189 & 1191.
1617/A	Brougham saloon	1936	Bentley 4¼-litre	Two bodies: 1196 & 1197.
1619	Four-door, four-light coupé de ville with dickey	1935	Bentley 3½-litre	One body: 1170.
1620	Pillarless saloon	1937	Bentley 4¼-litre	One body: 1268.
1624	Four-light fixed-head coupé	1935	Rolls-Royce 20/25	One body: 1183.
1628/A	Saloon; some with division	1935-1936	Rolls-Royce 20/25 Rolls-Royce 25/30	Seven bodies: 1184, 1192, 1198, 1207, 1208, 1209 & 1224.
1629	Four-light fixed-head coupé	1935	Hispano-Suiza 30hp	One body: 1182.
1632/A	Brougham saloon	1936	Rolls-Royce 20/25 Rolls-Royce 25/30	Three bodies: 1186, 1194 & 1195.
1641	Limousine de ville	1937	Rolls-Royce Phantom III	One body: 1223.
1643	Saloon	1935	Rolls-Royce 20/25	One body: 1187.
1645	Two-door, four-light 'Airline' saloon coupé	1936	Bentley 3½-litre	One body: 1190.
1691	Limousine de ville	1936	Rolls-Royce Phantom III	One body: 1201.
1698	Special light four-door cabriolet	1936	Hudson Terraplane 8	One body: 1204.
1700	Four-door, six-light saloon	1936-1937	Rolls-Royce Phantom III	Two bodies: 1199 & 1253.
1705	Saloon	1936	Rolls-Royce 25/30	One body: 1202.
1708	Four-door Speed Saloon (derived from 1601/A)	1936	Talbot 3½-litre	Two bodies: 1205 & 1206.
1722	Fixed-head coupé	1936	Bentley 4¼-litre	One body: 1211.
1731	Fixed-head coupé	1936	Bentley 4¼-litre	One body: 1212.
1737	Four-light sports saloon	1936	Daimler 3½-litre	One body: 1216.
1741	Sedanca de ville	1936	Rolls-Royce 25/30	One body: 1220.
1743	Six-light sports saloon	1936	Rolls-Royce 25/30	One body: 1218.
1751	Sedanca de ville	1937	Rolls-Royce Phantom III	One body: 1213.
1753	Brougham saloon	1936	Lagonda LG45	One body: 1215.
1755	Brougham saloon	1936-1938	Bentley 4¼-litre	Nine bodies: 1214, 1221, 1226, 1227, 1228, 1229, 1230, 1231 & 1245. See note in Chapter 4 about nos 1230 and 1245.
1760	Saloon with division	1936-1937	Rolls-Royce Phantom III	Three bodies: 1222, 1240 & 1257.
1761	Sedanca de ville	1936	Rolls-Royce 25/30	One body: 1219.
1763	Six-light saloon	1936	Rolls-Royce Phantom III	One body: 1200.
1765	Four-light saloon	1935	Alvis 4.3-litre	One body: 1217.
1774	Drophead sedanca coupé	1936	Rolls-Royce Phantom III	One body: 1225.

1775	Two-door, two-seat Brougham coupé	1937	Frazer-Nash BMW	One body: 1234.
1779	Two-door, two-light 'Brougham' coupé	1937	Bentley 4¼-litre	One body: 1232.
1782	Sports saloon	1937	Rolls-Royce Phantom III	One body: 1244.
1785/A	Brougham saloon	1937	Bentley 4¼-litre	One body: 1235.
1787	Drophead sedanca coupé	1937	Rolls-Royce Phantom III	One body: 1238.
1792	Sedanca de ville	1936	Rolls-Royce	Known only from a design drawing photographed on 11 November 1936; no bodies built.
1798	Three-position drophead coupé	1937	Rolls-Royce 25/30	One body: 1242.
1805	Saloon with division	1936	Rolls-Royce 25/30	One body: 1236.
1806	Brougham de ville	1937	Rolls-Royce 25/30	One body: 1243.
1809	Saloon with division	1937	Rolls-Royce 25/30	One body: 1239.
1811	Four-light saloon limousine	1937	Hispano-Suiza 30/120hp	One body: 1241.
1818	Sports saloon	1937	Bentley 4¼-litre	One body: 1251.
1821	Six-light saloon	1937	Rolls-Royce 25/30	One body: 1252.
1827	Saloon with division	1937-1938	Rolls-Royce 25/30	Eight bodies: 1248, 1249, 1250, 1254, 1255, 1258, 1259 & 1260.
1835	Touring saloon	1937-1938	Mercedes-Benz 540K	Two bodies: 1265 & 1280.
1837	Two-seat drophead coupé	1937	Bentley 4¼-litre	One body: 1256.
1851	Two-light fixed-head sedanca coupé	1937	Rolls-Royce 25/30	One body: 1247.
1867	Limousine (D-back)	1937-1938	Rolls-Royce 25/30	Three bodies: 1261, 1262 & 1279.
1869	Touring saloon	1937	Daimler 3½-litre	Two bodies: 1263 & 1333.
1874	Touring limousine	1937-1938	Daimler 4½-litre	Three bodies: 1264, 1285 & 1286.
1878	Touring saloon	1937	Daimler 3½-litre	One body: 1269.
1879	Touring saloon	1937	Daimler 3½-litre	Four bodies: 1267, 1270, 1271, 1272.
1880	Brougham saloon	1937-1940	Bentley 4¼-litre	Ten bodies: 1266, 1273, 1274, 1275, 1276, 1277, 1278, 1322, 1336 & 1337.
1910	Limousine	1938	Packard 8-cylinder	Two bodies: 1283 & 1284.
1919	Brougham saloon	1938	SS Jaguar 3½-litre	One body: 1281.
1928	Four-light saloon	1938	Mercedes-Benz 540K	One body: 1282.
1933	Coupé de ville	1938	Bentley 4¼-litre	One body: 1287.
1937	Two-door, two-light coupé de ville	1938	Rolls-Royce 25/30	One body: 1288.
1947	Six-light saloon	1938	Lagonda V12	Two bodies: 1289 & 1332.
1956	Four-door, four-light saloon	1938	Delage D6-70	12 bodies: 1290, 1291, 1292, 1293, 1294, 1295, 1296, 1297, 1298, 1299, 1300 & 1301.
1963	Touring saloon	1938	Mercedes-Benz 540K	One only: 1315.
1964	Two-door drophead coupé	1938	Delage D6-70	12 bodies: 1302, 1303, 1304, 1305, 1306, 1307, 1308, 1309, 1310, 1311, 1312 & 1313.
1968	Touring saloon	1938	Frazer-Nash BMW 326	One body: 1318.
1971	All-weather tourer	1938	Rolls-Royce Phantom III	One body: 1317.
1974	Touring saloon	1938	Daimler 4-litre	Two bodies: 1316 & 1319.
1993	Touring saloon with division	1939	Rolls-Royce Wraith	One body: 1341.
1996	Saloon	1939	Rolls-Royce Wraith	One body: 1330.
1998	Four-light touring saloon; some with division	1939	Rolls-Royce Wraith	Four bodies: 1326, 1327,1340 & 1344.
2001	Six-light semi-touring saloon	1939	Daimler 4-litre	Three bodies: 1328, 1329 & 1331.
2004	Six-light touring limousine	1939	Daimler 4½-litre	One body: 1321.
2005	Touring saloon	1939	Darracq T23	One body: 1323.
2007	Touring saloon	1938	Lagonda V12	One body: 1324.
2009	Sports saloon	1939	Bentley 4¼-litre	One body: 1320.
2026	Limousine	1939	Rolls-Royce Phantom III	One body: 1334.
2027	Saloon with division	1939	Rolls-Royce Wraith	One body: 1335.
2033	Six-light saloon	1939	Rolls-Royce Wraith	One body: 1325.
2034	Touring limousine	1939	Rolls-Royce Wraith	Two bodies: 1338 & 1339.
2044	Six-light touring limousine	1939	Daimler 4½-litre	One body: 1342.
2045	Six-light touring saloon	1939	Daimler 4-litre	One body: 1343.
2046	Touring saloon	1939	Lagonda V12	One body: 1345.
2049	Saloon	1939	Bentley Mk V	One body (not built): 1349.
2100	Four-light sedanca de ville	1945	Rolls-Royce Phantom III	One body: 1353.
3004	Saloon; Six-light saloon; Saloon with division	1947-1948	Rolls-Royce Silver Wraith	Six bodies: 1385, 1416, 1418, 1426, 1429 & 1430.
3004/A	Saloon with division	1947-1948	Rolls-Royce Silver Wraith	Five bodies: 1393, 1394, 1398, 1424 & 1432.
3004/A/2	Saloon with division	1947-1949	Rolls-Royce Silver Wraith	Three bodies: 1391, 1464 & 1468.
3004/A/2/F	Six-light saloon with division	1948	Rolls-Royce Silver Wraith	One body: 1475.
3004/A/3	Saloon with division	1947	Rolls-Royce Silver Wraith	One body: 1357.
3004/B	Saloon	1948-1949	Rolls-Royce Silver Wraith	Five bodies: 1422, 1435, 1440, 1459 & 1473.
3004/C	Saloon with division	1948-1949	Rolls-Royce Silver Wraith	Two bodies: 1392 & 1482.
3004/1	Four-light saloon	1947	Rolls-Royce Silver Wraith	One body: 1354.

3004/2	Six-light saloon	1949	Rolls-Royce Silver Wraith	Two bodies: 1454 & 1467.
3005	All-weather tourer	1947	Rolls-Royce Silver Wraith	One body: 1383.
3008	Foursome drophead coupé with concealed head	1947	Bentley Mk VI	One body: 1388.
3009	Saloon limousine	1946-1949	Daimler DE27	13 bodies: 1359, 1360, 1363, 1364, 1365, 1367, 1368, 1369, 1371, 1372, 1373, 1374 & 1375.
3009/A	Limousine	1946-1950	Daimler DE36	Five bodies: 1358, 1361, 1362, 1366 & 1370.
3010/A	Saloon	1947-1948	Bentley Mk VI	Eight bodies: 1399, 1400, 1402, 1405, 1406, 1413, 1414, 1417.
3010/B	Saloon	1947	Bentley Mk VI	One body: 1390.
3010/C	Saloon	1947	Bentley Mk VI	One body: 1389.
3010/D	Saloon	1947	Bentley Mk VI	Two bodies: 1355, 1356.
3010/E	Six-light saloon	1948-1949	Bentley Mk VI	Seven bodies: 1395, 1431, 1437, 1442, 1452, 1455, 1486.
3013	Saloon	1947	Bentley Mk VI	One body: 1387.
3014	Fixed-head coupé	1947	Rolls-Royce Silver Wraith	One body: 1384.
3027	Fixed-head coupé	1947	Bentley Mk VI	One body: 1386.
3029	Four-light saloon coupé	1947	Bentley Mk VI	One body: 1439.
3029/A	Four-light saloon coupé	1949	Bentley Mk VI	Two bodies: 1489 & 1497.
3029/C	Four-light saloon coupé	1949-1951	Bentley Mk VI	Four bodies: 1515, 1518, 1546 & 1565.
3030	Fixed-head coupé	1947	Bentley Mk VI	One body: 1408.
3030/A	Fixed-head coupé	1948	Bentley Mk VI	One body: 1427.
3031	Sports saloon	1949	Daimler DE36	One body: 1461.
3036/B	Fixed-head coupé	1948	Bentley Mk VI	One body: 1420.
3037/D	Fixed-head coupé	1949	Bentley Mk VI	One body: 1460.
3038	Saloon	1947-1949	Bentley Mk VI	12 bodies: 1403, 1404, 1409, 1446, 1447, 1456, 1457, 1470, 1479, 1484, 1498 & 1501.
3046	Six-light saloon	1948-1949	Bentley Mk VI	Four bodies: 1476, 1495, 1496, & 1499.
3046/C	Six-light saloon	1948-1952	Bentley Mk VI	18 bodies: 1463, 1509, 1512, 1516, 1517,1520, 1521, 1522, 1527, 1528, 1529, 1530, 1531, 1532, 1533, 1534, 1572 & 1590.
3046/C/F	Six-light saloon	1948-1951	Bentley Mk VI	21 bodies: 1535, 1536, 1537, 1538, 1540, 1548, 1552, 1553, 1554, 1558, 1562, 1564, 1570, 1581, 1582, 1592, 1600, 1603, 1605, 1612 & 1631.
3046/1	Six-light saloon	1948	Bentley Mk VI	One body: 1507.
3047	Saloon with division	1949	Rolls-Royce Silver Wraith	One body: 1500.
3047/B	Six-light saloon	1949-1950	Rolls-Royce Silver Wraith	Two bodies: 1438 & 1547.
3047/B/2	Six-light saloon	1949	Rolls-Royce Silver Wraith	One body: 1508.
3047/C	Six-light saloon	1952	Bentley Mk VI	One body: 1590.
3047/1	Saloon with division	1949	Rolls-Royce Silver Wraith	One body: 1494.
3047/2	Saloon with division	1949	Rolls-Royce Silver Wraith	One body: 1506.
3047/2/A	Six-light saloon limousine	1949	Rolls-Royce Silver Wraith	One body: 1487.
3050	Six-light saloon with division	1949	Rolls-Royce Silver Wraith	Two bodies: 1502 & 1510.
3050/A/B	Six-light saloon with division	1949	Rolls-Royce Silver Wraith	Four bodies: 1513, 1523, 1525 & 1544.
3050/A/C	Limousine	1952	Rolls-Royce Silver Wraith	One body: 1595.
3050/A/CE	Limousine	1951	Rolls-Royce Silver Wraith	One body: 1587.
3050/A/D	Limousine	1951	Rolls-Royce Silver Wraith	One body: 1626.
3050/B	Six-light saloon	1950-1951	Rolls-Royce Silver Wraith	Two bodies: 1524 & 1526.
3051	Four-light sports saloon	1949	Daimler DE36	One body: 1514.
3056	Drophead coupé	1949	Rolls-Royce Silver Wraith	One body: 1511.
3068	Estate car (utility)	1950	Rolls-Royce Silver Wraith	One body: 1541.
3070	Saloon	1951-1952	Rolls-Royce Silver Wraith	Two bodies: 1549, 1578.
3070/A	Saloon; some with division	1950-1953	Rolls-Royce Silver Wraith	Five bodies: 1540, 1567, 1615, 1616 & 1632.
3070/B	Saloon with division	1950	Rolls-Royce Silver Wraith	One body: 1539.
3070/E	Saloon	1952	Rolls-Royce Silver Wraith	One body: 1589.
3073	Four-light saloon coupé	1950-1953	Bentley Mk VI Bentley R type	Four bodies: 1542, 1550, 1551 & 1722.
3074/A/B	Limousine	1951	Rolls-Royce Silver Wraith	Two bodies: 1575 & 1583.
3077	Drophead coupé	1952	Bentley Mk VI	One body: 1642.
3077/A	Drophead coupé	1952	Bentley Mk VI	One body: 1638.
3077/A/P	Drophead coupé	1954	Bentley R Type	One body: 1748.
3081	Six-light saloon with division	1951-1952	Rolls-Royce Silver Wraith	One body: 1577.
3082/C	Six-light saloon	1951-1954	Bentley Mk VI Bentley R Type	21 bodies: 1580, 1585, 1588, 1611, 1619, 1629, 1623, 1625, 1627, 1628, 1629, 1637, 1640, 1647, 1650, 1656, 1693, 1723, 1727, 1730 & 1736.
3082/D	Six-light saloon	1952	Bentley R Type	One body: 1696.
3087	Fixed-head coupé	1952-1953	Rolls-Royce Silver Wraith	Two bodies: 1571 and 1663.
3090/B	Six-light saloon with division	1952	Rolls-Royce Silver Wraith	One body: 1697.
3091	Six-light saloon	1953	Rolls-Royce Silver Wraith	Two bodies: 1601 & 1717.

3091/A	Six-light saloon with division	1951-1954	Rolls-Royce Silver Wraith	Five bodies: 1573, 1593, 1610, 1721 & 1729.
3092	Six-light saloon	1952-1953	Rolls-Royce Silver Wraith	1951 Earls Court Show. Seven bodies (1574, 1609, 1617, 1636, 1671,1708, 1714).
3092/A	Six-light saloon with division	1952-1953	Rolls-Royce Silver Wraith	Two bodies: 1654 & 1728.
3093/A	Six-light saloon	1952-1954	Bentley Mk VI Bentley R Type	Twelve bodies: 1641, 1644, 1698, 1713, 1716, 1718, 1726, 1731, 1733, 1734, 1738 & 1742.
3093/A/L	Six-light Saloon	1954	Bentley R Type	Seven bodies: 1751, 1756, 1763, 1768, 1770, 1771 & 1775.
3107	Coupé	1952	Rolls-Royce Silver Wraith	Two bodies: 1691 & 1695.
3110/A	Limousine	1953	Rolls-Royce Silver Wraith	Two bodies: 1646 & 1709.
3110/A/L	Limousine	1953	Rolls-Royce Silver Wraith	One body: 1725.
3131/A	Four-light touring limousine	1953-1954	Rolls-Royce Silver Wraith	Two bodies: 1719 & 1761.
3131/A/L	Four- light touring limousine	1953-1955	Rolls-Royce Silver Wraith	Eight bodies: 1724, 1739, 1746, 1749, 1750, 1752, 1758, 1781.
3131/A/L/3	Six-light touring limousine	1956	Rolls-Royce Silver Wraith (LWB)	One body: 1785.
3131/L	Six-light saloon	1954	Rolls-Royce Silver Wraith	One body: 1754.
3132	Saloon	1953	Bentley R Type	One body: 1720.
3160	All-weather tourer	1954	Rolls-Royce Silver Wraith (LWB)	One body: 1745.
3163	Six-light saloon	1954-1955	Rolls-Royce Silver Dawn	Five bodies: 1740, 1755, 1757, 1765 & 1766.
3165	Six-light saloon	1954	Rolls-Royce Silver Dawn	One body: 1744.
3170/A	Limousine	1954	Rolls-Royce Silver Wraith	One body: 1743.
3171	Six-light touring limousine	1955	Rolls-Royce Silver Wraith	Two bodies: 1769 & 1774.
3171/A	Six-light touring limousine; also Four-light touring limousine	1954-1958	Rolls-Royce Silver Wraith	11 bodies: 1747, 1760, 1772, 1776, 1778, 1787, 1789, 1790, 1816, 1821, 1824
3171/M	Six-light touring limousine	1957	Rolls-Royce Silver Wraith	One body: 1820.
3183	Coupé	1954	Rolls-Royce Silver Wraith	One body: 1753.
3190	Limousine	1955	Rolls-Royce Silver Wraith	One body: 1764.
3191	Special Sports Saloon (six-light); Limousine on LWB chassis	1954-1958	Bentley R Type Rolls-Royce Silver Cloud (LWB)	Four bodies: 1762 & 1767 (R Type); 1826 & 1829 (LWB Silver Cloud). Drawings show the LWB bodies as 3191/LWB, but the order book does not.
3191/A	Special Sports Saloon (six-light)	1956	Bentley S Type	Eight bodies: 1779, 1783, 1784, 1786, 1792, 1793, 1801 & 1808.
3192/A	Saloon with division	1955	Rolls-Royce Silver Wraith	One body: 1759.
3193	Two-door, four-light saloon	1956	Rolls-Royce Silver Cloud	One body: 1796.
3194	Six-light saloon	1956	Rolls-Royce Silver Cloud	Two bodies: 1791 and 1797.
3199	Six-light saloon	1955-1958	Bentley S Type	Thirteen bodies: 1773, 1777, 1780, 1788, 1794, 1795, 1799, 1803, 1812, 1819, 1823, 1825 & 1832.
3206	Six-light saloon	1956-1958	Rolls-Royce Silver Cloud	Seven bodies: 1782, 1800, 1805, 1807, 1809, 1811 & 1828
3206/A	Six-light saloon	1956	Rolls-Royce Silver Cloud	One body: 1815.
3210/A	Coupé	1956	Rolls-Royce Silver Cloud	One body: 1804.
3222	Special limousine	1956	Rolls-Royce Silver Wraith	One body: 1813.
3224/SC	Six-light saloon	1956	Rolls-Royce Silver Cloud	One body: 1814.
3224/1	Six-light saloon	1956	Bentley S Type	One body: 1817.
3225	Limousine	1958	Rolls-Royce Silver Wraith	Two bodies: 1818 & 1830.
3230	Saloon with division	1957	Rolls-Royce Silver Wraith	One body: 3230.
3243/B	Two-seat sports drophead coupé	1957	Bentley S Type	One body: 1831.
3243/C	Two-seat sports drophead coupé	1957-1958	Rolls-Royce Silver Cloud	Two bodies: 1827 & 1833.

The order book records body number 1061, a Two-door, close-coupled saloon on a 1933 Delage D8 chassis as having design number 3786/A. This is presumably an error.

Index